SHAPE IT! 2

COMBO

CB030937

STUDENT'S BOOK
WITH DIGITAL PACK

Claire Thacker and Stuart Cochrane
with Andrew Reid and Daniel Vincent

CAMBRIDGE
UNIVERSITY PRESS

CONTENTS

STARTER

WELCOME!

VOCABULARY

Free Time and Hobbies

S.01 **1 Match verbs 1–10 with the words in the box to make phrases. Listen, check, and repeat.**

a bike ride	cookies/videos	online
a blog	friends	photos
an instrument	music	shopping
~~books/magazines~~		

1 read books/magazines
2 chat ______
3 go ______
4 go for ______
5 hang out with ______
6 listen to ______
7 make ______
8 play ______
9 take ______
10 write ______

S.02 **2 Listen and write the activities from Exercise 1.**

1 play an instrument
2 ______
3 ______
4 ______
5 ______
6 ______
7 ______

Sports

S.03 **3 Match the words with the pictures (1–8). Circle the two sports that aren't in the pictures. Listen, check, and repeat.**

basketball	☐	swimming	☐
gymnastics	1	table tennis	☐
hockey	☐	track and field	☐
rugby	☐	volleyball	☐
sailing	☐	windsurfing	☐

LEARN TO LEARN

Verb and Noun Phrases

We often use verbs and nouns together to make different phrases. Learn them together.

4 Complete the list with nouns from Exercises 1 and 3.

Verb	Noun
play	an instrument,
go	
make	
write	
read	

Use It!

5 Discuss the questions.

1 What is your favorite sport to watch on TV?
2 What is your favorite sport to do?
3 What isn't a good sport to do on your own?

Explore It!

Is the sentence *T* (true) or *F* (false)?

Rugby is popular in many countries, but it is the only sport in Exercise 3 that isn't played at the Summer Olympic Games. ☐

Find another interesting fact about sports and write a question for your partner to answer.

READING
A Blog Post

1 **Look at the photos in the blog post. What do you want to know about the people?**

S.04 **2** **Listen as you read the blog post. Do you learn the information you wanted to know in Exercise 1?**

3 **Find words in the blog post that mean:**

1 doing a lot of things ___busy___
2 difficult ____________
3 making you a little angry ____________
4 very bad ____________
5 very good ____________

4 **Read the blog post again and write the names of the people. Who …**

1 is a busy person? ___Rosie___
2 are Rosie's brother and sister? ____________
3 likes computer magazines and computer games? ____________
4 is not a good singer? ____________
5 are Sara and Fatima? ____________
6 thinks Rosie's blog is very good? ____________

Voice It!

5 **Discuss the questions.**

1 Are you like any of the people in Rosie's blog? If so, who and why?
2 Do you read blogs? Why / Why not?
3 What's your favorite blog? What's it about?

THOUGHTS FOR TODAY

Rosie Wilson

Hi everyone! Today, my blog is all about my hobbies, family, and friends. I'm always busy! So, what do I do?

I go swimming three mornings a week. I always get up at 5:30 a.m. 🥱. It's tough, but swimming is my favorite thing (after my blog – obviously!).

My Big Brother, Dan

He plays computer games, and he sometimes reads magazines (computer game ones!). He plays soccer every day with his friends, but he doesn't leave the house! 🙄

My Annoying Little Sister, Nora

She often does her homework and listens to music at the same time. Does she sing, too? Yes, she does – but she's a terrible singer! 😱

Best Friends Forever: Sara and Fatima ❤️❤️❤️

I don't see them during the week because we don't go to the same school. That isn't a problem because we usually hang out together on the weekend. They love taking selfies, and they post Snapchat stories every day!

What about you? Do you often read my blog? How do you spend your free time? **Let me know!**

COMMENTS:

Jody I read your blog in my free time. It's awesome!

LANGUAGE IN ACTION

Simple Present

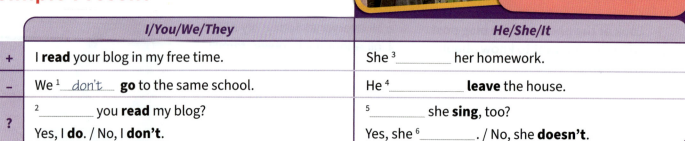

Watch video S.1
What does Zara do on the bus?
What does the vlogger do in the morning?

	I/You/We/They	*He/She/It*
+	I **read** your blog in my free time.	She [3] ________ her homework.
–	We [1] *don't* **go** to the same school.	He [4] ________ **leave** the house.
?	[2] ________ you **read** my blog? Yes, I **do**. / No, I **don't**.	[5] ________ she **sing**, too? Yes, she [6] ________. / No, she **doesn't**.

1 **Complete the examples in the chart above. Use the blog post on page 5 to help you.**

2 **Write simple present sentences.**

1 Rosie / get up / at 5:30 a.m. three mornings a week.
Rosie gets up at 5:30 a.m. three mornings a week.

2 Dan / play / computer games.
____

3 Rosie / not listen / to music when she / do / her homework. ________
____

4 Sara and Fatima / not see / Rosie during the week. ________
____

S.05 **3** **Complete the blog post with the simple present form of the verbs. Then listen and check.**

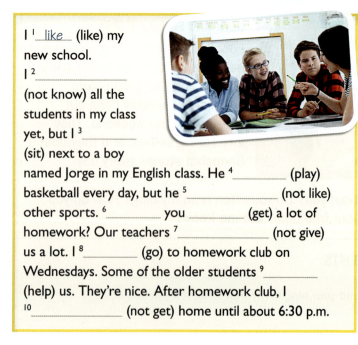

I [1] *like* (like) my new school. I [2] ________ (not know) all the students in my class yet, but I [3] ________ (sit) next to a boy named Jorge in my English class. He [4] ________ (play) basketball every day, but he [5] ________ (not like) other sports. [6] ________ you ________ (get) a lot of homework? Our teachers [7] ________ (not give) us a lot. I [8] ________ (go) to homework club on Wednesdays. Some of the older students [9] ________ (help) us. They're nice. After homework club, I [10] ________ (not get) home until about 6:30 p.m.

Adverbs of Frequency

Rosie is **always** busy.
Dan **sometimes** reads magazines.
Nora **often** listens to music when she does her homework.
Rosie **usually** hangs out with friends on the weekend.

4 **Complete the timeline with the adverbs of frequency in the chart above.**

0% [1] ________ [3] ________ 100%
never [2] ________ [4] ________

5 **Rewrite the sentences with the words in parentheses.**

1 I'm late for school. (never)
I'm never late for school.

2 I do my homework on the weekend. (always)
____

3 Do you go shopping with friends? (sometimes)
____

4 I'm tired after school. (often)
____

5 Do you take photos with your phone? (usually)
____

Use It!

6 **Discuss the sentences in Exercise 5. Are they true for you?**

Are you always late for school?

No, I'm never late for school!

VOCABULARY AND LISTENING

Personal Possessions

1

2

3

4

5

6
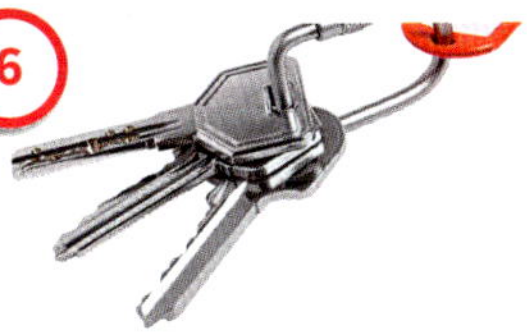
7

8

9

10

S.06 **1 Match the words with the photos. Listen, check, and repeat.**

bus pass	☐	money	☐
camera	☐	passport	☐
headphones	☐	phone	☐
keys	☐	portable charger	☐
laptop	☐	tablet	1

2 Complete the sentences with words from Exercise 1.

1 Where are my keys ? I can't open the door.

2 Martin is always late. Can I borrow your ________ to text him?

3 You can't go to France without your ________.

4 I want to take good photos. I need a nice ________.

5 That music is very loud. Use your ________.

LEARN TO LEARN

Making Vocabulary Cards

Make vocabulary cards to help you learn new words. Draw a picture on one side and write the word on the other.

3 Make your own vocabulary cards for the words in Exercise 1.

4 Test a partner. Show your cards. Can your partner say the words in English?

Use It!

5 Describe a possession from Exercise 1 for your partner to guess. Think about:

- when and where you use it
- what you use it for

I use it every day. I always keep it in my bag. I use it to get to school.

Is it your bus pass?

A Conversation

S.07 **6 Listen to the conversation. Circle the club Alex wants to go to.**

a the coding club b the photography club

S.07 **7 Listen again and circle the correct answers.**

1 Emma goes to the … club.
 a coding (b) photography

2 Alex … taking photos.
 a likes b doesn't like

3 Alex has a …
 a tablet. b laptop.

4 Mr. Adams …
 a is a good teacher. b knows Bill Gates.

5 In her free time, Libby writes …
 a a blog. b computer programs.

Voice It!

8 Do you go to any school clubs? Which ones? What school club would you like to go to?

GRAMMAR IN ACTION

Love, Like, Don't Mind, Hate + -ing

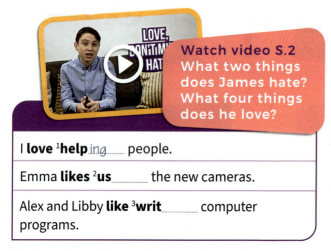

Watch video S.2
What two things does James hate? What four things does he love?

I **love** [1]**help**ing_____ people.
Emma **likes** [2]**us**_____ the new cameras.
Alex and Libby **like** [3]**writ**_____ computer programs.

1 **Complete the words in the chart above.**

2 **Write the sentences with the correct form of the verbs in parentheses.**

1 Emma likes meeting (meet) new people.
2 Alex doesn't like _____ (take) photos.
3 Libby doesn't mind _____ (help) Alex.
4 Mr. Adams loves _____ (tell) stories.

3 **Complete the blog post with the correct form of the verbs in the boxes.**

love 🙂🙂🙂 ~~like~~ 🙂 not mind 😐 not like ☹ hate ☹☹☹

do get up help ~~listen~~ speak

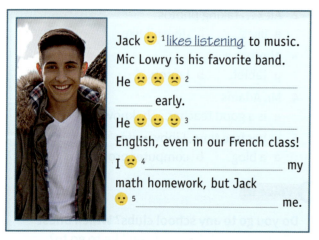

Jack 🙂 [1]likes listening to music. Mic Lowry is his favorite band.
He ☹☹☹ [2]_____________ _____ early.
He 🙂🙂🙂 [3]_____________ English, even in our French class!
I ☹ [4]_____________ my math homework, but Jack 😐 [5]_____________ me.

Use It!

4 **Think of five sentences using *love, like, don't mind,* and *hate*. Does your partner agree with you?**

I don't mind cleaning the kitchen. *I hate doing it!*

To Have

	I/You/We/They	He/She/It
+	We [1] have two new cameras.	She **has** a new camera.
–	I **don't have** a map of the school.	Alex **doesn't** [3] _____ a map of the school.
?	**Do** you **have** your own laptop? Yes, I **do**. / No, I [2] _____.	[4] _____ he **have** his own laptop? Yes, he [5] _____. / No, he **doesn't**.

5 **Complete the examples in the chart above.**

6 **Complete the sentences with the correct form of *to have*.**

1 Alex doesn't have his own laptop. ✗
2 Alex _____ a tablet. ✓
3 They _____ a lot of laptops at the club. ✓
4 Libby _____ her own computer. ✓
5 She _____ much free time. ✗

S.08 **7** **Complete the text with the correct form of *to have*. Then listen and check.**

We [1] have a new student in our class. Her name's Paola. What [2] _____ we _____ in common? A lot! She [3] _____ brown hair and blue eyes – just like me! [4] _____ she _____ any brothers and sisters? Yes, she [5] _____. She [6] _____ two little sisters, just like me. She [7] _____ any brothers. We [8] _____ the same phones and headphones! We [9] _____ school today because it's a holiday. I'd like to call Paola – but I [10] _____ her phone number. It's annoying!

Use It!

8 **Ask and answer questions using *to have*.**

Do you have any brothers or sisters?

WRITING
A Personal Profile

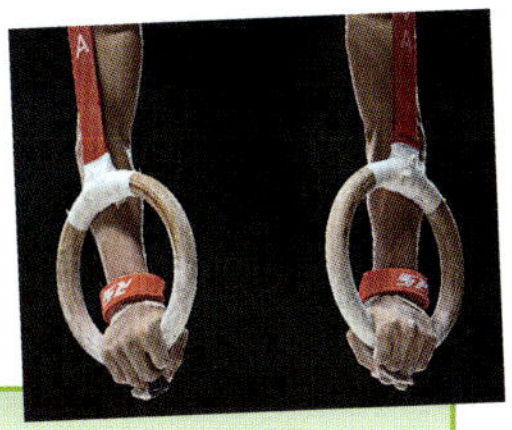

1 Look at the photo. What does Ernesto like doing? Read his profile and check.

1 Hi! 👋 My name's Ernesto Mendes and I'm 14 years old. I'm from Vancouver in Canada. I live with my mom and dad, my grandma, and my cat. My cat's name is Tiger 🐯. My best friends are Joel and Ruby.

2 My favorite free-time activity is gymnastics. I train every day. Training starts at 6:00 a.m. 😬. It's tough because I hate getting up early, but I love practicing.

3 I also like going for bike rides on my own. I have a new bike, and I usually go for a bike ride after school. I don't have much free time, but I always hang out with my friends on the weekend. We often go to Joel's place because he has a swimming pool.

2 Read the profile again. Answer the questions.

1 Where is Ernesto from?
He's from Vancouver in Canada.

2 Why does Ernesto get up early?
______

3 What does he like doing on his own?
______

4 What does he do on the weekend?
______

3 Look at the *Useful Language* box. Find and underline examples of apostrophes and commas in the profile. Match them with the correct use and write them in the box.

Useful Language

We use apostrophes:

- for contractions / short forms: name's ______
- to show possession: My cat's name ______

We use commas to indicate a pause:
my mom and dad, my grandma, and my cat
______

4 Rewrite the sentences with commas and apostrophes in the correct places.

1 Were from South Africa.
We're from South Africa.

2 Whats your history teachers name?
______

3 That isnt my tablet.
______

4 I have a cat three horses and a parrot!
______

5 My sisters friends very noisy!
______

PLAN

5 Plan your own personal profile. Take notes for each paragraph.

1 You, your family, and friends:
______
______

2 Your favorite free-time activity:
- what it is, where and how often you do it

______
______

3 Other free-time activities:
- what you like doing on your own or with friends
- when and where you do the activities

______
______

WRITE

6 Write your profile. Remember to include three paragraphs, the information in Exercise 5, the simple present, adverbs of frequency, *love*, etc. + *-ing*, and *to have*.

CHECK

7 Do you ...
- describe you, your family, and friends?
- describe your favorite free-time activity?
- describe other things you like doing?
- use apostrophes and commas correctly?

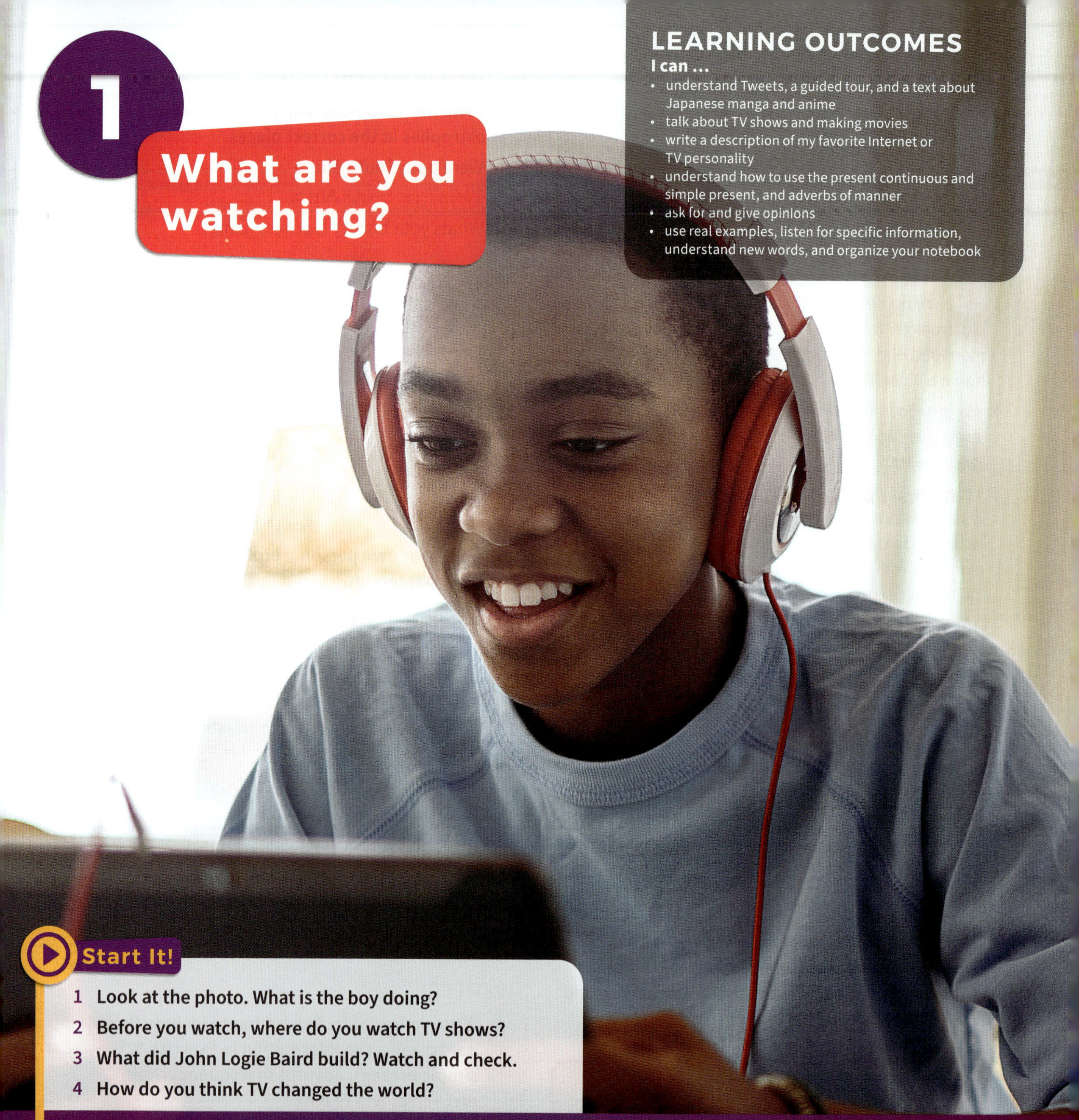

1 What are you watching?

LEARNING OUTCOMES

I can ...

- understand Tweets, a guided tour, and a text about Japanese manga and anime
- talk about TV shows and making movies
- write a description of my favorite Internet or TV personality
- understand how to use the present continuous and simple present, and adverbs of manner
- ask for and give opinions
- use real examples, listen for specific information, understand new words, and organize your notebook

Start It!

1 Look at the photo. What is the boy doing?
2 Before you watch, where do you watch TV shows?
3 What did John Logie Baird build? Watch and check.
4 How do you think TV changed the world?

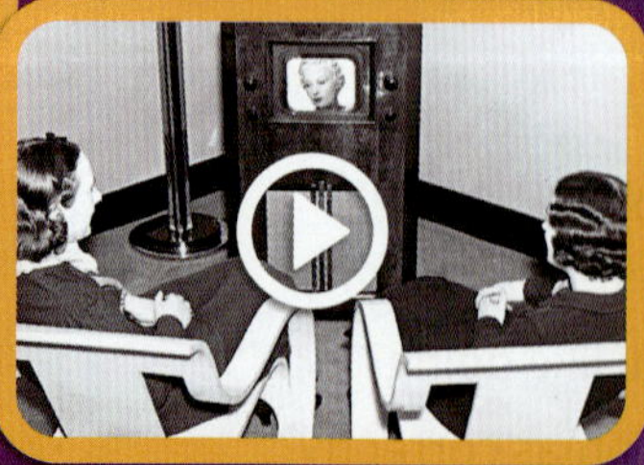

Watch video 1.1

p13

Grammar in Action 1.2

p15

Grammar in Action 1.3

p16

Everyday English 1.4

p18

Globetrotters 1.5

VOCABULARY
TV Shows

1.01 **1 Match eight of the TV shows in the box with the photos. Circle the four shows that aren't in the photos. Listen, check, and repeat.**

cartoon	☐	reality show	☐
comedy	☐	soap opera	1
cooking show	☐	sports show	☐
documentary	☐	streaming series	☐
drama	☐	talk show	☐
game show	☐	the news	☐

2 Match the sentences with TV shows from Exercise 1.

1 "Put your potatoes in a pan and add some salt." cooking show

2 "They're coming! We need to get out of here." ______

3 "Giant pandas are in danger. There are only about 1,800 left." ______

4 "We have some really interesting guests on tonight's show." ______

5 "Can they score in the last minute?" ______

6 "Today: A hurricane hits the city." ______

1.02 **3 Listen. Write the shows the people talk about.**

1 comedy
2 ______
3 ______
4 ______
5 ______
6 ______

LEARN TO LEARN
Using Real Examples

When you learn vocabulary, think of examples to help you remember it.

4 Think of an example of each type of TV show in Exercise 1.

5 Ask about your partner's TV shows. Can you guess what they are?

What type of show is it? *A sports show.*

Use It!

6 Complete the sentences so they are true for you. Tell your partner.

1 I love watching ______
2 My family often watches ______
3 My favorite TV show is ______
4 I hate ______

Explore It!

Guess the correct answer.

Which country in the world watches the most TV?

a Poland b U.S.A. c Japan

Find an interesting fact about TV. Then write a question for your partner to answer.

READING
Tweets

1 **Look at the pictures and titles. What do you think the Tweets are about?**

1.03 **2** **Read the Tweets. Match the people with the TV shows. Then listen and check.**

1 Jack a a comedy
2 Holly b the news
3 Rory c a streaming series

3 EXAM **Check (✓) the correct column.**

	Jack	Holly	Rory
1 likes different TV shows from their friend			
2 does media studies			
3 is with a friend now			
4 talks about a friend in a different place			

4 **Match the words with the definitions.**

average episode season subscribe

1 one individual show in a series ________
2 typical, normal ________
3 arrange to pay and receive something regularly ________
4 a period in which a show appears regularly on TV ________

Voice It!

5 **Imagine you are watching a famous event from history on the news. Discuss the questions.**

1 Where are you?
2 Who or what can you see?
3 How many people are there?
4 How do you feel?

Crazy about TV @crazyabouttv
Apart from sleeping, the average teenager spends more time in front of a television than doing any other free-time activity! So … are you watching TV right now? Where are you watching it and who with? We want to know! Tweet us and send us your photos. #crazyaboutTV

JackLong @JLo-o-o-ng
I'm learning about the history of TV in media studies this week. So for homework, I'm traveling back to 1969 to watch the news about Neil Armstrong, the first person on the moon.

Crazy about TV @crazyabouttv
@JLo-o-o-ng Amazing! Neil Armstrong and Buzz Aldrin are walking on the moon. Around 530 million people are watching them with you. We're over the moon, too! #crazyaboutTV

Holly Bardsley @HBards
At the moment, I'm sitting in my bedroom with my best friend @superfanz. We're watching our favorite streaming series, *Stranger Things*, on my new tablet. We're super fans and this episode is so scary!

Crazy about TV @crazyabouttv
@HBards Here's a cool fact for you. More than 100 million people around the world subscribe to Netflix, and you're one of them. Do you want to know about the next season of *Stranger Things*? Just ask us! Spoiler alert! #crazyaboutTV

Rory Green @RoryG
I'm waiting for my favorite comedy to start, so I'm taking a selfie and I'm messaging my friend @laughingboi at the same time! He isn't watching TV – he's listening to music. He doesn't like comedies.

Crazy about TV @crazyabouttv
@RoryG Believe it or not, if you're an average American teenager, you probably send about 128 instant messages a day! #crazyaboutTV

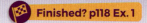

Finished? p118 Ex. 1

Watch video 1.2
What are Ben and Nick doing?
What two things is the vlogger doing?

GRAMMAR IN ACTION
Present Continuous

	I	*He/She/It*	*We/You/They*
+	I'**m sitting** in my bedroom.	He [1]'s **listening** to music.	Neil Armstrong and Buzz Aldrin [3] ______ **walking** on the moon.
–	I'**m not sitting** in class.	He [2] ______ **watching** TV.	We **aren't watching** the news.
?	**Am** I **listening** to music? Yes, I **am**. / No, I'**m not**.	**Is** Rory's friend **listening** to music? Yes, he **is**. / No, he **isn't**.	[4] ______ you **watching** TV right now? Where [5] ______ you **watching** it?

Pronunciation p141

Get It Right!

We don't usually use some verbs with the present continuous. For example, **know**, **understand**, **like**, **love**, **prefer**, **remember**.

Do you understand me? **NOT** *~~Are you understanding me?~~*

1 **Complete the examples in the chart above. Use the Tweets on page 12 to help you.**

2 **Write sentences with the present continuous.**

1 Jack / watch TV / with 530 million other people.
Jack is watching TV with 530 million other people.

2 Holly and her friend / not sit / in the library.
______

3 Holly and her friend / watch / a streaming series now.
______

4 Rory / not watch / his favorite comedy at the moment.
______

3 **Complete the blog with present continuous verbs.**

This week I [1]'m researching (research) my favorite subject – TV! I'm very happy because I [2] ______ (not do) it on my own. I [3] ______ (prepare) a presentation with my friend Saul.

At the moment, Saul [4] ______ (not talk) to me. He [5] ______ (watch) a new online series, and he [6] ______ (take) notes. I'm tired right now, so I [7] ______ (take) a break. But we [8] ______ really ______ (enjoy) this project.

4 1.06 **Complete the conversation with the present continuous form of the verbs. Then listen and check.**

call ~~do~~ give interview study talk watch

ROSA What [1] are you doing right now, Toni?
TONI I [2] ______ to you.
ROSA Ha, ha. Very funny. [3] ______ you ______ for the math test?
TONI No, I [4] ______ a talk show. Why [5] ______ you ______ me?
ROSA Well, this math homework [6] ______ me a headache. Can you help me?
TONI Sorry, Rosa. I can't talk now. They [7] ______ Ed Sheeran. I'll call you back, OK? Bye.
ROSA Great. Thanks a lot, Toni.

Use It!

5 **Write questions. Then ask and answer with a partner.**

1 what / you / wear?
What are you wearing?

2 what / your teacher / do / right now?
______

3 where / your best friend / sit / today?
______

What are you wearing? *I'm wearing ...*

Finished? p118 Ex. 2

VOCABULARY AND LISTENING

Making Movies

1.07 **1 Match the words with the people and things in the picture. Listen, check, and repeat.**

actor		lights	
camera operator		makeup artist	
costume		script	
(digital) camera		set	1
director		sound engineer	

2 (Circle) the correct word in each sentence.

1 It's too dark. We need extra (*lights*) / *cameras*.
2 They're building the *director* / *set* this week.
3 We can't start filming – the main *operator* / *actor* isn't here.
4 Who is writing the *script* / *lights*?
5 I'm not wearing that *costume* / *camera*. No way!
6 We can't hear the voices very well. Where's the *makeup artist* / *sound engineer*?

Use It!

3 Choose a job from Exercise 1 and describe what you're doing. Can your partner guess the job?

I'm sitting in my chair. I'm talking to the actors, and I'm looking at the set.

A Guided Tour

4 Look at the photos. Where do you think you can see these things? What are they?

1.08 **5 Listen and (circle) Matt's favorite movie.**

a *Thor* b *Avatar* c *The Lord of the Rings*

LEARN TO LEARN

Listening for Specific Information

Check what type of answer you need (a number, a name, a place, a job, etc.) before you listen.

6 Read the questions in Exercise 7. Write the type of answer you think you need to listen for.

1 a place
2 ______
3 ______
4 ______
5 ______
6 ______

1.08 **7 Listen again and answer the questions.**

1 Where does Matt live? Wellington
2 How many people visit movie locations in New Zealand each year? ______
3 What is Clara's job? ______
4 Where do the students go first? ______
5 How tall are some of the bigatures? ______
6 What is Martin's job? ______

Voice It!

8 What is on your dream movie studio tour?

GRAMMAR IN ACTION

Simple Present and Present Continuous

Watch video 1.3
What is he doing? Describe two tips he gives.

Simple Present	Present Continuous
More than 3 million people [1] ________ locations for movies here every year.	Today, I [2] ________ a movie workshop with my media studies class.
Time expressions: *always, sometimes, never, every day/week*, etc.	Time expressions: *(right) now, at the moment, today, this morning*, etc.

1 **Complete the examples in the chart above with the correct form of *visit*.**

2 **Circle the correct verbs.**

1. Matt *lives* / *is living* in Wellington. (*lives* circled)
2. They *wait* / *are waiting* for their tour guide.
3. Martin *works* / *is working* hard today.
4. Martin always *uses* / *is using* a digital camera.

3 (1.09) **Complete the text with the correct form of the verbs in parentheses. Then listen and check.**

Media studies [1] is (be) my favorite subject at school. I [2] ________ (love) it! This week, we [3] ________ (study) the history of film. We [4] ________ (learn) all about talkies, CGI, and lots more! I [5] ________ (not know) much about it. It [6] ________ (take) a long time and a lot of people to make a movie. Sorry! Time to go! My little brother [7] ________ (make) a lot of noise downstairs. I think he [8] ________ (watch) his favorite comedy with my mom and dad. They all [9] ________ (love) it, and they always [10] ________ (laugh) a lot! 😂

What [11] ________ you ________ (do) at school this week?

Use It!

4 **Write sentences with the verbs and time expressions. Use the correct tense.**

do / sometimes   drive / now   ~~watch / always~~

1. We / sports shows on the weekend.
   We always watch sports shows on the weekend.
2. They / their homework together.
   ____
3. My parents / me to the gym.
   ____

Adverbs of Manner

If I'm not explaining [1] clearly (clear), let me know!
Talk [2] ________ (quiet), please.
He's working [3] ________ (hard) today.

5 **Complete the examples in the chart above with the correct form of the words in parentheses.**

6 **Write the adverbs for adjectives 1–6. Circle the ones that don't use *-ly*.**

1. nice nicely
2. fast ________
3. beautiful ________
4. loud ________
5. happy ________
6. good ________

Use It!

7 **Write questions. Use the simple present or present continuous and the adverb form of the adjectives.**

1. you / always / make / new friends? (easy)
   Do you always make friends easily?
2. you / speak / English / today? (good)
   ____
3. your math teacher / explain / everything? (clear)
   ____
4. you / work / this term? (hard)
   ____

8 **Ask and answer the questions in Exercise 7.**

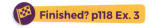

Finished? p118 Ex. 3

SPEAKING
Asking for and Giving Opinions

1.10 **1** **Listen to the conversation. Does Eva like the show?**

EVA	What are you doing?
ALEX	I'm watching the second episode of this new comedy series.
EVA	But it's lunchtime.
ALEX	I'm not having lunch today. Lunch can wait.
EVA	So, what [1] do you think of the show?
ALEX	I love it! Do you like comedies?
EVA	No, I don't. I'm not [2] ____________ them. I [3] ____________ documentaries and dramas.
ALEX	Everyone's watching this one. It's really cool! Why don't you watch it with me?
EVA	I'm not sure.
ALEX	I think you'll really like it.
EVA	OK. Let's see.
ALEX	Well? What do you think of it?
EVA	Actually, it's [4] ____________!

1.10 **2** **Complete the conversation with the phrases from the *Useful Language* box. Then listen and check.**

Useful Language

I prefer watching …
I'm not really into it/them.
It's great / good / not bad / awful.
What do you think of … ?

3 **Look at the *Everyday English* box. Find and underline the phrases in the conversation.**

Watch video 1.4
Everyday English

Actually …   It's really cool!
Let's see.   Well?

4 **Complete the conversations with the *Everyday English* phrases.**

1 A This actor is great, isn't he?
B ____________, I don't really like him.

2 A ____________? Do you like the show?
B Yes, I do. ____________!

3 A Come with us to the gym on Saturday.
B Maybe, but I'm not sure. ____________.

PLAN

5 **With your partner, choose two TV shows to talk about. Take notes about them.**

Which shows? ____________
____

What do you think of them?
____
____

Why? ____________
____

SPEAK

6 **Practice a conversation with your partner, asking for and giving opinions about TV shows. Remember to use the simple present and present continuous, vocabulary from this unit, and phrases from the *Useful Language* and *Everyday English* boxes.**

CHECK

7 **Work with another pair. Listen to their conversation and complete the notes.**

Which shows? ____________
____

What do they think of them?
____
____

Why? ____________
____

WRITING
A Description of a Celebrity

1 **Look at the photo. What is the woman holding? Read the description and find the answer.**

2 **Match topics a–c with paragraphs 1–3.**

a Why I like this person
b An introduction to the person and her show
c Typical episodes in the show

3 **Read Lidia's description again. Are the sentences *T* (true) or *F* (false)?**

Rosanna Pansino …

1 is from the U.S.A. ___
2 has a game show on the Internet. ___
3 likes trying other people's recipes. ___
4 makes unusual cakes. ___

4 **Find and <u>underline</u> examples of *and*, *but*, and *or* in Lidia's description. Complete the *Useful Language* box.**

Useful Language

We use [1] ________ to add similar information.
We use [2] ________ to show different information.
We use [3] ________ when there is a choice of two or more things.

5 **(Circle) the correct word.**

1 I don't like making cakes, *or* / (*but*) I love eating them!
2 Ryan Higa is my favorite Internet star, *and* / *but* I often watch his videos.
3 Do you prefer watching comedies *and* / *or* soap operas?
4 Lots of people love talk shows, *and* / *but* I think they're boring.

My Favorite Internet Star

By Lidia Suarez

1 ☐ Rosanna Pansino is my favorite Internet star. She's an American actor, but she also has a cooking show – *Nerdy Nummies*. She bakes fantastic cakes. I love the show and trying her recipes. She has more than 10 million subscribers, and every month her show gets 75 million views.

2 ☐ In each episode, she explains how to make her cakes. But they aren't normal cakes! They look like characters or objects from TV shows, video games, movies, or books. This week, she's making Batman cakes.

3 ☐ I like her because she's a great cook and because she makes the videos herself, too. She uses her own computer, camera, and lights. She always explains her recipes clearly. They're easy to follow and the cakes taste great!

PLAN

6 **Plan a description of your favorite Internet or TV personality. Take notes for three paragraphs.**

1 Who the person is: ________
What they do: ________
2 What they do in each episode: ________
____
What they are doing in this week's episode: ________
____
3 Why I like this person and the show: ________
____

WRITE

7 **Write your description. Remember to include three paragraphs, the correct present tenses, adverbs, and *and*, *but*, and *or*.**

CHECK

8 **Do you …**

- use sentences with *and*, *but*, and *or*?
- give information about what the person usually does and is doing now?
- explain why you like the person?

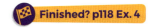

Finished? p118 Ex. 4

AROUND THE WORLD

READING
An Online Article

1 **Look at the photos. What kinds of movies can you see? What country are the movies from?**

1.11 **2** **Read the article and check your answers.**

3 **Read the article again. Answer the questions in your notebook.**

1. What is the difference between anime and manga?
2. How are manga comics different outside of Japan?
3. Why does the article mention *Howl's Moving Castle* and *Ponyo*?
4. Who is Hayao Miyazaki?
5. What does the number 170,000 refer to?

Globetrotters

Watch video 1.5 Bollywood

- How many movies does India produce a year?
- Where does the name Bollywood come from?
- How many different movies can actors be in at the same time?

Voice It!

4 **Discuss the questions.**

1. Teamwork is an important part of making a movie. Why?
2. What skills do you need to work as a team?
3. What teamwork skills do you have?

Magical Pictures – from Manga to Anime

Are you familiar with *anime*? *Anime* usually refers to Japanese animated cartoons. They often use *manga* (comic book) characters and stories. Manga and anime have a style that is popular around the world, with series such as *Naruto* and *Dragon Ball Z*.

People read Japanese manga comics from right to left. Outside of Japan, some printers change the direction of reading on the page so people can read the stories from left to right.

You may already like anime! Do you like *Howl's Moving Castle* (2004) or *Ponyo* (2008)? Studio Ghibli, an animation studio in Tokyo, Japan, produced these movies. The director, Hayao Miyazaki, is famous for beautiful anime movies. A single movie can take up to eight years and thousands of hours to produce! But what is the process like?

Hayao Miyazaki

First, screenwriters develop a script for the story. Then they think about the characters. What do they look like? What are their personalities like? What do we learn about the characters in the story? What do they learn about themselves?

After this, concept artists draw the characters, their expressions, and their clothes. Next, storyboard artists use the script to **sketch** a **storyboard**. A storyboard shows all the important **scenes** in the movie. Voice actors read the characters' lines in a recording studio, and animators draw the characters and the **backgrounds**. To animate a scene, they make tiny changes to each picture. When they play the **frames** as a video, the characters come alive. It requires a lot of pictures. The movie *Ponyo* has 170,000 frames, and artists animated every scene by hand, not with a computer. The final result is a movie that people everywhere can experience and enjoy.

LEARN TO LEARN

Understanding New Words

Don't worry if you don't understand some words. First, try to get a general understanding of the article. Then guess the meaning of the new words.

5 Look at the words in bold in the article. Try to guess their meaning. Then check in a dictionary.

- Look at the words before and after the word.
- Think of similar words in your language.
- Look at any pictures to help you understand.
- Look for other examples of the word in the article.

6 Think of your own sentences with the new words. Say each sentence, but don't say the new word. Can your partner guess it?

Explore It!

Guess the correct answer.

Spirited Away is a famous Studio Ghibli film. The location for the movie is in …

a Taiwan. **b** Tokyo. **c** Seoul.

Find three more interesting facts about animated movies. Choose your favorite fact and write a question for your partner.

SHAPE IT!

CULTURE PROJECT

An Infographic

An infographic has illustrations to present information in a clear and memorable way. Make an infographic about a movie-making job.

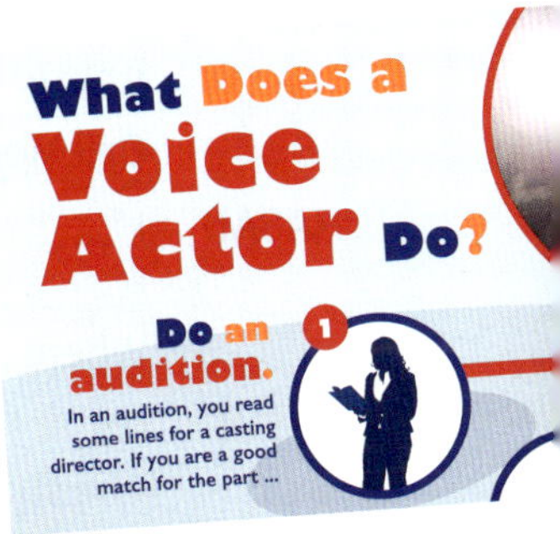

Teacher's Resource Bank

1 REVIEW

VOCABULARY

1 The TV shows are wrong. Write the correct ones.

1 My little sister loves **soap operas**. Her favorite character is Sponge Bob. ______
2 That new **documentary** is so exciting, and it's only the second episode! ______
3 This **sports show** is about dolphins.
______
4 Which guests are on the **soap opera** tonight?
______
5 Only one person can win the car and the money on this **drama**. ______

2 Write the TV and movie words for the definitions.

1 clothes that actors wear in movies ______
2 a person who changes the actors' appearance
______
3 the words for a movie ______
4 the place where they film a TV show
______
5 the person who tells actors what to do
______

GRAMMAR IN ACTION

3 Complete the conversation with the present continuous form of the verbs.

HASAN Hey, Yusuf. Are you at home?
YUSUF Yes, I [1] ______ (watch) last night's music show. Where [2] ______ you ______ (call) from?
HASAN I [3] ______ (stand) outside the house. I don't have my keys.
YUSUF Call Mom.
HASAN I [4] ______ (call) you because Mom [5] ______ (not answer) her phone. Where are you?
YUSUF I [6] ______ (sit) in the backyard. The sun [7] ______ (shine), the birds [8] ______ (sing).
HASAN Yusuf, can you let me in, please? NOW!

4 Complete the sentences with the simple present or present continuous.

1 The actor ______ the script at the moment. (not read)
2 ______ you usually ______ your friends after school? (meet)
3 The students ______ for their drama exam this week. (study)
4 Simon always ______ TV after school. (watch)

5 Rewrite the sentences with adverbs of manner.

1 The children are talking in the library. (quiet)
______
2 Are you writing in your notebooks? (careful)
______
3 The teacher is explaining the activity. (clear)
______
4 We're studying for our exams. (hard)
______

6 Complete Kim's blog with the simple present, present continuous, and adverbs of manner.

My friend Ava often [1] ______ (come) to my place on Saturday afternoons, and we [2] ______ (listen) to music together. This Saturday is different. My dad [3] ______ (drive) us to a movie premiere. There's a lot of traffic, so we [4] ______ (not move) [5] ______ (quick). I usually [6] ______ (write) my blog on Saturday evening in my bedroom, but today I [7] ______ (type) it [8] ______ (slow) on my phone in the car!

Self-Assessment

I can talk about TV shows.
I can talk about making movies.
I can use the simple present and present continuous.
I can use adverbs of manner.

LEARN TO ... ORGANIZE YOUR NOTEBOOK

When you organize your notebook, it helps you to study better.

1 Ask and answer with a partner.

1. What do you usually write in your notebook?
2. How often do you use your notebook when you study at home?
3. How can you organize your notebook better?

2 Look at Irina's notebook. Match the tips (1–5) with a–e.

1. Divide your notebook into sections so that you can find things quickly. ☐
2. Use different color pens for different things (for example, adjectives can be red, numbers can be green). ☐
3. Highlight or underline important notes, words, and facts. ☐
4. When you write a text, make a plan on the left and then write on the right. ☐
5. Write all your homework notes (what page, what exercise) in the same place so that you don't forget what you have to do. ☐

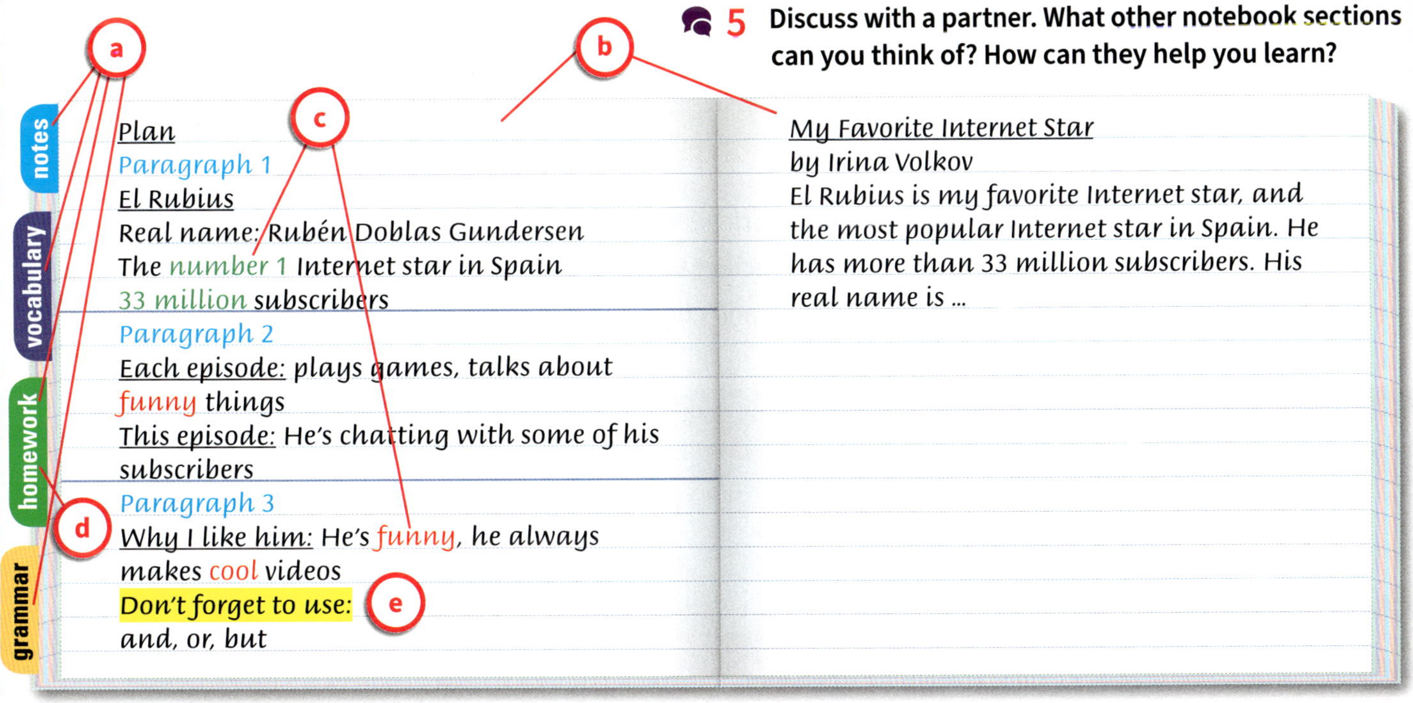

a
b
c
d
e
notes
vocabulary
homework
grammar
Plan
Paragraph 1
El Rubius
Real name: Rubén Doblas Gundersen
The number 1 Internet star in Spain
33 million subscribers
Paragraph 2
Each episode: plays games, talks about funny things
This episode: He's chatting with some of his subscribers
Paragraph 3
Why I like him: He's funny, he always makes cool videos
Don't forget to use:
and, or, but
My Favorite Internet Star
by Irina Volkov
El Rubius is my favorite Internet star, and the most popular Internet star in Spain. He has more than 33 million subscribers. His real name is ...

3 Look at the tips in Irina's notebook again. Complete the sentences.

1. Highlighting and underlining help you see the __________ information.
2. You can use the __________ on the left when you're writing.
3. The __________ notes help you remember what to do at home.
4. You can use different color pens for __________ things. It's your choice!
5. You can find notes quickly when you use different __________.

SHAPE IT!

4 Follow the plan to organize your notebook.

1. Divide your notebook into sections.
2. Choose different color pens for your notes.
3. Get a highlighter for important information (or you can underline it instead).
4. Start using your notebook today!

5 Discuss with a partner. What other notebook sections can you think of? How can they help you learn?

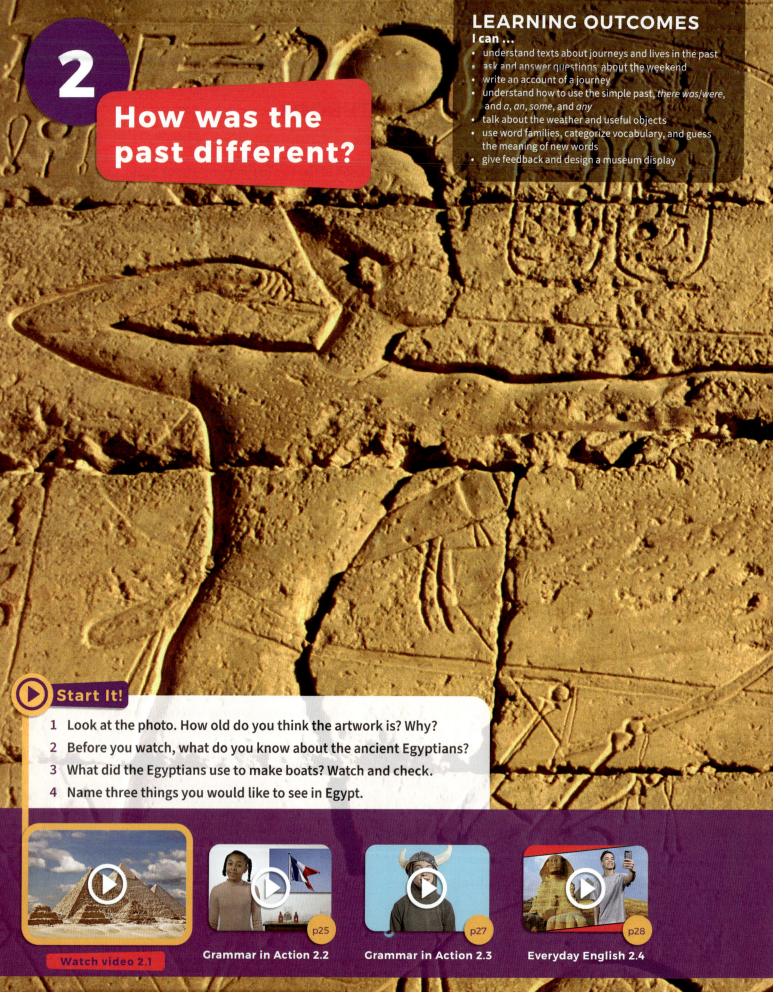

2 How was the past different?

LEARNING OUTCOMES

I can ...

- understand texts about journeys and lives in the past
- ask and answer questions about the weekend
- write an account of a journey
- understand how to use the simple past, *there was/were*, and *a*, *an*, *some*, and *any*
- talk about the weather and useful objects
- use word families, categorize vocabulary, and guess the meaning of new words
- give feedback and design a museum display

Start It!

1 Look at the photo. How old do you think the artwork is? Why?

2 Before you watch, what do you know about the ancient Egyptians?

3 What did the Egyptians use to make boats? Watch and check.

4 Name three things you would like to see in Egypt.

Watch video 2.1

p25

Grammar in Action 2.2

p27

Grammar in Action 2.3

p28

Everyday English 2.4

VOCABULARY
The Weather

1 2.01 **What is the weather like in the photos? Circle the weather words that aren't in the photos. Listen, check, and repeat.**

cloudy cold ~~dry~~ foggy ~~hot~~ icy rainy snowy stormy ~~sunny~~ warm wet windy

1 dry, hot, and sunny
2 ______
3 ______
4 ______
5 ______

1

2

3

4

5

2 Complete the sentences with adjectives from Exercise 1.

1 It's today. cloudy
2 Is it all year? ______
3 August is usually . ______
4 We love weather! ______
5 It isn't . It's . ______

LEARN TO LEARN
Word Families (1)

Build your vocabulary by learning words from the same family. Many adjectives ending in *-y* come from a noun.

3 Write the adjective forms.

1 cloud cloudy
2 fog ______
3 ice ______
4 rain ______
5 snow ______
6 storm ______
7 sun ______
8 wind ______

Use It!

4 Complete the sentences with your own ideas. Tell your partner.

1 When it's foggy, it's difficult to ______.
2 In hot, sunny weather, I always wear ______.
3 On wet days, I hate ______.
4 I think cold, snowy weather is ______.

Explore It!

Is the sentence *T* (true) or *F* (false)?

Snow isn't always white – sometimes there is pink snow in the Sierra Nevada mountains in the U.S.A. ☐

Find another interesting fact about the weather. Then write a question for your partner to answer.

READING
Diary Extracts

1 **Look at the photos. What do you think the girl is writing about?**

2.02 **2** **Read the text. Check your answer to Exercise 1.**

3 **Read the text again and find these things:**

1 two American states ______
2 two types of furniture ______
3 five weather adjectives ______
______
4 two musical instruments ______
5 two animals ______

4 **Match the highlighted words with the definitions.**

1 a long trip to another place ______
2 wet and dirty after rain ______
3 a difficult task ______
4 not deep ______
5 vehicles with four wheels to transport heavy things ______
6 large animals like cows that can pull heavy things ______

5 **Complete the sentences with words from the text.**

1 People on the Oregon Trail were called ______.
2 Oregon is on the ______ coast of the U.S.A.
3 The adults and children didn't usually travel in the ______.
4 Louisa traveled across the country with her ______.
5 One of Louisa's brothers played the ______.

Voice It!

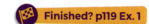

6 **Discuss the questions.**

1 Do you think diaries are important?
2 What challenges do you face each day?

Finished? p119 Ex. 1

The Oregon Trail

Between 1843 and 1869, more than 500,000 pioneers left their homes in the east of the U.S.A. to travel more than 3,000 km west to Oregon and California. Some people wanted to find gold and others wanted to start a new life.

The pioneers used wagons to cross the country. They took things like tables, chairs, tents, and food – and also things they loved, like pianos! Oxen pulled the heavy wagons, but the adults and children usually walked or rode horses. The journey took between four and six months.

Louisa, age 14

Louisa Evans made the journey with her parents and two brothers, Samuel and Jesse. These are extracts from her diary.

<u>April 8, 1850</u>

I got up at 5:30 a.m. with Mother, and we made johnnycakes for breakfast. Then we cleaned up the wagon and we left at 7 a.m. We didn't stop until 5 p.m. After dinner, Samuel played his violin, and we sang songs and danced. It was a warm, dry day.

<u>May 1, 1850</u>

Last night it was cold and rainy, and my clothes got wet. I didn't sleep well, and I felt tired all day. It wasn't easy to walk on the muddy ground. We didn't travel far today, and we faced a new challenge: a river. It was high because of the rain and it looked dangerous. Did we cross it? Yes, we did. We found a shallow part and walked across. We were lucky, but other people weren't.

Watch video 2.2
How did she travel?
What happened on the way back?

GRAMMAR IN ACTION
Simple Past

	Other Verbs	To Be	
	I/You/He/She/It/We/They	I/He/She/It	You/We/They
+	I **got up** at 5:30 a.m.	It **was** cold and rainy.	We [4] ________ lucky.
–	We **didn't stop** until 5 p.m.	It [2] ________ easy to walk.	Other people **weren't** lucky.
?	**Did** we cross it? Yes, we [1] did . / No, we **didn't**.	**Was it** a hot day? Yes, it [3] ________ . / No, it **wasn't**.	**Were** all the people lucky? Yes, they **were**. / No, they [5] ________ .

Pronunciation p141

1 **Complete the examples in the chart above. Use the text on page 24 to help you.**

2 **Rewrite the sentences in the simple past.**

1 More than 500,000 people leave the east coast.
More than 500,000 people left the east coast.

2 The journey takes between four and six months.
____

3 April 8 is a warm, dry day.
____

4 They don't stop until 5 p.m.
____

2.05 **3** **Complete the text with the simple past form of the verbs. Then listen and check.**

On September 6, 1620, 102 people [1] left (leave) England to travel 4,500 km to North America. They [2] ________ (not agree) with some of the religious views in Europe at that time, so they [3] ________ (decide) to start a new life.

They [4] ________ (travel) on a ship called the *Mayflower*, and the journey [5] ________ (take) 66 days. The first half of the journey [6] ________ (go) well. Then the weather [7] ________ (change), and it [8] ________ (be) very cold and stormy. People got sick and some of them [9] ________ (not survive).

In December, they [10] ________ (arrive) in Plymouth Bay. They [11] ________ (not know) anything about this new land, but the local Wampanoag people [12] ________ (help) them find food and build houses.

4 **Put the words in the correct order to make questions. Then ask and answer.**

1 last / your friends / you / see / Did / weekend / ?
Did you see your friends last weekend?

2 you / did / after school / What / yesterday / do / ?
____

3 night / Were / asleep / at 10:30 p.m. / last / you / ?
____

4 any homework / your English teacher / Did / last week / give / you / ?
____

5 Was / hot / yesterday / the weather / ?
____

Use It!

5 **Think of questions to interview Louisa or a person from the *Mayflower* about their journey. Use the ideas below or your own ideas.**

new friends | the challenges | the date
the food | the other people | the weather

6 **Take turns asking and answering your questions.**

When did you leave?

I left on April 2 with my family.

Finished? p119 Ex. 2

VOCABULARY AND LISTENING

Useful Objects

2.06 **1 Match the words with the pictures. Listen, check, and repeat.**

blanket	☐	hairbrush	☐	plate	☐
bowl	☐	knife	☐	scissors	☐
comb	☐	lamp	☐	spoon	☐
cup	☐	mirror	☐	toothbrush	☐
fork	1	pillow	☐		

2.07 **2 Listen. Write the objects the people are using.**

1 toothbrush
2 ______
3 ______
4 ______
5 ______
6 ______

LEARN TO LEARN

Categorizing

Recording new words in groups in your notebook can help you remember them.

3 Write the words in Exercise 1 in the chart. Can you add any more words?

Appearance	comb,
Bedtime	blanket,
Meals	bowl,

Use It!

4 Choose an object in Exercise 1. Ask questions to guess your partner's object.

Do you use it every day? *Yes, I do.*

A Radio Show

2.08 **5 Listen to an interview about a discovery from the Bronze Age. What can you see in the photo?**

2.08 **6 Listen again and complete the text.**

This is the Egtved Girl. She's [1] 3,000 years old. Archaeologists found her body in [2] ______, in Egtved, a small village in southern [3] ______. . . . We know she died in [4] ______ BCE when she was between 16 and [5] ______ years old. And we know she died in the [6] ______ because there were some summer flowers with her body.

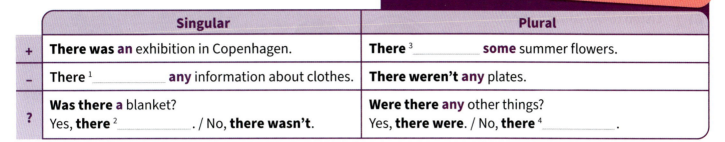

Watch video 2.3
Was the Viking Age peaceful?
Were there any coins in the exhibition?

GRAMMAR IN ACTION
There Was/Were

	Singular	Plural
+	**There was an** exhibition in Copenhagen.	**There** [3] ______ **some** summer flowers.
–	There [1] ______ **any** information about clothes.	**There weren't any** plates.
?	**Was there a** blanket? Yes, **there** [2] ______ . / No, **there wasn't**.	**Were there any** other things? Yes, **there were**. / No, **there** [4] ______ .

1 Complete the examples in the chart above with *was*, *wasn't*, *were*, or *weren't*.

Get It Right!

We use **some** and **any** with plural countable nouns and uncountable nouns.

some/any plates **NOT** ~~*some/any plate*~~
some/any information **NOT** ~~*an information*~~

2 Correct the sentences about the Egtved girl.

1 There wasn't an exhibition about the Egtved girl.
There was an exhibition about the Egtved girl.
2 There weren't any flowers with her body.
______
3 There weren't any useful objects with her body.
______
4 There was a hairbrush.
______
5 There weren't a lot of travelers in northern Europe.
______

3 Ask and answer about the information in Exercise 2.

Was there was an exhibition about the Egtved girl?

Yes, there was.

4 Circle the correct words.

1 There were *some* / *any* students at the talk.
2 There was *an* / *some* interesting exhibition last week.
3 There weren't *some* / *any* audio guides.
4 Was there *some* / *any* snow in the mountains?
5 There wasn't *a* / *any* documentary on TV last night.

5 Write and circle to complete the sentences. Then answer the quiz.

DID YOU KNOW ... ?

1 There were ✓ *some* / *any* humans in ... 250,000 years ago.
a Portugal b Africa
2 There ______ ✗ *a* / *an* alphabet with letters in ... society.
a Aztec b Roman
3 There ______ ✓ *some* / *any* university courses for students in ... in 1095.
a Paris b Oxford
4 There ______ ✗ *some* / *any* ... for eating food in ancient Greece.
a forks b knives
5 There ______ ✓ *a* / *some* famous Roman ... named Apicius.
a emperor b cook

6 Discuss your answers to the quiz. Then listen and check. 2.09

Use It!

7 In pairs, choose a photo from Units 1 and 2 and look at it for one minute. Close your books. What can you remember?

Were there any clouds in the sky?

Yes, there were. There were some white clouds.

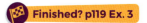

Finished? p119 Ex. 3

SPEAKING

Talking About Your Weekend

2.10 **1 Listen to the conversation. Why was Andy in the country?**

CARLA Hi Andy. ¹How was your weekend?

ANDY ²__________ OK, thanks.

CARLA What ³__________?

ANDY I went to the country for my grandpa's 70th birthday.

CARLA Cool! What ⁴__________ like?

ANDY It was cold, wet, and windy.

CARLA That's a shame. ⁵__________?

ANDY We stayed on my grandpa's farm.

CARLA What was it like?

ANDY Well, there wasn't any Wi-Fi, and there were a lot of noisy sheep outside.

CARLA Really?

ANDY Yes, really. That region has more sheep than people.

CARLA Wow. You learn something new every day!

ANDY What ⁶__________? What did you do?

CARLA Nothing much. I watched TV and made some cupcakes.

ANDY Sounds good!

2.10 **2 Complete the conversation with the phrases from the *Useful Language* box. Then listen and check.**

Useful Language

How was your weekend?
It was (OK/good/great/amazing/awful), thanks.
What about you?
What did you do?
What was the weather like?
Where did you stay?

3 Look at the *Everyday English* box. Find and underline the phrases in the conversation.

Watch video 2.4
Everyday English

Nothing much. Sounds good!
That's a shame.
You learn something new every day!

4 Which *Everyday English* phrase do we use to respond to …

1 negative news? __________
2 interesting facts? __________
3 positive news? __________
4 a question? __________

PLAN

5 Think about something you did in the past, and take notes.

Where you went: __________
What you did: __________
____
The weather: __________
Any problems you had: __________
____

SPEAK

6 Practice a conversation with your partner about what you did. Remember to use the simple past and *there was/were*, vocabulary from this unit, and phrases from the *Useful Language* and *Everyday English* boxes.

CHECK

7 Work with another pair. Listen to their conversation and take notes.

Where they went: __________
What they did: __________
____
The weather: __________
Any problems they had: __________
____

WRITING
An Account of a Journey

1 **Look at the photos. Where do you think the man wanted to go? Read the account and check your answer.**

A Difficult Journey

Fridtjof Nansen was a Norwegian explorer. He wanted to be the first person to reach the North Pole. He set off on June 24, 1893, from Oslo on a ship with 12 men.

At first, things went well, but by November, the weather was foggy and icy. The ship moved slowly through the ice for a year. Then Nansen and another man, Johansen, decided to cross the ice on skis.

The two men left the ship in March 1895, but there were a lot of problems. They couldn't reach the Pole and turned south. The weather was warm, so the ice melted, and it was difficult to travel. They built a shelter and waited there for eight months.

Finally, on June 17, a British explorer found them. They arrived home safely on August 13, 1896.

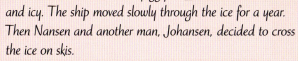

2 **Read the account again. Are the sentences *T* (true) or *F* (false)?**

1. Nansen left Norway in June 1893. ___
2. He started the journey on his own. ___
3. The weather was bad in November. ___
4. Nansen and Johansen didn't have any problems. ___
5. Nansen was the first person to reach the North Pole. ___
6. Nansen returned to Norway one year after he left. ___

3 **Read the phrases in the *Useful Language* box. In what order do they appear in the account?**

Useful Language

☐ At first, …	☐ (He) set off on …
☐ Finally, …	☐ There were a lot of problems.

4 **Put the sentences in the correct order (1–4).**

a ☐ Finally, we arrived back safely at 9 p.m.
b [1] We set off from home early one morning.
c ☐ At first, we made good progress.
d ☐ There were a lot of problems.

PLAN

5 **Plan an account of a journey. Take notes for four paragraphs.**

1. Who made the journey: ______
   When it started: ______
2. The first part of the journey: ______
   The weather: ______
3. How the journey continued: ______
   Any problems: ______
4. The end of the journey: ______

WRITE

6 **Write your account. Remember to include the simple past, *there was/were*, and phrases from the *Useful Language* box.**

CHECK

7 **Do you …**

- use the simple past to talk about the past?
- explain what the journey was like?
- put the events in the correct order?

Finished? p119 Ex. 4

HISTORY PROJECT

A Museum Display

1 Discuss the questions.

1 What museums do you know?
2 What can you see in them?
3 What makes a museum interesting?

2 Read the texts. Then read the sentences and write *S* (scissors), *M* (mirror), *L* (lamp), or *B* (bowl).

1 The way of making this object is the same today as it was in the 1600s. S
2 It's black, but you can see things in it. ___
3 Only rich people had objects like this. ___
4 This type of object first appeared in Egypt. ___
5 There was probably water in this. ___
6 This object had two uses. ___
7 It took a long time to find this object after a natural disaster. ___
8 This had connections with weather. ___

3 Read the texts again. Underline the information with the correct colors.

name of object year or time period
location material use

How to Give Feedback

2.11 **4 Read the tips about giving feedback. Then listen to the conversation. What kind of display are Sophie and Leo talking about?**

1 Read the text.
2 Talk about the things you like or find interesting.
3 Point out possible problems:
- Is any important information missing?
- Is the information in a logical order?
- Is anything unclear?

4 Make suggestions for improving the text.

2.11 **5 Listen again. Answer the questions.**

1 What event are they at?
___
2 Whose display did they like?
___
3 What did they like about it?
___
4 What information was missing?
___
5 How did Oliver respond to the feedback? What is he going to do?
___

USEFUL OBJECTS DISPLAY

SCISSORS, STEEL, AND IRON, 1628
Yi County, Anhui Province, China

The ancient Egyptians invented scissors, and today scissors are one of the most common objects in a home. This is one of the first pairs of scissors from Zhang Sijia's shop. Zhang Sijia opened the first scissors shop in China in 1628. He made all of the scissors by hand and followed the same 72 steps to make them. Customers bought the scissors to cut cloth, plants, and even metal. There is still a scissors factory in Hangzhou, China, and the workers use the same process today as in the 1600s.

SHAPE IT!

MIRROR, OBSIDIAN, AROUND 4,000 BCE
Çatalhöyük, South-Central Turkey

Archaeologists found this mirror in Çatalhöyük. It was one of the first cities in the world, and 8,000 people lived there. The mirror is made from a special black stone called obsidian, and it was one of the first mirrors in the world. People used these mirrors to look at themselves and also to look at the sun.

LAMP, BRONZE, 79 CE
Pompeii, Southern Italy

Archaeologists found this oil lamp in the ancient city of Pompeii in 1752, but it is much older than that. A volcanic eruption destroyed Pompeii in 79 CE. This oil lamp is in the shape of a dolphin, and it is made of bronze. Bronze objects were expensive, so this lamp probably belonged to a rich family. People needed oil lamps to light rooms and hallways at night.

TLALOC BOWL, TERRACOTTA, 3RD–8TH CENTURY
Veracruz, Mexico

This bowl was probably for holding water. The face shows one of the faces of the Aztec figure Tlaloc, from ancient Central Mexico. People believed he sent good rain when he was happy to help plants grow, and he sent bad rain and storms when he was unhappy.

PLAN

6 Work in groups. Choose four historical objects. Then complete the steps below.

- Decide on the object that each student will research.
- Research your object and write a short text to use in the display.
- Find a photo or draw a picture of your object.
- Read each other's texts and give feedback.
- Make any changes or improvements.
- Work in your group and make your display.

PRESENT

7 Put your display on your classroom wall. Remember to follow the tips in *How to Give Feedback*, and include correct facts, photos or pictures, and an attractive design.

CHECK

8 Look at your classmates' displays. Do they explain the four historical objects well? Give feedback to other groups on their displays.

2 REVIEW

VOCABULARY

1 Complete the sentences with the adjective form of the nouns in the box.

cloud	fog	ice	rain	storm	wind

1 I don't like it when it's ______ because it's dark and noisy.
2 It's dangerous to drive when it's ______ and you can't see well.
3 Take an umbrella. It's ______ today.
4 It's ______ outside. The trees are moving.
5 It's ______ today, so we can't sunbathe.
6 Watch out! It's ______ outside. Don't slip.

2 Complete the sentences.

1 I need a ______ to stir my drink.
2 I have a ______, so I can read in bed.
3 You can use a ______ or a ______ to make your hair look better.
4 Do you have any ______ to cut this paper?
5 I slept on my friend's sofa last night without a ______ or a ______!

GRAMMAR IN ACTION

3 Complete the text with the simple past.

Meriwether Lewis [1] ______ (want) to explore more of North America in the early 1800s. He and William Clark [2] ______ (leave) on May 14, 1804, to go to the west of Mississippi. It [3] ______ (not be) an easy journey. They [4] ______ (meet) a lot of people, but they [5] ______ (not speak) their language. At times, they [6] ______ (not have) enough food, and it [7] ______ (be) difficult to survive. After two years and more than 13,000 km, the men finally [8] ______ (complete) their journey in September 1806.

4 Complete the review with *there was(n't)* or *there were(n't)* and *a, an, some,* or *any*.

I went to my local museum last week.
✓ [1] ______ amazing exhibition about Egypt.
✓ [2] ______ amazing things to see, like bronze mirrors and beautiful necklaces.
✓ [3] ______ board game called Senet. It was so much fun to play.
✗ [4] ______ Egyptian mummies!
✗ [5] ______ café. I was hungry.
? [6] ______ good exhibitions in your town last week?

5 Complete the conversation with simple past verbs or *there was(n't)/were(n't)*. Circle *a, an, some,* or *any*.

CHLOE What [1] ______ you ______ (do) on the weekend?
MAX I [2] ______ (go) to my grandma's town. [3] ______ [4] *a / an* outdoor film festival.
CHLOE Cool! [5] ______ you ______ (watch) [6] *some / any* movies?
MAX Yes, I [7] ______. [8] ______ [9] *some / any* excellent movies, but the weather [10] ______ (be) rainy.
CHLOE Oh, no. When [11] ______ you ______ (get) home?
MAX This morning.
CHLOE You [12] ______ (not text) me.
MAX I know. [13] ______ [14] *a / any* problem with my phone.

Self-Assessment

I can talk about the weather.
I can talk about useful objects.
I can use the simple past.
I can use *there was/were*.

LEARN TO ... GUESS THE MEANING OF NEW WORDS

When you don't know a word, the beginning of the word, the end of the word, and the rest of the sentence can help you guess the meaning.

1 Circle the answer that is true for you. Compare and discuss your answer with a partner.

When I see a word I don't know, I usually ...

1 guess the meaning from the rest of the sentence.
2 see if I can understand part of the word.
3 ask the teacher what it means.
4 look in a dictionary.
5 write it in my notebook.

2 Read the text. Then tell your partner three things that surprise you.

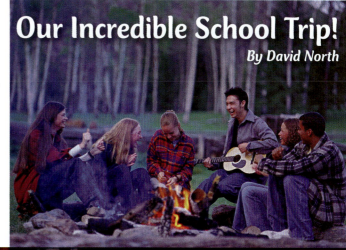

Our Incredible School Trip!

By David North

Last February, I went on a field trip to Oregon.

The weather was very **unusual** for that time of year. Normally, it's wet and windy, but it didn't rain once! It was a little cold, so we wore jackets or sweaters every day.

Our bus set off very early on the first day, at about 5:15 a.m. The campground was over 320 km away, and it took almost four hours. We couldn't take phones or tablets with us, so we chatted and played games instead.

When we saw the campground for the first time, we were really happy. There was a small store, and a room with table tennis and a TV. We hung out there in the evenings.

We did a lot of **enjoyable** activities. We went hiking and sailing, and I tried windsurfing for the first time. My favorite activity was survival skills. We collected wood in the forest, and then we built a small shelter. Clara and Ben saw some spiders and **ran away** – they hate things like spiders and bugs. In the evening, we cooked over a campfire. That night, we didn't sleep in a cabin. We slept in tents, and I shared a **tent** with my best friends.

It was an **unforgettable** experience, and I was very sad to leave.

SHAPE IT!

3 Read the text again. Discuss the questions about each of the words in bold with a partner. Take notes in your notebook.

1 Is the word a noun, verb, or adjective?
2 What clues about the meaning can you find in the text?
3 Do any parts of the word give you clues to the meaning?
4 What do you think the word means?

I think "unusual" is an adjective.

"Unusual" describes the weather. The text says "Normally it's wet and windy, but it didn't rain once!"

Yes. It starts with "un-" which means "not."

I think "unusual" means "not usual."

4 Check the meanings of the words in a dictionary or with your teacher. Did the questions in Exercise 3 help you guess correctly?

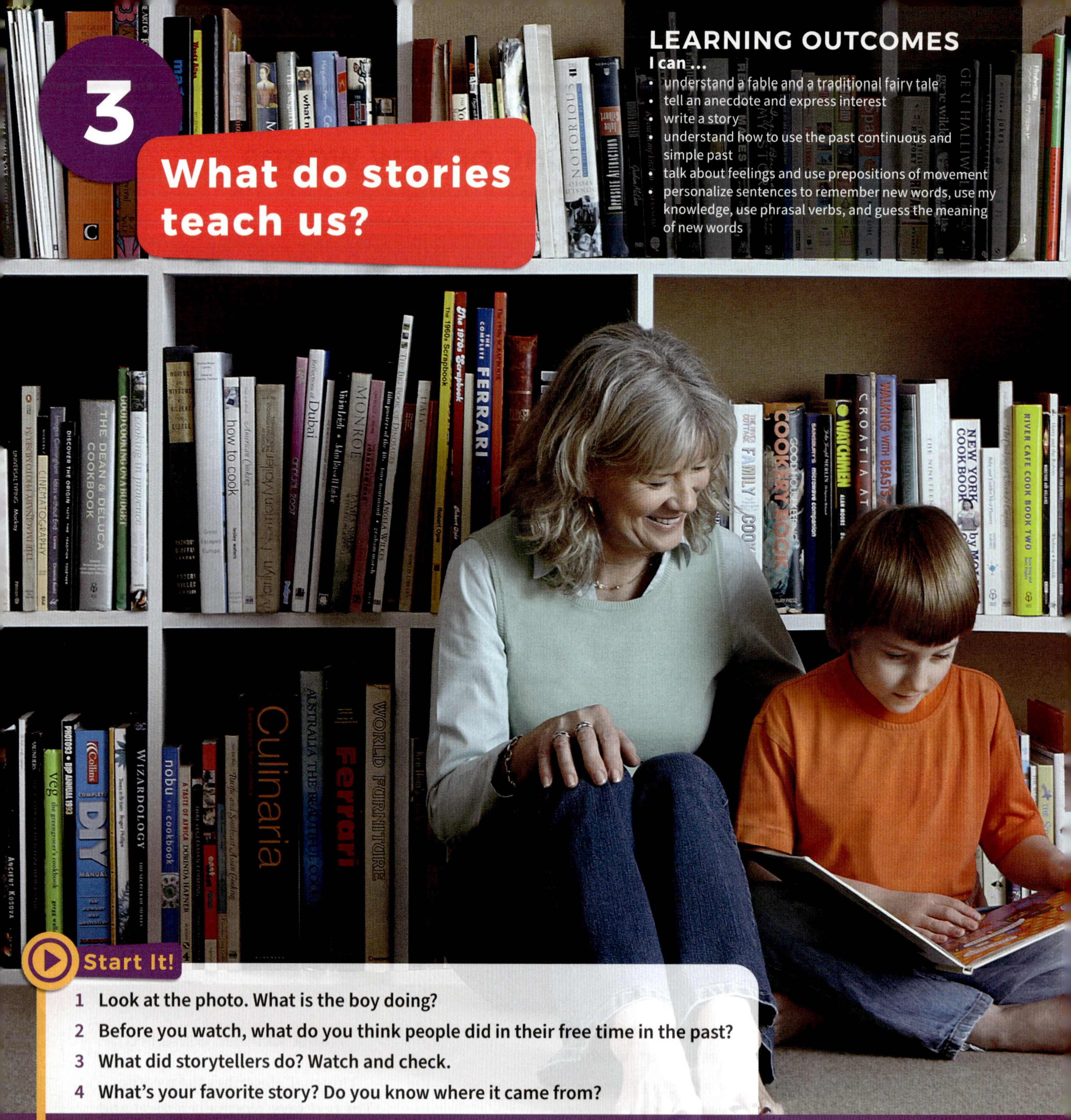

3 What do stories teach us?

LEARNING OUTCOMES

I can ...

- understand a fable and a traditional fairy tale
- tell an anecdote and express interest
- write a story
- understand how to use the past continuous and simple past
- talk about feelings and use prepositions of movement
- personalize sentences to remember new words, use my knowledge, use phrasal verbs, and guess the meaning of new words

Start It!

1 Look at the photo. What is the boy doing?

2 Before you watch, what do you think people did in their free time in the past?

3 What did storytellers do? Watch and check.

4 What's your favorite story? Do you know where it came from?

Watch video 3.1

p37

Grammar in Action 3.2

p39

Grammar in Action 3.3

p40

Everyday English 3.4

p42

Globetrotters 3.5

VOCABULARY
Adjectives of Feeling

3.01 **1 Circle the adjectives to describe the people in the photos. Listen, check, and repeat.**

1
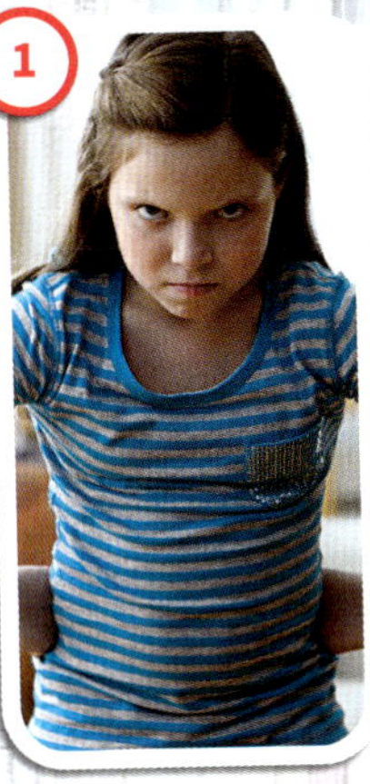
angry / bored

2

embarrassed / tired

3

surprised / worried

4

lonely / tired

5

afraid / upset

6

excited / nervous

Pronunciation p141

2 Complete the sentences with adjectives from Exercise 1.

1 Sam's ___afraid___ of dogs, so he doesn't want to walk through the park.

2 I felt so ____________ when I dropped the glasses. My face went red.

3 I'm ____________ about my exams. What should I do?

4 It's Ana's birthday! She's very ____________.

5 I'm ____________. This documentary isn't very interesting.

LEARN TO LEARN
Personalizing

You can write a sentence that is true for you to help you remember new words.

I often feel tired in the evening.

3 Write a personal sentence for six of the adjectives from Exercise 1.

1 ____________
2 ____________
3 ____________
4 ____________
5 ____________
6 ____________

4 Read your sentences aloud, but don't say the adjectives. Can your partner guess the adjectives?

I feel ... when I forget someone's name.

Embarrassed?

Use It!

5 Choose an adjective from Exercise 1 and tell your partner about a time when you felt like that. Ask questions to find out more.

I felt angry when my brother took my bike because he didn't ask me.

When did that happen?

Explore It!

Guess the correct answer.

If you have didaskaleinophobia, you are afraid of ...

a cheese. b spiders. c school.

Find another unusual thing people are afraid of. Then write a question for your partner to answer.

READING

A Fable

1 Read the introduction and discuss the questions.

1 What is special about fables?

2 Why do you think Aesop's stories are still important today?

Aesop's Fables

Aesop was a writer from ancient Greece. He wrote a lot of short stories called fables. Fables usually have a moral message. The main characters are often animals, but they act like humans.

3.04 **2 Read the fable. Circle the best title.**

a The Fox's Dance b The Monkey as King

One day, all the animals from the jungle were sitting in a circle. They felt excited because this was the day to choose their new king.

The animals took turns giving speeches about why they wanted to be king. When the fox was giving his speech, a lot of the other animals were getting bored, and they weren't listening. Then it was the monkey's turn, but he didn't give a speech. He danced, made silly faces, and made the other animals laugh. They decided to make the monkey king.

The fox knew it was a bad decision, and he was angry. The monkey didn't have the right qualities to be a good king. He decided to play a trick on the monkey. "I have a present for you!" he said. "Follow me." The monkey followed him. All the animals were watching.

As they were walking through the jungle, the fox pointed toward a tree. "Look at all those bananas!" he said. As the monkey was running to the tree, he fell into a trap. "Help! Help!" he shouted. He wasn't dancing now.

"How can the monkey take care of us and be our king?" asked the fox. "He can't even take care of himself." The animals realized that they were wrong. "You are our king now," they told the fox. "You are clever and you can protect us."

3 Find words in the story that mean:

1 a warm place with a lot of trees and other plants ________

2 not clever or sensible ________

3 something that people give you on a special occasion ________

4 a hole in the ground to catch animals or people ________

5 to keep people safe ________

4 EXAM Circle the correct answers.

1 What did the animals take turns doing?
- A giving speeches
- B telling jokes
- C looking for food

2 Who didn't give a speech?
- A the fox
- B the monkey
- C the bear

3 Why did the animals choose the monkey to be their king?
- A He danced and made them laugh.
- B He was the best animal.
- C He found food for them.

4 What happened at the end?
- A The fox gave bananas to the monkey.
- B The monkey played a trick on the animals.
- C The fox became the king.

Voice It!

5 Discuss the questions.

1 What is the moral of the story?

2 What do you think a good leader needs?

3 Which other fables do you know?

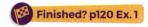

Finished? p120 Ex. 1

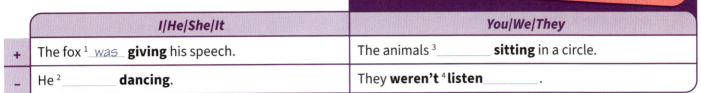

Watch video 3.2
Why was Sophia's first vlog bad?
How many people follow her?

GRAMMAR IN ACTION

Past Continuous: Affirmative and Negative

	I/He/She/It	You/We/They
+	The fox [1] was **giving** his speech.	The animals [3] ______ **sitting** in a circle.
–	He [2] ______ **dancing**.	They **weren't** [4] **listen**______.

1 **Complete the examples in the chart above. Use the story on page 36 to help you.**

2 **Complete the sentences with *was/were* or *wasn't/weren't*.**

1 The animals weren't standing in a circle. They were sitting.
2 The fox wasn't quiet. He ______ giving a speech.
3 The animals ______ watching each other. They were watching the fox and the monkey.
4 The monkey ______ walking to the tree. He was running.

3.05 **3** **Complete the story with the past continuous form of the verbs. Then listen and check.**

One day, a hare [1] was telling (tell) the other animals how fast he could run. At that moment, a tortoise [2] ______ (walk) past. He heard the hare, and he offered to race him.

The race began. At first, the hare [3] ______ (run) very fast and the tortoise [4] ______ (go) very slowly. The hare was soon near the end of the race. The other animals [5] ______ (not watch), so he decided to stop for a rest. He soon fell asleep. The tortoise continued to walk slowly while the hare [6] ______ (sleep).

Finally, just as the tortoise [7] ______ (finish) the race, the hare woke up. The tortoise was the winner!

The moral of the story is: don't be too sure that something is easy. Sometimes things are more difficult than you think.

4 **Complete the sentences with the past continuous form of the verbs in the box.**

make	not live	not work	
~~read~~	take	travel	watch

1 At 9 p.m. last night, I was reading a book.
2 Leo ______ selfies this morning.
3 Esma ______ a cake when I called.
4 My parents ______ at 10 p.m. last night. They ______ TV.
5 Sandra ______ at home this time last year. She ______ around the world!

Use It!

5 **Think of true sentences about things you were doing at these times. Use the activities in the box or your own ideas.**

at … o'clock yesterday morning/afternoon/evening
at … o'clock last Monday/Tuesday
this time two days/months/years ago
this time last week/month/year

chat with friends   do my homework   get up
go to bed   have breakfast/lunch/dinner
play basketball / computer games
walk home / to school   sleep

6 **Compare your sentences with a partner.**

At eight o'clock yesterday morning, I was walking to school. What about you?

I wasn't walking to school. I was brushing my teeth.

Finished? p120 Ex. 2

VOCABULARY AND LISTENING

Prepositions of Movement

3.06 **1 Match the prepositions with the pictures. Listen, check, and repeat.**

across	☐	into	☐	past	☐
along	☐	off	☐	through	☐
between	☐	out of	☐	under	☐
down	1	over	☐	up	☐

3.07 **2 (Circle) the correct prepositions. Then listen and check.**

1 Be careful! Don't fall *over* / *(down)* the stairs.
2 Who is that coming *out of* / *under* Bruno's house? Is it Carla?
3 Let's jump *into* / *up* the water together! Are you ready?
4 Don't cross the road *through* / *between* those cars. It's dangerous.
5 Why don't we swim *across* / *off* the lake to the other side? It isn't far.
6 Laura walked *along* / *past* me without saying hello.

Use It!

3 In your notebook, write about your trip to school today using prepositions from Exercise 1. Compare with a partner.

First, I went out of my house. Then I walked down the street and over the bridge.

A Radio Phone-in

LEARN TO LEARN

Using your Knowledge

Before you listen, think about what you already know about the topic and words you might hear.

4 Look at the photos and think about words you might hear.

3.08 **5 Listen to Melissa's story. How many of your words from Exercise 4 do you hear?**

3.08 **6 Listen again and put the events in the correct order.**

a ☐ A boy fell into the lake in the park.
b ☐ A photographer was taking a photo of Clayton's wife.
c ☐ Clayton and his wife were in a park.
d 1 Clayton Cook got married.
e ☐ Clayton jumped into the water and rescued the boy.
f ☐ Some children started shouting.

7 Close your book. Take turns telling the story. Can you remember the events in order?

GRAMMAR IN ACTION
Past Continuous: Questions

Watch video 3.3
What were they doing in the country?
What was her sister holding?

I/He/She/It	You/We/They
Was he **wearing** his wedding clothes?	[3] ______ the children **standing** close to the lake?
Yes, he [1] ______. / No, he [2] ______.	Yes, they [4] ______. / No, they **weren't**.

1 **Complete the examples in the chart above.**

3.09 **2** **Write the conversations using the past continuous form of the verbs. Then listen and check.**

1 A you / TV at 8 p.m. last night? (watch)

Were you watching TV at 8 p.m. last night?

B ✓

Yes, I was.

2 A What / you / yesterday? (wear)

______

B jeans and a hoodie

______

3 A your brother / at 5 p.m. yesterday? (chat online)

______

B ✗ play basketball

______

4 A Where / Alice and her family / in 2017? (live)

______

B in Mexico City

______

Simple Past and Past Continuous

When Clayton **jumped** into the water, he [1] ______ (wear) his wedding clothes.
While the photographer [2] ______ (prepare) his camera, Clayton **noticed** three children.

3 **Complete the examples in the chart above with the correct form of the verbs in parentheses.**

Get It Right!

We can use **when**, **while**, and **as** + past continuous for a longer action in progress.

We use the simple past for a short action that interrupts a longer action in the past continuous.

simple past

past continuous

3.10 **4** **Complete the text with the simple past or past continuous. Then listen and check.**

I [1] was walking (walk) to the bus stop one afternoon when I [2] ______ (fall) down on the icy street. I [3] ______ (carry) a heavy bag with all my school things, and I [4] ______ (break) my glasses. I [5] ______ (feel) very embarrassed. Other people [6] ______ (wait) for the bus, but they [7] ______ (not help) me. However, one woman [8] ______ (pick up) my bag and glasses, and she [9] ______ (find) an empty seat for me. While I [10] ______ (sit) there, she [11] ______ (clean) my face and gave me some water. But when I [12] ______ (look) for her a few minutes later, there was no one there.

Use It!

5 **Work in pairs. Continue and finish the story below. Use the simple past and past continuous.**

While I was walking to school this morning, I saw …

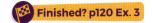

Finished? p120 Ex. 3

SPEAKING
Telling an Anecdote

3.11 **1 Listen to the conversation. Who is the story about, and what was the person doing?**

DAVID ¹Guess what happened yesterday.
LAURA No idea. What?
DAVID Well, it didn't happen to me. ² ______ Adrian.
LAURA Go on.
DAVID He was at the new shopping mall.
LAURA You're kidding! ³ ______ a shopping mall? He hates shopping.
DAVID He was looking for new sneakers.
LAURA ⁴ ______
DAVID Yes, really. Now please stop interrupting. While he was looking at the sneakers, someone bumped into him.
LAURA Who was it?
DAVID It was LeBron James!
LAURA No way! ⁵ ______
DAVID I know.
LAURA Did he take a photo?
DAVID No, he didn't. He was too embarrassed. Can you believe it?
LAURA What a great story!

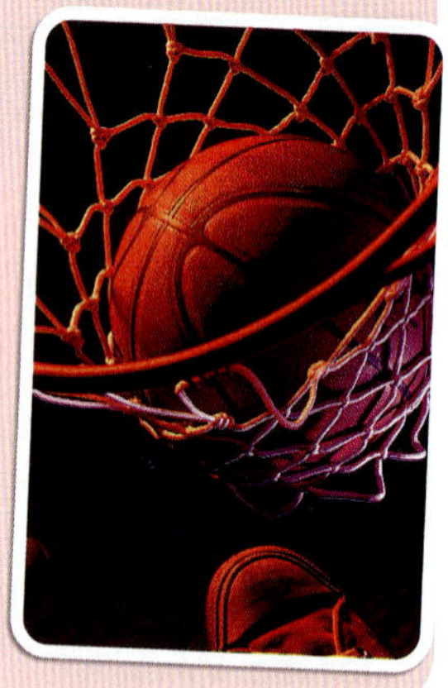

3.11 **2 Complete the conversation with the phrases from the *Useful Language* box. Then listen and check.**

Useful Language

Guess what happened (yesterday).
It happened to …
Really?
That's amazing/incredible!
What was (he) doing (at) … ?

3 Look at the *Everyday English* box. Find and underline the phrases in the conversation.

Watch video 3.4
Everyday English

Go on. No idea. What a great story! You're kidding!

4 Which *Everyday English* phrases do you use when you …

1 don't know? ______
2 hear something surprising? ______
3 want someone to continue? ______
4 liked someone's story? ______

PLAN

5 Think of something funny or unusual that happened, and take notes.

Who it happened to: ______
What the person was doing when it happened: ______
What happened: ______

SPEAK

6 Practice telling your anecdote to your partner. Remember to use the simple past and past continuous, vocabulary from this unit, and phrases from the *Useful Language* and *Everyday English* boxes.

CHECK

7 Work with another pair. Listen to one of their anecdotes and complete the notes.

Who the story happened to: ______
What the person was doing when it happened: ______
What happened: ______

WRITING
A Story

1 **Look at the photo. What do you think Alison's story is about? Read the story and check your answers.**

A Silly Story By Alison Dunmire

Last Sunday, I was feeling bored and decided to ride my bike. I went to the garage to get it, but it wasn't there! At first, I thought maybe it was in the yard. I was looking for it outside when Mom came out and said, "If you left it outside, maybe someone stole it." I was really angry.

The next day, while I was walking to school, I saw a bike exactly like mine in front of the supermarket. I didn't have time to investigate. In the afternoon, I was busy and forgot all about it. The next morning, the bike was still there! I took a look, and it was my bike – with my bike lock on it and everything!

Suddenly, I remembered! I was riding home last week when it started to rain, so I decided to leave my bike at the supermarket!

2 **Read the story again and answer the questions.**

1 When did the events in the story happen?

____

2 Where did Alison look for her bike?

____

____

3 Where was the bike?

____

4 Did someone steal it? What really happened?

____

____

____

3 **Complete the sentences in the *Useful Language* box with time and sequencing phrases from the story.**

Useful Language

1 ______________________, I was feeling bored.
2 ______________________, I thought it was outside.
3 ______________________, I saw a bike exactly like mine.
4 ______________________, I was busy and forgot all about it.
5 ______________________, the bike was still there!
6 ______________________, I remembered!

PLAN

4 **Plan a story about a time when something interesting, funny, or scary happened to you. Take notes for three paragraphs.**

1 What was happening before the main events started: ______________________________

____

What happened first: ______________________________

____

2 The main events of the story: ______________________________

____

____

3 What happened in the end: ______________________________

____

WRITE

5 **Write your story. Remember to include time and sequencing phrases, the simple past and past continuous, and vocabulary from this unit.**

CHECK

6 **Do you ...**

- use phrases from the *Useful Language* box?
- explain the main events?
- explain what happened in the end?

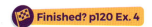

Finished? p120 Ex. 4

AROUND THE WORLD

READING

A Turkish Fairy Tale

1 **Look at the pictures. What is happening in each picture? What do you think the story is about?**

3.12 **2** **Read the fairy tale. Put the pictures in the order of the story.**

a ☐

b ☐

c ☐

3 **Read the fairy tale again. Answer the questions in your notebook.**

1 Why did the boy start his journey?
2 How did he feel when he started the journey?
3 What did the ogre try to do?
4 What did the boy do when he heard the people on the ship?

Globetrotters

Watch video 3.5
A Bee's Story

- Where are bees very busy?
- What is honey used for?
- Who did artists in the 18th century paint?

Voice It!

4 **Discuss the questions.**

1 How does the boy face fear in the story?
2 What causes fear? How can it affect your life?
3 How can fear be good?

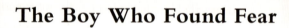

The Boy Who Found Fear

Once upon a time, a woman and her son lived in a small house in a forest. They didn't have any neighbors, and the lonely boy stayed at home with his mother every day.

One winter's evening, they were having dinner when a storm started. The wind blew the door open and the mother said, "Close the door. I feel fear."

"What is fear?" asked the boy.

"Fear is when you feel afraid," she replied.

"I don't understand. I want to find fear."

So the next morning, the boy set off confidently. While he was looking for fear, he met a lot of different people and he faced a lot of challenges. First, there was a group of robbers. They made him do dangerous and difficult things, but he wasn't afraid. He continued his journey.

LEARN TO LEARN

Phrasal Verbs

A phrasal verb is a verb + a small word like *for* or *on*. They have a special meaning that is different from the verb on its own.

5 Find phrasal verbs in the story that mean:

1 to start a journey ____________
2 to try to find ____________
3 to find by accident ____________
4 to arrive or reach ____________
5 to continue ____________

6 Complete the sentences with the phrasal verbs in Exercise 5.

1 Are we all ready to go? Let's ____________ now before it gets too hot.
2 A I don't think it's a good idea to ____________ in the dark.
  B OK. Let's camp here for the night.
3 Can you help me ____________ my phone? I don't know where it is.
4 A How long did it take you to ____________ the beach?
  B Ages! It was really far away.
5 While I was doing some research, I ____________ this photo of our street in 1885.

Next, he came across an angry ogre who tried to attack him, but the boy ran away. After that, he got to the ocean. There was a terrible storm, and he saw a ship in great danger. The people on the ship were terrified, and they were shouting for help, so he jumped into the water and saved them. He wasn't afraid at all.

He went on until finally he got to a city. There were people everywhere, and it was very busy. One man told the boy that the people were sad because their king was dead, but today they were choosing a new king. Just then, three beautiful doves flew down from a tower, and they sat on the boy's head. The people were excited. "This is the sign! You are our king!"

At that moment, he saw into the future: he was the king, he was trying to make everyone happy, but the people were angry. And he suddenly realized what fear was, and he was afraid.

Explore It!

Is the sentence *T* (true) or *F* (false)?

The story of *Cinderella* first appeared in a Chinese book around the year 850. ☐

Find another interesting fact about a fairy tale. Write a question for your partner to answer.

SHAPE IT!

CULTURE PROJECT

A Comic Strip

A comic strip uses words and pictures to tell a story. Make a comic strip using a traditional story from around the world.

Teacher's Resource Bank

3 REVIEW

VOCABULARY

1 Complete the sentences with the adjectives.

afraid	embarrassed	surprised	tired	upset

1 Elsa looks ________ and she's crying.
2 I can't believe I won! I'm really ________ .
3 My dad is ________ of heights. He hates being in very tall buildings.
4 I forgot David's birthday. I was so ________ !
5 I'm really ________ . I didn't sleep much.

2 Complete the story with the prepositions.

across	between	down	into	out of	through	under	up

Tiger the cat went [1] ________ the front door and walked [2] ________ the road [3] ________ two cars. He went [4] ________ the park and climbed [5] ________ a tree. Then a mouse appeared. "Lunch!" thought Tiger. He climbed [6] ________ the tree and followed it. The mouse ran [7] ________ the grass and then disappeared [8] ________ a rock. "Maybe I'll have lunch at home today," said Tiger.

GRAMMAR IN ACTION

3 What was happening at 10:30 a.m. yesterday? Write two sentences in the past continuous.

1 it / not snow – rain
____

2 I / not study – sleep
____

3 Alex / not read / a book – listen / to music
____
____

4 Eva and Helen / not talk – have / a snack
____
____

4 Write past continuous questions. Then match them with the answers (a–d).

1 you / wear / jeans / yesterday? ☐
____

2 Lidia / work / at 10 p.m. last night? ☐
____

3 where / they / go / last Saturday at 7 p.m.? ☐
____

4 what / I / do / an hour ago? ☐
____

a They were going to the movies.
b Yes, she was.
c You were taking photos.
d Yes, I was.

5 Complete the text with the simple past or past continuous form of the verbs.

Suzanne Collins [1] ________ (work) in television when she [2] ________ (meet) children's author James Proimos. After talking with him, she [3] ________ (decide) to try writing books, too. She [4] ________ (think) about the story of *Alice in Wonderland* when she [5] ________ (have) the idea for her first novel, *Gregor the Overlander*. She [6] ________ (want) to change Alice's story to a modern adventure, set in a city. The book was very successful, and she [7] ________ (write) four more books about Gregor. The series [8] ________ (win) a lot of prizes. While she [9] ________ (write) the series, she also [10] ________ (complete) a picture book for children. Now she is most famous for her *Hunger Games* books and movies.

Self-Assessment

I can use adjectives to talk about feelings.

I can use prepositions to talk about movement.

I can use the past continuous in sentences and questions.

I can use the simple past and past continuous together.

LEARN TO LEARN

LEARN TO ... GUESS THE MEANING OF NEW WORDS

You can help your partner learn vocabulary by writing sentences with missing words for them to guess.

1 Erin writes sentences with missing words for a friend to guess. Can you guess what the words are? Discuss with a partner.

OK, the first one. Is it an adjective?

Yes, it is.

Is it "happy"?

No. Try again!

1 I was ______ because my soccer team was winning.

2 The plane flew ______ the city.

3 The boy felt ______ when he called his teacher "Mom."

2 Choose five words from the box. Write five sentences with missing words like the sentences in Exercise 1.

between	bored	jungle	nervous	protect
surprised	tired	trap	under	worried

1

2

3

4

5

SHAPE IT!

3 Show your sentences to your partner. Can they guess the missing words?

4 Why is it a good idea to learn words in sentences? Discuss with your partner.

5 Close your book. Take turns saying the five words you chose in Exercise 2. Can your partner remember your sentences?

The word was "bored." What was the sentence?

"I feel bored when ... ." No, sorry, can you help me?

OK. It starts, "I was bored because ... ."

I remember! "I was bored because ..."

4

What do you value most?

LEARNING OUTCOMES

I can ...

- understand texts about money and caring jobs
- make and respond to requests
- write an opinion essay
- understand how to use *could*, comparative and superlative adjectives, *too*, *too much*, *too many*, and *(not) enough* + noun
- talk about money and caring jobs
- remember similar words, identify key information, and organize my homework
- reach agreement as a group and make a poster

Start It!

1 Look at the photo. How does the boy feel?
2 Before you watch, how do you help other people?
3 How can helping others be good for you? Watch and check.
4 Which of the ways to help in the video do you like best?

Watch video 4.1

p49

Grammar in Action 4.2

p51

Grammar in Action 4.3

p52

Everyday English 4.4

VOCABULARY
Money Verbs

1 **Look at the verbs in bold. Then match the sentences with the photos.**

1 Don't worry. I can **pay** for you, too. [g]

2 He **spends** all his money on video games. He should **save** it for something he needs. [ ]

3 Friendships don't **cost** money. They're free! [ ]

4 I want to **earn** money. Can I wash your car? [ ]

5 I **owe** my friend $50. I can **sell** my bike. [ ]

6 **A** Could you **lend** me some money?

B How much do you want to **borrow**? [ ]

7 I want to **change** this money, please. [ ]

4.01 **2** **Listen to the verbs in Exercise 1 and repeat.**

4.02 **3** **Listen and write the correct verb from Exercise 1 for each situation. Sometimes there is more than one possible answer.**

1 ___pay___

2 ________

3 ________

4 ________

5 ________

LEARN TO LEARN
Similar Words

Many words have similar meanings. Think of ways to help you understand the differences.

You lend money to someone (it's yours).
You borrow money from someone (it isn't yours).

4 **Look at these pairs of verbs. Think of more ways to remember the different meanings.**

spend / buy   earn / win

5 **Compare with a partner. How does your partner remember the meanings?**

Use It!

6 **Complete the sentences in your notebook with your own ideas. Tell your partner.**

1 A good way to earn money is to …

2 The last time I borrowed money was …

3 I spend most of my money on …

Explore It!

Is the sentence *T* (true) or *F* (false)?

In Zimbabwe, there was a $100 trillion bill. At that time, bread cost $300 billion. [ ]

Find another interesting fact about money. Then write a question for your partner.

READING

A Newspaper Article

1 **Look at the photos. What do you think the man did?**

2 **Skim the article and choose the correct summary.**

a A man sold his home and bought an RV to travel around the world for three years.

b A man lived without money for three years.

4.03 **3** **Read the article and answer the questions.**

1 Where did Mark live after he sold his own home?

2 How did he use his laptop without electricity?

3 Which three things were difficult for him at first?

4 What did he buy after his time without money?

Voice It!

4 **Imagine you can interview Mark Boyle after his three years without money. Write questions to ask him using the ideas below.**

Family and friends:

Clothes:

Food:

Work:

Travel:

5 **Take turns being Mark Boyle and the interviewer and do the interview.**

How often did you see your family?

When did you see your friends?

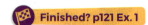

Finished? p121 Ex. 1

A Different Life

Can you imagine living for a day without money? Mark Boyle, from Ireland, did that for three years.

Mark had a good job and he earned a lot of money. One day, a friend challenged him to live without money. Mark decided he could change his life and do it.

First, he sold his houseboat, and he went to live in an RV on a farm. He kept his laptop and cell phone – he knew he could use solar power to charge them. He couldn't make any calls, but he could receive them.

The first few months were the worst – simple things were more difficult than before. Mark couldn't buy food, take a shower, or travel easily. But he soon found his own food – usually vegetables, fruit, and other plants. He made a stove to cook outside, and he collected wood to use as fuel. He washed in a river, and he used plants to clean himself. He even made his own toothpaste! He walked or cycled everywhere, so he was fitter and healthier than he was before.

So, was life without money better for Mark than life with money? Yes, it was. He was happier than before, and the best thing was that he felt

more alive. He also discovered that friendship is more important than money.

The biggest and most difficult decision for Mark was to return to a life with money. After three years without money, what was the first thing he bought? A pair of sneakers from a thrift store!

GRAMMAR IN ACTION

Could

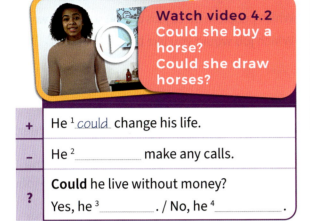

Watch video 4.2
Could she buy a horse?
Could she draw horses?

+	He [1] could change his life.
–	He [2] ________ make any calls.
?	**Could** he live without money? Yes, he [3] ________ . / No, he [4] ________ .

1 **Complete the examples in the chart. Use the article on page 48 to help you.**

2 **Complete the sentences with *could* or *couldn't* and the verbs in parentheses. Check your answers in the article.**

1 Mark could receive calls on his phone. (receive)
2 He ________ food. (buy)
3 He ________ his laptop with solar power. (charge)
4 He ________ a shower. (take)

Use It!

3 **Complete the sentences. Use *could* or *couldn't* and the ideas in the box.**

buy my own clothes make my own lunch ride a bike use a laptop

1 When I was five, I ________
____
2 When my grandparents were young, they ________
____
3 A year ago, I ________
____

4 **Ask and answer with a partner.**

Could you buy your own clothes when you were five?

Comparative and Superlative Adjectives

	Adjective	Comparative	Superlative
Short Adjective	fit	[1] fitter	the fittest
	happy	[2] ________	the happiest
Long Adjective	important	[3] ________	the most important
	difficult	[4] ________	the most difficult
Irregular Adjective	good	[5] ________	the best
	bad	worse	[6] ________

5 **Complete the examples in the chart above. Use the article on page 48 to help you.**

Get It Right!

We use **than**, not **that**, to compare two things.
My sister is fitter than me. **NOT** ~~My sister is fitter that me.~~

6 **Complete the sentences with the comparative or superlative form of the adjectives.**

1 Life for Mark without money was better (good) than before.
2 ________ (good) thing was that he felt more alive.
3 ________ (difficult) decision was to return to a life with money.

4.04 **7** **Complete the text with the comparative or superlative form of the adjectives. Then listen and check.**

It's the fourth Friday in November and it's Black Friday. It's [1]the busiest (busy) shopping day of the year. Things are [2] ________ (cheap) than usual today. Shoppers can get [3] ________ (good) prices for [4] ________ (late) gadgets or [5] ________ (stylish) sneakers. In my opinion, Black Friday is [6] ________ (bad) day of the year. People seem to be [7] ________ (interested) in shopping than anything else! I think we could all be [8] ________ (happy) without spending money all the time.

Use It!

8 **Choose a topic from the box or use your own. Discuss with a partner. Use comparatives and superlatives.**

math / history / science market / shopping mall / online shopping

History is more difficult than … but … is the most difficult.

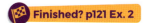

Finished? p121 Ex. 2

VOCABULARY AND LISTENING
Caring Jobs

4.05 **1 Match eight jobs with the photos. Circle the jobs that aren't in the photos. Listen, check, and repeat.**

caregiver	☐	paramedic	☐
firefighter	☐	police officer	☐
garbage collector	☐	preschool teacher	☐
lawyer	☐	surgeon	☐
lifeguard	☐	vet	1
nurse	☐	volunteer	☐

1
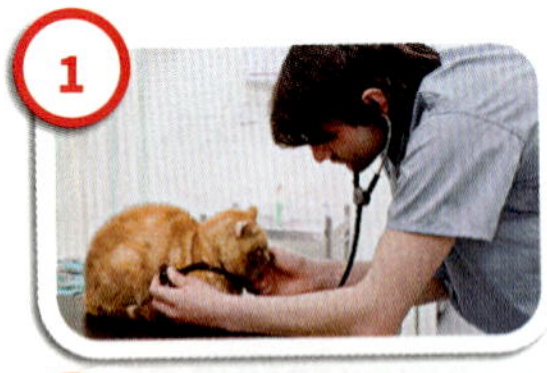
2

3

4

5

6
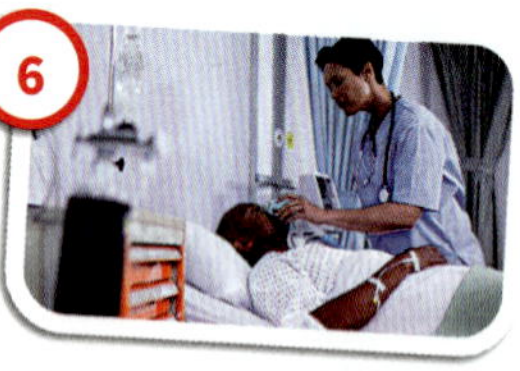
7

8
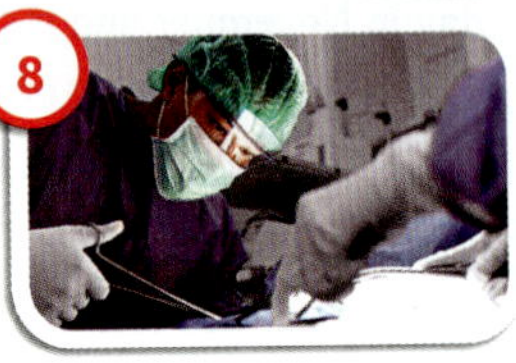

Pronunciation p141

2 Write which person you need in these situations.

1 You're at the swimming pool. Your friend has a problem. lifeguard
2 There's a fire at your school. ______
3 Your grandma needs help at home. ______
4 Your cat has a problem with its eye. ______
5 Your friend is in the hospital. This person is doing an operation on them. ______

Use It!

3 Work with a partner. Discuss the questions.

1 What do the jobs in Exercise 1 have in common?
2 Which people in these jobs do you see every week?
3 Which job would you like to do?

Job Profiles

4 What do you think are the best and worst things about doing a caring job? Discuss with a partner.

4.08 **5 EXAM Listen to the job profiles and match the speakers with their jobs. There are two extra jobs.**

Speaker 1 ___
Speaker 2 ___
Speaker 3 ___
Speaker 4 ___

a lifeguard
b paramedic
c volunteer
d nurse
e vet
f lawyer

LEARN TO LEARN
Identifying Key Information

When you are matching people with information, check key words before you listen. This helps you to focus on the information you need.

6 Read the questions in Exercise 7. Circle the key words you need to listen for.

4.08 **7 Listen again. Write *1*, *2*, *3*, or *4*.**

Who …

a usually takes care of dogs and cats? ___
b wants people to follow rules? ___
c collects clothing and blankets? ___
d drives an ambulance? ___
e only works during the summer? ___
f serves meals to people? ___

8 Imagine you have one of the jobs in Exercise 1. In your notebook, write five sentences about your day. Read your sentences aloud, but don't say the job. Can your partner guess?

I sometimes work all night.

Are you a nurse?

Watch video 4.3
Say three reasons why some people don't volunteer.
How does volunteering help the vlogger at school?

GRAMMAR IN ACTION
Too, Too Much, Too Many

Too + Adjective	*Too Much* + Uncountable Noun	*Too Many* + Plural Countable Noun
I'm **too** [1] ________ to have lunch.	Some kids make **too much** [2] ________.	I have **too many** [3] ________.

1 **Complete the examples in the chart above with the words in the box.**

busy clothes noise

2 **Read the sentences about the people you listened to on page 50. Circle the correct words.**

1 The hours were (too) / *too much* / *too many* long in the paramedic's last job.
2 The volunteer thinks people own *too* / *too much* / *too many* books.
3 Sometimes the pool is *too* / *too much* / *too many* noisy for the lifeguard.
4 The vet spends *too* / *too much* / *too many* time at work.

3 **Complete the questionnaire with *too*, *too much*, or *too many*.**

All About You!

Do you have …
1 too much homework this week?
2 ________ clothes?

Do you …
3 spend ________ money on clothes?
4 buy ________ snacks?

Are you …
5 ________ busy to listen to your friends?
6 ________ young to drive a car?

Use It!

4 **Work with a partner. Ask and answer the questions in Exercise 3.**

(Not) Enough + Noun

I can't volunteer. I don't have [1] ________ ________ (time).	He can invite 20 people. He has [2] ________ ________ (chairs).

5 **Complete the examples in the chart above with the words in parentheses and *enough*.**

6 4.09 **Complete the text with the words in the box. Then listen and check.**

enough chairs enough space enough time too many animals too many people too much information too noisy ~~too young~~

I'm [1] too young to have a full-time job, but every Saturday I'm a volunteer with a local vet. I help the receptionist when she doesn't have [2] ________ to do everything. Last week, there were [3] ________ in the waiting room – we didn't have [4] ________ for them to sit on! Sometimes it gets [5] ________ for me, especially when there are [6] ________ and there isn't [7] ________ in the waiting room.

The best thing: I love animals and I can spend all day with them! 🙂

The worst thing: Sometimes there's [8] ________ for me, and I don't understand it all.

Use It!

7 **Imagine a day doing your dream job. Take notes. Then compare with a partner.**

- What the job is: ________
- The best thing: ________
- The worst thing: ________

My dream job is to be a firefighter. It's an exciting job, but it can be dangerous.

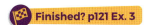

Finished? p121 Ex. 3

SPEAKING
Making Requests

4.10 **1 Listen to the conversation. Who lends Rita some money?**

BILLY Hey, Rita. What's up? You look worried.

RITA I am. [1] Could you do me a favor ?

BILLY [2] ______________. What do you need?

RITA [3] ______________ lending me $20?

BILLY Oh. [4] ______________. I spent too much money on the weekend.

RITA OK, no problem. What about you, Greg?

GREG Maybe. What's it for?

RITA I want to buy a bag for Maisie's birthday. There's a really cute one that I want to get her, but I don't have enough money.

GREG When's her birthday?

RITA Yesterday! Please, Greg.

GREG [5] ______________, since you asked so nicely. There you go.

RITA Thanks, Greg. You're the best! I owe you one.

GREG Actually, you owe me 20!

4.10 **2 Complete the conversation with the phrases from the *Useful Language* box. Then listen and check.**

Useful Language

Could you do me a favor?
I'm sorry, I can't.
It depends.
Sure.
Would you mind …ing … ?

3 Look at the *Everyday English* box. Find and underline the phrases in the conversation.

Watch video 4.4
Everyday English

cute   I owe you one.
There you go.   What's up?

4 Complete the conversations with the *Everyday English* phrases.

1 A ______________, Kate?
B I need a favor.

2 A Thanks for paying. ______________.
B Any time.

3 A Can I borrow your phone for a second?
B Sure. ______________.

4 Look at that little dog! It's so ______________.

PLAN

5 Work in groups of three. One person wants to borrow something. One friend can't lend it, but the other can. Take notes.

What the person wants to borrow and why:
____
____

Why one friend can't lend it: ______________
____
____

SPEAK

6 Practice a conversation making requests in your group. Remember to use (*not*) *enough* and *too*, *too much*, *too many*, vocabulary from this unit, and phrases from the *Useful Language* and *Everyday English* boxes.

CHECK

7 Work with another group. Listen to their conversation and complete the notes.

What the person wanted to borrow and why:
____
____

Why one friend couldn't lend it: ______________
____

WRITING
An Opinion Essay

1 **Read Min-Seo's essay. Does she agree with the statement?**

Professional sports stars earn too much money. Do you agree?

By Lim Min-Seo

1 *Nowadays, sports stars can earn a lot of money. Some basketball players earn more than $40 million every year. In my opinion, this is too much.*

2 *First of all, sports stars work less than other people. They only entertain people for a short time each week. Also, they have long vacations.*

3 *Personally, I think that other jobs are more important. For example, nurses, like my dad, save lives. I also think it's easier to live without sports or sports stars than to live without nurses and firefighters.*

4 *In conclusion, I believe that some sports stars earn too much money, and people with important life-saving jobs don't earn enough. We need to find a better and fairer way to pay those people more.*

2 **Circle the correct words.**

1 According to Min-Seo, sports stars earn *enough* / *too much* money.

2 Min-Seo thinks sports stars *help* / *entertain* people.

3 In Min-Seo's opinion, sports stars have *more* / *less* important jobs than firefighters.

4 It is *easier* / *more difficult* to live without nurses than without sports stars.

5 People with life-saving jobs *don't earn enough* / *earn too much* money.

3 **Complete the phrases in the *Useful Language* box.**

Useful Language

1 __________ opinion,
2 __________ of all,
3 __________, I think (that)
4 In __________,
5 I __________ (that)

4 **Put the words in the correct order.**

1 need / less / think / Personally, /we / homework / I / that __________

2 students / homework / In / too much / have / opinion, / my __________

3 work / all, / enough / in class / do / we / of / First __________

PLAN

5 **Plan your own opinion essay. Choose one of these topics and take notes for four paragraphs in your notebook.**

- Pop stars earn too much money.
- Money can't buy happiness.

1 Introduce the topic and give your opinion.
2 Give a reason for your opinion.
3 Give a second reason.
4 Summarize your opinion.

WRITE

6 **Write your opinion essay. Remember to include (*not*) *enough* and *too*, *too much*, *too many*, and phrases from the *Useful Language* box.**

CHECK

7 **Do you ...**

- have four paragraphs?
- give reasons for your opinions?
- summarize your opinion at the end?

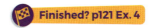

Finished? p121 Ex. 4

SOCIAL STUDIES PROJECT

A Poster

1 What is the purpose of the poster? Read and check (✓).

a to encourage more people to use a local park ☐

b to ask for more volunteers to clean the park ☐

c to tell people about a charity event ☐

2 Read the poster again. Under which heading can you find this information?

1 the place for the activity *Where?*

2 the type of activity ______

3 the people organizing the activity ______

4 the reasons it is a useful thing to do ______

5 the time and place to meet ______

6 why volunteers enjoy the activity ______

How to Agree as a Group

3 Read the tips on how to agree as a group. Put them in the best order.

a ☐ Ask other people for their opinions.

b ☐ Make a decision as a group. Check that everyone agrees.

c ☐ Introduce the decision you need to make.

d ☐ Give your own opinion politely.

e ☐ Interrupt politely if you want to comment.

f ☐ Summarize all the opinions.

4.11 **4 Listen to the students. Write *Y* (Yusuf), *L* (Lara), or *T* (Thiago).**

Who …

1 suggests ideas (two people)? ___ ___

2 interrupts politely? ___

3 asks other people for their opinion and summarizes the opinions? ___

Could you be a volunteer with us?

Do you have enough time to help us? All ages are welcome.

Don't give us your money – give us your time!

Together we can make our park better!

Your Community Needs You!

WHAT?

Help us to make the park a cleaner space for the whole community.

WHERE?

Greenhill Park

WHO?

We have a team of five volunteers, but there's too much work for us. We need more volunteers.

WHEN?

10 a.m. every Saturday.
Meet at the park café.

WHY?

It helps your community!
There aren't enough people using the park. We want more people to use it.

WHAT ARE THE BENEFITS?

We need only an hour of your time once a week.
You can get fitter and have fun.
It's one of the best ways to make new friends and make a difference!

PLAN

5 Work in groups. Plan a poster for a volunteer project. Follow the steps below.

- Choose one of these ideas for a volunteer project, or use your own idea.

> Teaching older people how to use the latest gadgets.
> Helping at an after-school or local sports club for younger students.
> Working in an animal shelter.

- Think of what you can say to inform and attract volunteers.
- Organize your material under headings.
- Add photos to create an attractive design.

PRESENT

6 Display your poster on your classroom wall. Remember to include photos and useful information for volunteers, and to follow the tips in *How to Agree as a Group*.

CHECK

7 Look at your classmates' posters. Would you like to work on their projects? Discuss in your group and then vote on the best poster.

4 REVIEW

VOCABULARY

1 Complete the conversations with the pairs of verbs in the box.

borrow / owe	pay / lend	spend / save	sell / earn

1 A Can you ________ me $5 for coffee?
  B Don't worry. I can ________ for yours.
2 A Those people ________ hats at the market.
  B Yes, but they don't ________ much money.
3 A Should I ________ my money for the future?
  B No! Why don't you ________ it now? Let's go shopping.
4 A Could I ________ some money for the bus?
  B Sure, but you now ________ me $5!

2 Read the descriptions and write the correct job.

1 I give my free time to help people. I don't earn any money, but I love my job. ________
2 I have a difficult job in a hospital. I'm not a normal doctor or a nurse. ________
3 I keep our community safe. I can arrest people who are breaking the law. ________
4 I treat very sick people at home and then take them to the hospital. ________

GRAMMAR IN ACTION

3 Complete the quiz with the comparative or superlative form of the adjectives. Then decide if the sentences are *T* (true) or *F* (false).

1 Basketball players are usually ________ than soccer players. (tall) ____
2 ________ place on Earth is in Antarctica. (dry) ____
3 Chris Hemsworth is ________ than Chris Evans. (old) ____
4 The Istanbul Cevahir shopping mall is ________ in the world. (big) ____
5 A hippo is ________ than a lion. (dangerous) ____
6 New York is ________ city to live in. (expensive) ____

4 Put the words in the correct order.

1 lifeguard / you're / too / be / young / to / a
____
2 a / money / I / soda / to / don't / have / enough / buy
____
3 room / there / too / people / were / the / many / in
____
4 much / week / I / last / spent / too / money
____

5 Complete the blog with *too* + adjective, *too much* / *too many* or *enough*, or a comparative or superlative adjective.

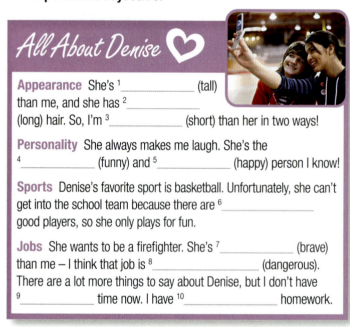

All About Denise

Appearance She's [1] ________ (tall) than me, and she has [2] ________ (long) hair. So, I'm [3] ________ (short) than her in two ways!

Personality She always makes me laugh. She's the [4] ________ (funny) and [5] ________ (happy) person I know!

Sports Denise's favorite sport is basketball. Unfortunately, she can't get into the school team because there are [6] ________ good players, so she only plays for fun.

Jobs She wants to be a firefighter. She's [7] ________ (brave) than me – I think that job is [8] ________ (dangerous). There are a lot more things to say about Denise, but I don't have [9] ________ time now. I have [10] ________ homework.

Self-Assessment

I can talk about money.

I can talk about caring jobs.

I can use *could* and *couldn't*.

I can use comparative and superlative adjectives.

I can use *too*, *too much*, *too many*, and (*not*) *enough*.

LEARN TO ... ORGANIZE YOUR HOMEWORK

When you organize your homework, you study and use your time better.

1 Do the quiz. Find out your score. Do you agree with what it says about you? Discuss the results with a partner.

Homework Superstar?

Knowing What to Do

When your teacher gives you homework, do you …

a write it in your notebook or homework planner?
b write it on your hand?
c listen but then forget?

Organizing Your Time

When do you do your homework?

a After school or on the weekend.
b Sometimes after school, sometimes before.
c Always while I'm having breakfast!

Deciding What Comes First

You have too much homework and not enough time. Do you …

a do the most important things first?
b do the easiest things first?
c look at your books but never start?

Concentrating

While you're doing your homework, do you …

a put your phone on silent?
b try not to look at your phone?
c spend a lot of time checking your phone?

Results

a = 2 points **b** = 1 point **c** = 0 points

6–8: You're a superstar! You organize your homework well.
3–5: Not bad! You try to organize your homework, but our advice can help.
0–2: Oh, no! You really need our advice!

2 Complete Esma's homework planner with the words in the box.

difficult | first | For when? | Homework | hours | Notes | Other things | Subject

Date	[1] ______	[2] ______	[3] ______	[4] ______
Mon Feb. 11	English	Page 27, Exercise 4	Mon Feb. 18	🙂 Nice and easy!
Tues Feb. 12	Science	Label the parts of plants.	Thurs Feb. 14	It's [5] ______ – ask Jo for help.
Wed Feb. 13	History Math	Page 36 Study for the test.	Thurs Feb. 14 Fri Feb. 15	Do math [6] ______ – there's a LOT to study!
Thurs Feb. 14	English	Write story.	Tues Feb. 19	I need about two [7] ______.
Fri Feb. 15		No homework!		
[8] ______ : Remember Zoe's party on Saturday afternoon! 🙂				

SHAPE IT!

3 Copy Esma's design for a homework planner in your notebook , using the same headings. Then complete the planner with your homework for next week.

5 What is your dream house?

LEARNING OUTCOMES

I can ...

- understand texts about different homes and doing household chores
- describe a photograph
- write a description of a house
- understand how to use (*not*) *as* + adjective + *as*, (*not*) + adjective + *enough*, and *have to* / *don't have to*
- talk about furniture and household chores
- make spidergrams to record vocabulary, use techniques to answer multiple-choice questions, use word families, and a memory journey

Start It!

1 Look at the photo. Would you like to live in this house?

2 Before you watch, where do you live?

3 Why did people build homes in mountains? Watch and check.

4 What other unusual homes are there?

Watch video 5.1

p61

Grammar in Action 5.2

p63

Grammar in Action 5.3

p64

Everyday English 5.4

p66

Globetrotters 5.5

VOCABULARY

Furniture

5.01 **1** **Match the words in the box with 1–13 in the pictures. Listen, check, and repeat.**

armchair	☐	floor	☐
bookcase	☐	fridge	☐
carpet	☐	picture	☐
ceiling	1	shelves	☐
chest of drawers	☐	sink	☐
cupboard	☐	wardrobe	☐
desk	☐		

5.02 **2** **Listen and match the speakers (1–4) with the rooms in the box. There is one extra room.**

bathroom	☐	kitchen	☐	study	☐
bedroom	☐	living room	☐		

5.02 **3** **Listen again and circle the words in Exercise 1 that you hear.**

LEARN TO LEARN

Using Spidergrams

Recording words in different ways will help you remember them. One way is to create spidergrams.

4 **Complete the spidergram using words from Exercises 1 and 2 and your own ideas.**

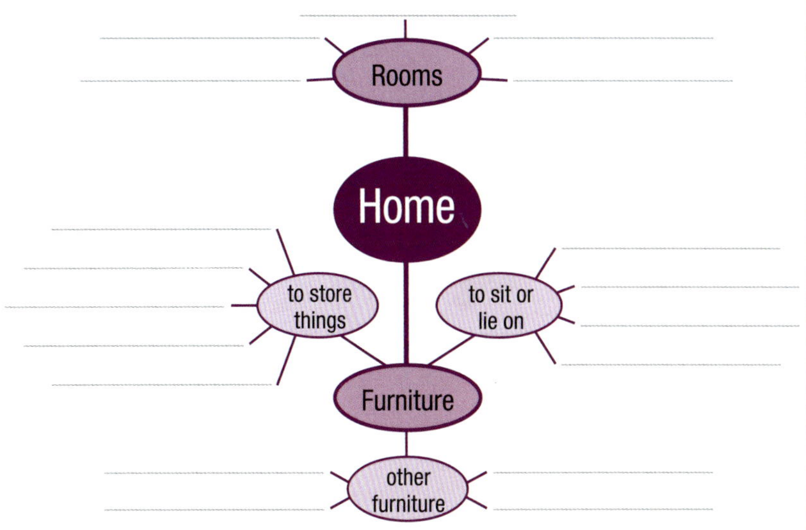

Use It!

5 **Describe the furniture in a room in your home. Your partner listens and draws the room.**

My bedroom has a wardrobe, a chest of drawers, and two pictures on the wall ...

Explore It!

Guess the correct answer.

The oldest bookcases in the world are ... years old.

a 200 **b** 400 **c** 600

Find another interesting fact about furniture. Then write a question for your partner.

READING
A Magazine Article

1 Look at the pictures. Discuss the questions.

1 What's unusual about these homes?

2 Who do you think lives in them?

5.03 **2 Read the article. Match the pictures with the houses.**

Amazing Homes

Everyone's home is special, but some homes are really amazing...

Keret House, Poland

A Polish architect designed this house for an Israeli author. [1]**It**'s in a space between two apartment buildings in Warsaw. To enter the house, you climb through a trap door in the floor of the living room. The living room is wide enough for a small sofa, but the back of the house is only as wide as a large armchair! There's a tiny bathroom upstairs and a tiny kitchen with a sink and a fridge ... but you need to stand in another room to open [2]**it**!

Nautilus House, Mexico

Nautilus House isn't as tiny as Keret House, but it's also very strange. Its owners – a Mexican couple and their two children – thought ordinary houses weren't close enough to nature. [3]**They** wanted their home to feel like a beautiful, colorful shell. Everything in Nautilus House is curved: the floors, the ceilings, and, of course, all the furniture.

The PAS House, U.S.A.

Lots of kids love skateboarding, but not many kids are as crazy about [4]**it** as Pierre André Senizergues. Senizergues learned to skateboard at school in France and later became the world champion. He designed the PAS House as a dream home for skateboarders. You can skate in every room. You can even skate on the furniture [5]**there**, and your mom won't yell at you!

3 Read the article again and correct the sentences.

1 The entrance to Keret House is through the kitchen.
The entrance to Keret House is through the living room.

2 Five people live in Nautilus House.

3 The rooms in Nautilus House have straight walls.

4 The PAS House is in France.

5 An architect had the idea for the PAS House.

4 Look at the words highlighted in the text. What do they refer to? Circle the correct answers.

1 a Polish architect / Keret House

2 the fridge / the sink

3 ordinary houses / the owners

4 the PAS house / skateboarding

5 the PAS House / France

5 Match the words with the definitions.

1 architect	a a home for a sea animal
2 author	b a door in the floor
3 apartment building	c a writer
4 trap door	d not straight
5 shell	e a building with homes in it
6 curved	f a person who designs buildings

Voice It!

6 Discuss the questions.

1 Which house do you like most?

2 Why do you like it?

3 Do you know any other unusual houses? Describe them.

Finished? p122 Ex. 1

Watch video 5.2
What's wrong with bedroom 1? Why does the vlogger prefer bedroom 3?

GRAMMAR IN ACTION

(Not) As ... As, (Not) ... Enough

	(Not) As + Adjective + *As*	*(Not)* Adjective + *Enough*
+	The back of the house is only [1] ___ (wide) a large armchair.	The living room is [3] ___ (wide) for a small sofa.
–	Nautilus House isn't / is not [2] ___ (tiny) Keret house.	They thought ordinary houses weren't / were not [4] ___ (close) to nature.

1 **Complete the examples in the chart above with *as ... as* or *enough* and the words in parentheses. Use the article on page 60 to help you.**

2 **Circle the correct words. Check your answers in the article on page 60.**

1 Keret House *is* / *isn't* as wide as other houses in Warsaw.
2 *It's* / *It's not* large enough for a kitchen.
3 The owners of Nautilus House think that straight walls *are* / *are not* as interesting as curved walls.

Get It Right!

We never put adjectives after **enough**.
I'm not tall enough. **NOT** ~~*I'm not enough tall.*~~

3 **Complete the sentences with *as ... as* or *enough* and the adjective in parentheses.**

1 My bedroom isn't *as big as* my sister's. (big)
2 I'm not ___ to reach the top shelf. (tall)
3 Is this sofa ___ for three people? (wide)
4 That phone is ___ a laptop! (expensive)

4 **Complete the second sentence so that it has the same meaning as the first. Use (*not*) *as ... as* or *enough* and the adjective in parentheses.**

1 We can't put a sofa in this small room.
This room *isn't large enough* for a sofa. (large)
2 My room is neater than my sister's room.
My sister's room ___ mine. (neat)
3 A microwave is quicker than a stove.
A stove ___ a microwave. (quick)
4 Enes is 18 now, so he can drive a car.
Enes ___ to drive a car. (old)

5.04 **5** **Complete the text using *as ... as* or *enough* and the adjectives in parentheses. Then listen and check.**

Kids' toys aren't cheap these days, but not many toys are [1] *as expensive as* (expensive) the Astolat Dollhouse Castle. It's [2] ___ (tall) a small Christmas tree and [3] ___ (heavy) a horse.

The castle was the idea of an American artist, Elaine Diehl, and it took 13 years to build. It isn't really a toy. It's a work of art, and it's [4] ___ (good) to be in a museum.

The furniture is [5] ___ (small) to fit in your hand, and it's [6] ___ (beautiful) the furniture in a real palace. The tiny sofas and beds are [7] ___ (soft) the real things. The books on the shelves aren't [8] ___ (large) to read, but they have real pages. One thing that isn't small is the price – over $8 million! Are you [9] ___ (rich) to buy it?

Use It!

6 **In your notebook, write one true sentence and one false sentence about places in the world with (*not*) *as ... as* or (*not*) *... enough*.**

The Amazon River is as long as the Nile River.

7 **Say your sentences. Can your partner guess which sentence is true?**

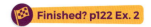

Finished? p122 Ex. 2

VOCABULARY AND LISTENING

Household Chores

5.05 **1 Match the phrases in the box with the pictures. Listen, check, and repeat.**

do the dishes	☐	make the bed	1
do the ironing	☐	mop the floor	☐
do the laundry	☐	sweep the floor	☐
dust (the furniture)	☐	vacuum (the carpet)	☐
load/empty the dishwasher	☐		

5.06 **2 Complete the note with verbs from Exercise 1. Then listen and check.**

Hi kids. Can you please help with some things around the house while I'm out?

Ollie: Please [1] mop the floor and [2] ________ the dishwasher with the plates and cups from breakfast. Can you also [3] ________ the furniture in the living room, please, and [4] ________ the carpet?

Mia: [5] ________ your bed and [6] ________ the floor in your bedroom. Then can you please [7] ________ the ironing for me?

Thanks, kids. I'll see you this evening. Love, Dad

Use It!

3 How often do you do the chores in Exercise 1? Compare with your partner.

I do the dishes every day!

Street Interviews

4 Look at the results of a survey in the UK. Does the information surprise you?

Do teenagers help with household chores?

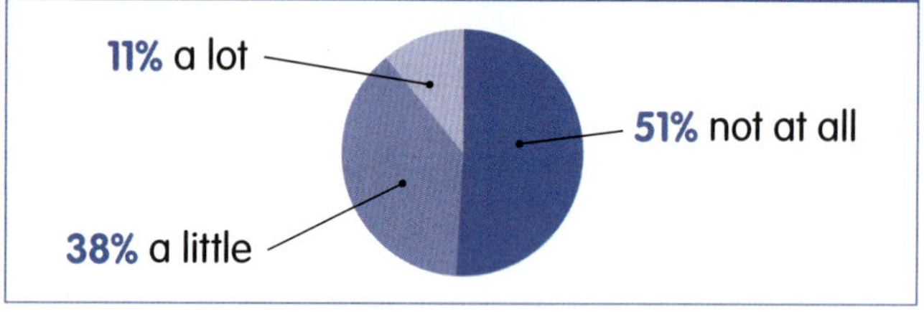

LEARN TO LEARN

Answering Multiple-Choice Questions

Before you listen, read the questions and options carefully, and try to guess the answers.

5 Read the questions in Exercise 6. Discuss with a partner which answers are probably wrong.

5.07 **6** EXAM **You will hear some people talk about doing chores. Listen and circle the correct answers.**

1 What does Cindy do in the kitchen?
   A She cooks dinner.
   B She loads the dishwasher.
   C She does the dishes.

2 When do Kim and her sister do household chores?
   A every morning B on the weekend
   C during school vacations

3 What doesn't Kim like?
   A cleaning the bathroom
   B vacuuming the living room
   C practicing the piano

4 When Adam does the ironing, what else does he like doing?
   A listening to music B moving around
   C doing his homework

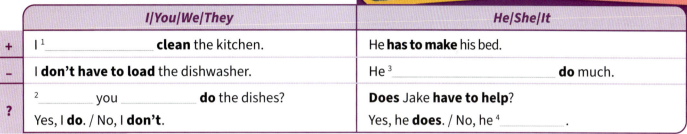

Watch video 5.3
How does Syd from Brazil help in the restaurant? What does Harumi have to clean?

GRAMMAR IN ACTION

Have To

	I/You/We/They	*He/She/It*
+	I [1] ______ **clean** the kitchen.	He **has to make** his bed.
–	I **don't have to load** the dishwasher.	He [3] ______ **do** much.
?	[2] ______ you ______ **do** the dishes? Yes, I **do**. / No, I **don't**.	**Does** Jake **have to help**? Yes, he **does**. / No, he [4] ______.

Pronunciation p141–142

1 **Complete the examples in the chart above with the correct form of *have to* / *don't have to*.**

2 **Complete the sentences with the correct form of *have to*.**

1 Cindy has to (+) clean the kitchen.
2 Kim and Maisie ______ (+) do a lot of homework.
3 They ______ (–) do housework on school days.
4 Jake ______ (–) help a lot.
5 Adam ______ (+) do the ironing.

3 **Circle the correct answer.**

1 I … do the gardening this weekend because my parents are on vacation.
a has to b doesn't have to c have to

2 … to do a lot of homework on weekends?
a Does you have b Do you has c Do you have

3 We … go to school on Monday because it's a national holiday.
a don't have to b have to c doesn't have to

4 Dad … do the cooking in the evenings because Mom works then.
a has to b doesn't have to c have to

4 **Complete the sentences with the correct form of *have to* and a verb from the box.**

do	help	~~go~~	work

1 The children don't have to go to school in summer.
2 Sam ______ with chores because he's only four.
3 I ______ the ironing on Saturdays, and it's so boring.
4 ______ your mom ______ on weekends?

5.10 **5** **Complete the text with the correct form of *have to* and the verbs in parentheses. Then listen and check.**

[1] Do you have to help (help) with the housework? [2] ______ you ______ (make) your bed or clean the kitchen? Martha Pinter and her brother, Ben, [3] ______ (do) more than most young people their age. They live on a farm in Queensland, Australia, and the whole family [4] ______ (share) the work. Martha [5] ______ (get up) early to milk the cows. In spring, she also [6] ______ (take) care of the new lambs – that's her favorite job. Ben [7] ______ (collect) the hens' eggs before breakfast. But Martha and Ben [8] ______ (not catch) the bus to school every day. There isn't a school near their farm, so they [9] ______ (have) all their lessons at home.

Use It!

6 **Think of questions to ask your partner using *have to*. Ask and answer your questions.**

Does your dad have to do the ironing on the weekend?

No, he doesn't. I have to do it!

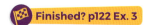

Finished? p122 Ex. 3

SPEAKING
Discussing a Photo

5.11 **1 Listen to the conversation. Who likes the room more, Oscar or Nina?**

OSCAR Hey, Nina. Look at this photo – it's Liam's bedroom in his new house.
NINA Oh! It looks big enough for two people. Does he have to share it?
OSCAR No, it's all his. Actually, it isn't as big as it looks. There's a large mirror in the [1] background, so it looks bigger.
NINA Oh, yes, I see. [2] __________ thing on the wall?
OSCAR It's a clock. What do you think of the color of the walls?
NINA Hmm. I'm not convinced.
OSCAR Really? I think it looks awesome! I don't think much of those curtains, though.
NINA: Me neither. And what's that [3] __________ the bottom? Is it a carpet?
OSCAR Yes, I think so. I like it. And I love those pictures [4] __________ the left.
NINA Me too. They look great.

5.11 **2 Complete the conversation with phrases from the *Useful Language* box. Then listen and check.**

Useful Language

at the bottom/top
on the left/right
in the background
What's that … ?

3 Look at the *Everyday English* box. Find and underline the phrases in the conversation.

Watch video 5.4
Everyday English

I'm not convinced.
It looks awesome!
Me neither.
Me too.

4 Match the phrases in the *Everyday English* box with the phrases that mean the same.

1 I feel the same way (after a positive statement). __________

2 I feel the same way (after a negative statement). __________

3 I don't think I like it. __________

4 It looks great. __________

PLAN

5 Write about a room. Take notes about the photo below or your own photo.

Who the room belongs to: __________

What is in it: __________

____

____

SPEAK

6 Practice discussing your room with your partner. Remember to use adjectives with (*not*) *as* … *as* and *enough*, *have to* / *don't have to*, vocabulary from this unit, and phrases from the *Useful Language* and *Everyday English* boxes.

CHECK

7 Work with another pair. Listen to their conversation and complete the notes.

Who the room belongs to: __________

What is in it: __________

____

____

WRITING
A Description of a House

1 **Look at the information about the competition and the photo. What can you guess about Olivia's dream house? Discuss with a partner.**

2 **Read Olivia's description of her dream house. Match the topics a–c with paragraphs 1–3.**

a What does the house have?

b Where is the house?

c What is the best thing about the house?

Describe Your Dream House and Win a Digital Camera!

1 ☐ I'd like to tell you about my dream house. It's near the beach on a sunny island. It has to be near the ocean because I love swimming.

2 ☐ The house has big windows and a fantastic view of the ocean. There's a lovely yard, too. It's large enough for people to play outdoor games, and it also has a swimming pool. As well as a pool, there's a skatepark. Inside the house, there's a huge fish tank. It's full of beautiful tropical fish.

3 ☐ But the really special thing about my house is the technology. There are robots in every room. I think they're as intelligent as humans. They cook the meals and do the dishes. They make my bed, and they vacuum the living room as well. I don't have to do any chores.

Olivia Reed (13), Newcastle

3 **Read the description again. Draw Olivia's house and yard in your notebook.**

4 **Find and underline the *Useful Language* phrases in the description. Answer the questions.**

1 Which go at the end of a sentence? ____________, ____________

2 Which goes before a noun? ____________

3 Which often goes before a verb? ____________

Useful Language

also as well as well as too

PLAN

5 **Plan a description of your own dream house. Take notes for three paragraphs.**

1 Where your house is: ____________________

____

2 What rooms, furniture, and other things it has: ____________________

____

____

3 What the best thing in the house is: ____________

____

WRITE

6 **Write your description. Remember to include adjectives with (*not*) *as ... as*, *enough*, *have to* / *don't have to*, and phrases from the *Useful Language* box.**

CHECK

7 **Do you ...**

- have three paragraphs?
- describe what the house has?
- describe one special thing in the house?

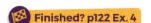

Finished? p122 Ex. 4

AROUND THE WORLD

READING
An Encyclopedia Entry

1 **Look at the photos of homes on page 67. Where are these homes? What do you know about them?**

5.12 **2** **Read the entry. Check your answers.**

3 **Read the entry again. Match headings a–e with paragraphs 1–5.**

a Why Use Igloos?
b Keeping Warm
c Who Are the Inuit?
d Life Inside an Igloo
e How to Build an Igloo

Globetrotters

Watch video 5.5 Living in a *Ger*

- What does "ger" mean in Mongolian?
- Would you like to live in a *ger*?

Voice It!

4 **Discuss the questions.**

1 Nomadic people have temporary houses, so "home" isn't a permanent building in a place. How else can people define "home"?
2 Besides your house, how do you define "home"?
3 How can you appreciate and celebrate your home?

LIFE IN AN INUIT IGLOO

1 ☐ The Inuit are the native people of the Arctic Circle. Today, they usually live in modern houses in small villages. Until recently, however, they still used their famous houses made of snow – igloos.

2 ☐ The Arctic isn't warm enough to farm, so the Inuit had a nomadic life. This means they traveled during the year to find food. Every winter and summer, the Inuit traveled thousands of kilometers across the frozen Arctic ocean. All nomads have to make temporary homes while they travel, and in summer, the Inuit lived in tents made from animal skins, called *tupiqs*. Igloos were their traditional winter homes.

3 ☐ Snow is a perfect material for building. It's as light as wood and easy to cut. The snow has to be dry and hard enough to make good blocks because wet snow doesn't have the strength an igloo needs. The Inuit make a dome shape by putting the snow blocks in a spiral. This is quick to build and creates a very strong structure.

4 ☐ The heat inside an igloo comes from people's bodies only, but this is warm enough to keep the igloo comfortable. This is because snow is a good insulator. In other words, it keeps the cold out and the warmth in. The entrance is a tunnel that goes under the walls. The heavy, cold air always stays in the tunnel and the light, warm air stays in the igloo.

5 ☐ Igloos don't have windows, but there are small holes in the walls. These let in clean air and let out dangerous smoke from the small oil lamps. Traditionally, the Inuit didn't have any furniture, but a platform of snow just below the ceiling provided a simple sofa and bed in the warmest part of the igloo. Inuit families spent all winter in small igloos with no furniture, no bathroom … and no Internet. Just imagine that!

LEARN TO LEARN

Word Families (2)

Many nouns have a related adjective. We usually form the related adjective or noun by adding extra letters. We sometimes need to change other letters, too.

Noun	Adjective	Extra Letters
beauty	beauti**ful**	-ful
tru**th**	true	-th

5 **Complete the chart. Use the encyclopedia entry to help you.**

Noun	tradition	2 ______	comfort	4 ______	danger
Adjective	1 traditional	strong	3 ______	warm	5 ______

6 **Complete the sentences with the correct form of the words in parentheses. Use the extra letters in the box.**

-ful -ic ~~-ly~~ -ous -th

1 My neighbor isn't very friendly. (friend)
2 Andy's room is full of photos of ______ people. (fame)
3 Nadir found a ______ website for his homework. (help)
4 Ava's yard is the ______ of a soccer field! (long)
5 My sister runs a lot. She's really ______. (athlete)

Explore It!

Guess the correct answer.

The Inuit live in Canada, Alaska, and …

a Iceland. **b** Greenland. **c** Norway.

Find three more interesting facts about the Inuit. Choose your favorite fact and write a question for your partner.

SHAPE IT!

CULTURE PROJECT

A Poster

A poster uses words and pictures to display information.

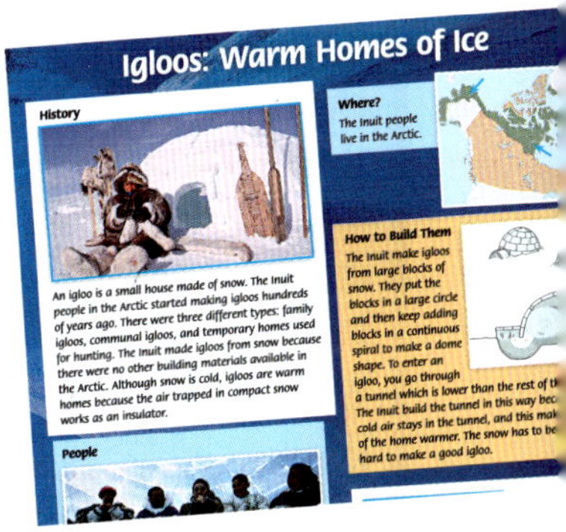

Teacher's Resource Bank

5 REVIEW

VOCABULARY

1 Complete the sentences.

1 The ________ on my walls are full of books.
2 This room needs some nice ________ on the walls.
3 Can you put this milk back in the ________ please?
4 I do all my homework at the kitchen table because I don't have a ________ in my room.
5 We painted the ________ blue. Look up!
6 There's a lovely, soft ________ on the floor.

2 Complete the "to do" list from John's mom.

- *Please clean your bedroom and make your* [1] ________  .
- *After breakfast, load the* [2] ________  .
- *Please do the* [3] ________  *, but don't do the* [4] ________  *! I'll do that when I get home.*

GRAMMAR IN ACTION

3 Complete Katy's email with *as … as* or *enough* and the adjective in parentheses.

Hi Lily,

I'm living in a new house. It isn't [1] ________ (large) our old one, but it's [2] ________ (big) for all of us, and we love it. We're in the middle of the country, but the nearest town is [3] ________ (close) to go shopping or to the movies. We have a big yard. It isn't [4] ________ (beautiful) yours, but I like it! Anyway, it's [5] ________ (good) for our pet rabbit. He's [6] ________ (happy) a baby, running around in the sunshine.

Write soon with your news.

Katy

4 Complete the conversation. Use the words in parentheses with *as … as*, *enough* or the correct form of *have to / don't have to*.

RENA Have you seen Bianca's new house? She told me it isn't [1] ________ (nice) her old one.

MIKE Really? The yard's amazing. It's [2] ________ (large) a soccer field!

RENA Wow!

MIKE Well maybe it's not that big. But it's [3] ________ (big) to play soccer, anyway.

RENA So why isn't she [4] ________ (happy) she was in her old house?

MIKE Because now she [5] ________ (share) her room with her little sister.

RENA I have a little sister, so I know how she feels! [6] ____ she still ________ (take) the bus to school?

MIKE No, her new house is [7] ________ (close) for her to walk. She and her sister are pleased because they [8] ________ (wake up) as early as before.

Self-Assessment

I can talk about rooms and furniture in a home.			
I can talk about household chores.			
I can use (*not*) *as* + adjective + *as*.			
I can use (*not*) adjective + *enough*.			
I can use *have to / don't have to*.			

LEARN TO … USE A MEMORY JOURNEY

A memory journey connects images with words. It can help you remember lists of vocabulary.

1 **Imagine you're going to use a memory journey to learn the words in the box for a test. Put steps a–d in order.**

awesome	beautiful	dangerous
famous	traditional	warm

a ☐ Imagine walking around your house, looking at those pieces of furniture.

b ☐ Think of an image for each word you need to learn, and put it with one of the pieces of furniture. Be creative!

c ☐ Think of six pieces of furniture in your house, for example, the shelves in your bedroom, the living room carpet, the kitchen sink.

d ☐ Think of your house.

2 **Read the example memory journey below. Which steps are included from Exercise 1? Discuss with a partner.**

First, I walk through the front door and into the living room. My dad and brother are having an awesome game of soccer on the carpet. Then I go into the kitchen. I see a famous singer cleaning the sink. After that, I go up to my bedroom. There's a dangerous snake on one of the shelves. Next …

3 **Follow the steps in Exercise 1 to make your own memory journey for the words in the box.**

4 **Describe your memory journey to your partner. Who has the strangest or funniest images?**

SHAPE IT!

5 **Use rooms and objects in your school to make a memory journey for the words in the box.**

comfortable	curved	friendly
helpful	nervous	strong

6 **Close your book. Can you remember the words from Exercise 5? Describe your memory journey to your partner.**

7 **What other places could you use for memory journeys? Discuss with a partner.**

6 How can I stay safe?

LEARNING OUTCOMES

I can ...

- understand texts about dangers at the beach and in the desert
- make suggestions
- write a blog post
- understand how to use *should/shouldn't*, *must/must not*, the zero conditional, and the first conditional
- talk about accidents and injuries and parts of the body
- use places to remember words, use pictures to predict a story, and give opinions about your partner's English
- work in a group and make an information pamphlet

Start It!

1 Look at the photo. What dangerous thing can you see?
2 Before you watch, when do you not have your phone with you?
3 Where are there special smartphone lanes? Watch and check.
4 Do you use your phone while walking down the street?

Watch video 6.1

p73

Grammar in Action 6.2

p75

Grammar in Action 6.3

p76

Everyday English 6.4

VOCABULARY
Accidents and Injuries

6.01 **1 Complete the phrases with the words in the box. Listen, check, and repeat.**

break	bruise	burn	~~cut~~	fall off	get bitten
get stung	hit	scratch	slip	sprain	trip over

1
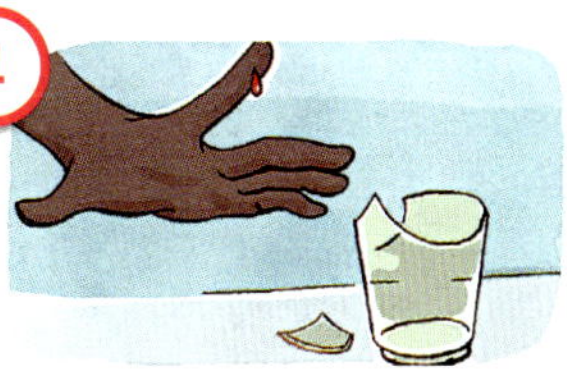
cut your finger

2

____

3
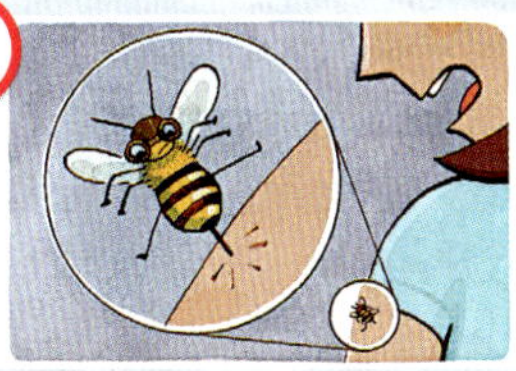
________ by a bee

4
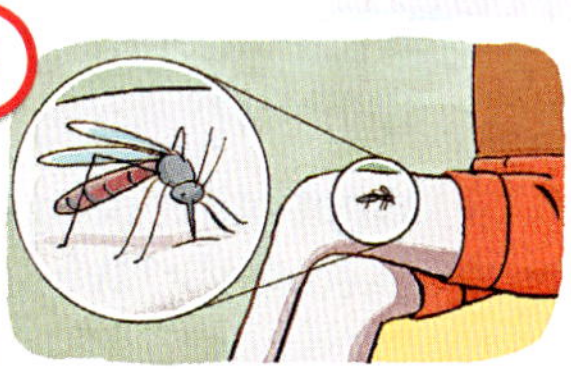
________ by a mosquito

5

________ your head

6
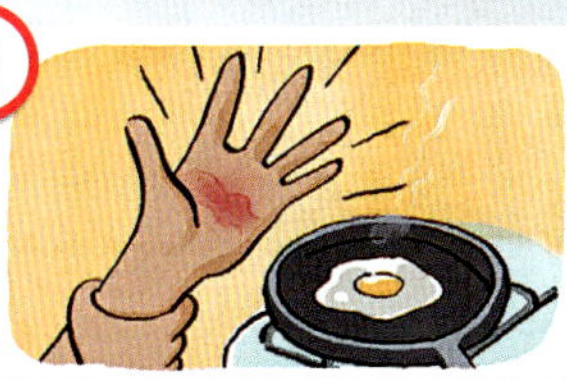
________ your hand

7

________ your arm

8

________ your leg

9

________ a chair

10

________ your horse

11
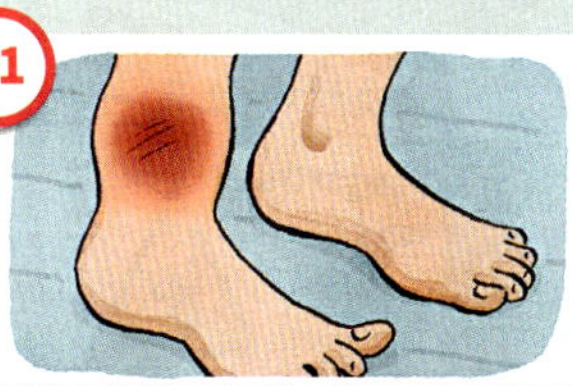
________ your ankle

12
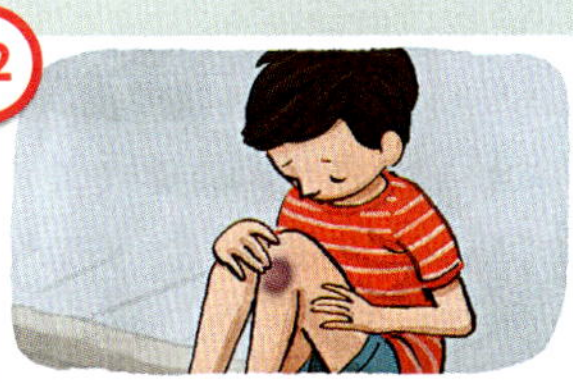
________ your leg

Get It Right!

We usually use words like **my**, **your**, **his**, **her** when we talk about parts of the body.

*I hit **my** head. Did Lisa burn **her** hand?*

6.02 **2 Listen. Write the accidents and injuries from Exercise 1 that you can hear.**

1 ________ 4 ________

2 ________ 5 ________

3 ________

LEARN TO LEARN
Using Places to Remember Words

It can help you to remember new words if you think of where they might happen.

3 Think of a place where each accident in Exercise 1 might happen.

trip over a chair – in the classroom

4 Test your partner. Say a place that you thought of in Exercise 3. Your partner guesses the accident or injury you thought of.

The kitchen. *Cut your finger?*

Use It!

5 Think about a time when one of the accidents or injuries happened to you or someone you know. Tell your partner about it.

My sister sprained her ankle last month.

How did that happen?

Explore It!

Is the sentence *T* (true) or *F* (false)?

All bees can sting. ☐

Find another interesting fact about an animal that bites or stings. Then write a question for your partner to answer.

READING
An Online Article

1 **Check the meaning of the words in the box. Can you see some of these things in the photos?**

animals that sting	broken glass	large waves
quicksand	rip currents	shark attack

6.03 **2** **Read the article. Which danger in Exercise 1 is <u>not</u> in the article?**

3 **Find words in the article that mean …**

1 difficult to find (para. 1) ________
2 quickly (para. 2) ________
3 something dangerous from an animal (para. 4) ________
4 move your body to get free (para. 5) ________
5 when the ocean goes in and out at different times of the day (para. 5) ________

4 **Are the sentences *T* (true) or *F* (false)?**

1 Some beaches are more dangerous than others. ___
2 Rip currents move away from the beach. ___
3 Crocodiles don't live near the ocean. ___
4 The blue-ringed octopus is a large and ugly animal. ___
5 One blue-ringed octopus can kill a lot of people. ___
6 All British beaches are safe. ___

Voice It!

5 **Discuss the questions.**

1 What other dangers at the beach can you think of?
2 What other dangerous places do some people like to visit? Why do they go there?

Finished? p123 Ex. 1

DANGERS AT THE BEACH

Beaches promise sun, sand, and fun and are usually safe places to go, but accidents can happen. You can slip and break your leg, or step on some glass and cut your foot. Ouch! Some beaches around the world have hidden dangers, however, and you should take extra care.

HAWAII

It's great for surfing, but beaches in Hawaii also have dangerous rip currents. Rip currents happen when water moves swiftly away from the beach. They are difficult to see and can move very fast. They can take people far out to sea, so swimmers must not try to swim against them. Instead, they should swim sideways along the beach until they get to safer waters.

AUSTRALIA

Everyone knows that huge sharks sometimes swim near Australian beaches, and crocodiles can also come very near. You must always be careful. Never swim when there isn't a lifeguard on the beach.

Sharks and crocodiles aren't the only danger on Australia's beaches. The beautiful Australian blue-ringed octopus, for example, is as small as your hand. But you must not go near them. They have enough venom to kill ten people!

UK

The sand can be as unsafe as the ocean, and on some British beaches it can kill! Dangerous quicksand is full of water, and it's very easy for people to sink in it. You shouldn't kick or struggle. You must move very slowly and carefully to get out … before the tide comes in!

Watch video 6.2
What should you do if you get burnt?
What should you do with a sprained ankle?

GRAMMAR IN ACTION

Should/Shouldn't and *Must/Must not*

	***Should* for Advice**	***Must* for Strong Advice or a Rule**
+	You [1] should **take** extra care.	You [3] ______ always **be** careful.
–	You [2] ______ **kick** or struggle.	Swimmers [4] ______ **try** to swim against them.

Pronunciation p142

1 **Complete the examples in the chart above with *should/shouldn't* or *must/must not*. Use the article on page 72 to help you.**

2 **Correct the sentences about the article on page 72.**

1 You shouldn't wear sandals on the beach.
You should wear sandals on the beach.

2 In a rip current, you must swim toward the beach.
______
______

3 You should swim near the blue-ringed octopus.
______
______

4 In quicksand, you should kick and jump to get out.
______
______

3 **Circle the correct words.**

1 You *should* / *shouldn't* swim here. The water isn't clean.

2 You *must* / *must not* speak while you're doing an exam.

3 I think everyone *should* / *must* play a sport. Exercise is good for you.

4 You *must* / *should* wear a seatbelt in the car. It's the law.

5 I think you *should* / *must* learn to speak another language.

6 You *shouldn't* / *must not* go outside in shorts. It's cold today.

6.07 **4** **Complete the teacher's message with *should/shouldn't* or *must/must not*. Then listen and check.**

Mrs. Harrison <jharrison@WGhighschool.org>
To: All students
Subject: Cycling

Hi everyone,

Now that spring is here, I think you [1] should all think about walking or cycling to school if you can.

Cycling is fun and healthy, but you [2] ______ be careful. For example, you [3] ______ ride when the weather is bad, and you [4] ______ wear a helmet. That's extremely important. However, you also [5] ______ forget that there are rules on the road for cyclists, and you [6] ______ learn these rules.

The school website has some good advice, such as which clothes you [7] ______ wear when riding your bike, and I think all cyclists [8] ______ read it carefully.

One more thing: we need to know which students are cycling to school, so you [9] ______ tell Mrs. Jones if you plan to ride your bike. That's a school rule, so you [10] ______ forget!

Use It!

5 **In your notebook, write rules and advice for staying safe while doing these activities.**

ice skating   mountain biking   rock climbing   surfing

6 **Read your rules and advice to your partner, but don't say the activities. Can your partner guess them?**

You should wear a wetsuit to do this. But you must not do it in bad weather. What is it?

Surfing?

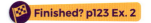

Finished? p123 Ex. 2

VOCABULARY AND LISTENING

Parts of the Body

6.08 **1 Match the words in the box with 1–12 in the photo. Listen, check, and repeat.**

cheek		forehead	1	shoulder	
chest		heel		teeth	
chin		knee		toe	
elbow		neck		wrist	

2 Complete the sentences with words from Exercise 1.

1 Your wrist is between your hand and your arm.
2 People have ten fingers and ten ________.
3 Children have 20 ________ and adults have 32.
4 Your ________ is just above your eyes.
5 Your ________ is in the middle of your leg.
6 Your ________ is at the top of your arm.

Use It!

3 Point to a part of the body from Exercise 1. Name the part your partner points to.

A Radio Interview

LEARN TO LEARN

Using Pictures to Predict a Story

Before you listen, look carefully at any pictures and use them to imagine a story.

4 Look at the pictures in Exercise 6. With your partner, choose one picture from each set of three and use them to make a story.

6.09 **5 Listen to the interview. What parts of your story were the same?**

6.09 **6 Listen again. Circle the correct answers.**

1 What job does Pam do?

2 What was Jamie doing before his accident?

3 What did Jamie do?

4 What injuries did Jamie get?

7 Work with your partner to tell Jamie's story. Use the pictures to help you.

8 EXAM Look again at the pictures in Exercise 6. Write Jamie's story in your notebook. Use 35 words or more.

GRAMMAR IN ACTION

Zero Conditional and First Conditional

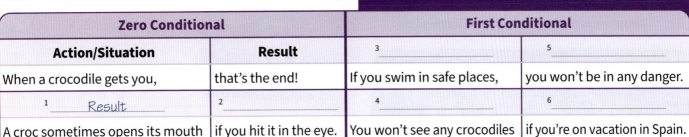

Watch video 6.3
How can you fall off a skateboard safely?
Is this a good way to fall?

Zero Conditional		First Conditional	
Action/Situation	Result	3 ________	5 ________
When a crocodile gets you,	that's the end!	If you swim in safe places,	you won't be in any danger.
1 Result	2 ________	4 ________	6 ________
A croc sometimes opens its mouth	if you hit it in the eye.	You won't see any crocodiles	if you're on vacation in Spain.

1 **Complete the headings in the chart above with *Action/Situation* or *Result*.**

2 **Match 1–5 with a–e. Then complete the results with the correct form of the verb in parentheses.**

1 When people aren't careful, a
2 If you don't go near a crocodile, ___
3 If a crocodile grabs you, ___
4 When a crocodile wants to cool down, ___
5 If a crocodile loses a tooth, ___

a accidents happen (happen).
b it ________ (try) to pull you under the water.
c another one ________ (grow).
d it ________ probably ________ (ignore) you.
e it ________ (open) its mouth.

6.10 **3** **Complete the email with the correct form of the verbs in parentheses. Then listen and check.**

So you're going to visit Queensland. Great idea! If you [1] like (like) beaches and forests, you [2] ________ (love) Port Douglas. It's amazing. It usually [3] ________ (take) about an hour to get there if you [4] ________ (take) a bus from the airport. Buses are frequent, so if you [5] ________ (miss) one, you [6] ________ (not have) a long wait. Of course, if you [7] ________ (not mind) spending more money, there [8] ________ (be) always taxis at the airport, too! If you [9] ________ (visit) Four Mile Beach, you [10] ________ (have) a great time surfing. But be careful! If you [11] ________ (not see) anyone else in the water, it probably [12] ________ (mean) there are sharks or jellyfish in the ocean!
Have fun and take care!

4 **Complete the information about the Amazon jungle. Use the words in the box.**

go   have   hide   run away

Snakes
Snakes [1] ________ if they hear people coming.
Most snake venom isn't fatal if you [2] ________ straight to the hospital.

Bigger Animals
You probably won't see any jaguars because they [3] ________ ________ when they feel threatened. However, if a jaguar [4] ________ young cubs, it is more dangerous.

5 **Imagine you're planning a jungle vacation. Write what you will do if the following things happen.**

1 If I see a snake on the path, I'll wait for it to go away.
2 If I'm very hot and I find a river, ________
3 If I get bitten by a spider, ________
4 If I get lost, ________

Use It!

6 **Say the second half of your sentences from Exercise 5. Can your partner guess the first half?**

I'll look for a river to follow.   *If I get lost?*

Finished? p123 Ex. 3

SPEAKING
Making Suggestions

6.11 **1** **Listen to the conversation. Who knows more about mountain bikes, Dan or Hayley?**

DAN Awesome mountain bike, Hayley.
HAYLEY Thanks, Dan.
DAN I'd like to get one, too. Do you think I should buy one online?
HAYLEY Not really. Some online stores aren't reliable. Their bikes aren't very safe. Anyway, [1]make sure you don't buy one without trying it first. [2] ______ try The Bike Shack in town? They're really good.
DAN OK. I'll have a go at it.
HAYLEY And [3] ______ buy a good helmet, too. You can really hurt yourself if you fall off, so you must not ride without one.
DAN Good idea. I think I should find some buddies to ride with, too. What do you think?
HAYLEY Sure. [4] ______ joining my bike club? We go out every weekend.
DAN Yeah! Good job, Hayley. I'll do that.

6.11 **2** **Complete the conversation with the phrases from the *Useful Language* box. Then listen and check.**

Useful Language

How about …ing … ?	Why don't you … ?
Make sure you don't …	You should definitely …

3 **Look at the *Everyday English* box. Find and underline the phrases in the conversation.**

Watch video 6.4
Everyday English

Awesome	buddies
I'll have a go at it.	Good job

4 **Complete the sentences with the *Everyday English* phrases.**

1 ______ snowboard, Maya!
2 Skateboarding? That sounds hard, but ______ ______ .
3 You remembered your camera! ______ , Beth!
4 That's Alfie. He's one of my surfing ______ .

PLAN

5 **Work in pairs. Choose a sport and think of advice for someone trying it for the first time. Take notes.**

What you should or must do: ______
______
What you shouldn't or must not do: ______
______

SPEAK

6 **Practice a conversation asking for and giving advice about the sport. Remember to use *should/shouldn't* and *must/must not*, vocabulary from this unit, and phrases from the *Useful Language* and *Everyday English* boxes.**

CHECK

7 **Work with another pair. Listen to their conversation and complete the notes.**

What you should or must do: ______
______
What you shouldn't or must not do: ______
______
The best suggestion: ______
______

WRITING
A Blog Post

1 **Look at the photo. What do you think the blog post is about? Read it and check.**

MATT'S BLOG

Thanks for all your comments on my posts. Here are my answers to your questions.

1 ☐
There are cheap boards, but it's best to avoid them. If you want a good board, you need to spend more. I'd say at least $100. Also, make sure you get the right size deck. If you have small feet, you'll need a narrow deck. If it's too wide, you won't be able to control the board.

2 ☐
Yes! When you're a beginner, accidents happen. That's why you need a helmet. It must be a proper skateboarder's helmet, and it must be the right size. If it moves when you shake your head, it's too big.

3 ☐
If you ask me, the street is too dangerous. A skatepark is the best place, but if there isn't one near you, any park will be good.

That's all for now. Have fun, but stay safe!

2 **Match questions a–c with paragraphs 1–3.**

a Can I skate in the street?
b What board should I buy?
c Should I wear a helmet?

3 **Read the blog post again. Which of these opinions does Matt have?**

1 Cheap skateboards aren't very good. ✓
2 You won't get a good skateboard for less than $100. ☐
3 For some people, narrow skateboards are best. ☐
4 Your helmet shouldn't move when you wear it. ☐
5 The only safe place for skateboarding is a skatepark. ☐

4 **Complete the phrases in the *Useful Language* box with words that Matt uses for giving advice.**

Useful Language

1 ________ say	3 ________ why
2 ________ sure	If you 4 ________ me

5 **Complete the sentences with the *Useful Language* phrases.**

1 If you fall off a board, you can really hurt your head. ________ skateboarders wear helmets.
2 If ________, all skateboarders should wear knee and elbow pads as well.
3 ________ you keep your board in good condition.
4 Many people skate on their own, but ________ it's more fun and safer to skate with friends.

PLAN

6 **Plan a blog post to give safety advice. Choose an activity and think of three questions about doing it safely. Take notes for the answers.**

1 ________
2 ________
3 ________

WRITE

7 **Write your blog post. Remember to include an introduction, three questions and answers, an ending, and phrases from the *Useful Language* box.**

CHECK

8 **Do you ...**

- answer each question?
- use *should/shouldn't* and *must/must not*?
- use vocabulary from this unit?

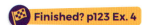

Finished? p123 Ex. 4

SCIENCE PROJECT

An Information Pamphlet

1 **Look at the information pamphlet. What is it about?**

a The dangers of the desert

b How animals live in the desert

2 **Read the pamphlet again. Are the sentences *T* (true) or *F* (false)?**

1 All deserts are hot and dry. F

2 Birds can help you in the desert. ___

3 If you drink water, you won't get heat cramps. ___

4 A *haboob* is a desert animal. ___

5 You shouldn't wear sandals in the desert. ___

6 Scorpions live in dark places. ___

3 **Complete the chart. Put the five dangers in the desert in the correct groups.**

Desert Animals	Desert Weather	Our Bodies in the Desert
		thirst

How to Work in Groups

6.12 **4** **Listen and decide which student worked in these ways. Write *J* (John), *I* (Isla), or *P* (Poppy).**

1 The group decided what the different jobs were for the project. Each person did a different job. ___

2 The group shared the writing on the project. Each person wrote a different section. ___

3 Each person worked alone first. Then they chose different sections of each person's work to make their poster. ___

5 **Which of the ways of working do you think is best? Why? Share your ideas with a partner.**

Desert Survival

Fact File

- A desert is a place with less than 250 mm of rain per year.
- Around 30% of the land on the Earth is desert.
- Only 20% of deserts are sandy. Some have snow.
- Highest temperature in a desert: 56.7°C (Death Valley, U.S.A.)
- Lowest temperature in a desert: – 89.2°C (Antarctica)

Deserts are extremely big, extremely dry, and extremely dangerous! If you are lost in one, here are some of the dangers you should know about.

Thirst

What's the danger?

You can't live without water for more than three days.

What should you do?

Walk slowly and rest often. If you don't, you'll lose a lot of water as sweat.

Drink a little and often.

If you see birds, follow them. They'll take you to the nearest water.

Heat Cramps

What's the danger?

As well as water, your body needs salt. When you sweat, you lose a lot of salt. If you lose too much, your legs and arms will begin to hurt. This is called heat cramp, and in the desert it can be dangerous.

What should you do?

Make sure you carry salt tablets with you. They can save your life!

Sandstorms

What's the danger?

When it gets windy in the desert, sandstorms happen. In Arabic, these huge walls of sand are called *haboob*. They are sometimes more than a kilometer high and can move at 40 kilometers per hour.

What should you do?

If a *haboob* is coming, you must hide. Sandstorms usually last for a few minutes, but sometimes they last three hours!

Snakes

What's the danger?

If you're in the Arizona Desert and you hear a rattle, it's probably a rattlesnake, and its bite can kill.

What should you do?

Wear strong boots, not sandals. If you see a snake, move carefully away. If it bites you, you must find a doctor as soon as you can.

Scorpions

What's the danger?

There are 2,000 different types of scorpions and 30 of them can kill.

What should you do?

Scorpions live under rocks, so you should be careful where you put your hands!

PLAN

6 Work in groups to plan an information pamphlet. Choose a remote place. Then follow the steps below.

- Decide how your group will work together.
- Decide on the sections your information pamphlet will include.
- Decide what images and diagrams you could include.
- Make a first draft of your pamphlet.
- Share your first draft with another group to get their feedback.

PRESENT

7 Display your information pamphlet on your classroom wall. Remember to include different sections, interesting facts and pictures, and the tips in *How to Work in Groups*.

CHECK

8 Ask different groups how they worked. Did they work in the same way as you? Who worked in a group best?

6 REVIEW

VOCABULARY

1 Circle the correct words.

1 Sue touched a hot pan and *burned* / *sprained* her fingers.
2 Juan *slipped* / *scratched* on some ice.
3 Jane *bruised* / *fell off* her bike.
4 Andy got *bitten* / *stung* by a bee.
5 Masha *fell off* / *tripped over* a plant in the garden.
6 I *cut* / *broke* my finger with a knife.

2 Match the words in the box with the descriptions. You can use the words more than once.

cheek	chin	elbow	forehead	
heel	knee	shoulder	toe	wrist

1 We have two or more of these.
____
____
2 These are parts of your arm.
____
3 These are parts of your leg and foot.
____
4 These are parts of your face.
____

GRAMMAR IN ACTION

3 Complete the sentences with *should/shouldn't* or *must/must not* and the verbs in the box.

sleep	stay	talk	wear

1 You ______________ a seatbelt in the car.
2 You ______________ in the sun too long.
3 You ______________ for eight hours at night.
4 You ______________ on your phone while you're riding a bike.

4 Complete the sentences with the zero or first conditional.

1 If you ______________ (not be) more careful, you ______________ (have) an accident.
2 When Gina ______________ (go) skateboarding, she always ______________ (wear) a helmet.
3 If someone ______________ (break) a leg, it ______________ (hurt) a lot.
4 If the weather ______________ (get) worse, the climbers ______________ (be) stuck on the mountain.
5 Snakes ______________ usually ______________ (not bite) you if you ______________ (not disturb) them.

5 Circle the best words to complete the notes.

Stay Safe in the Forest

Before you go, you [1]*should* / *shouldn't* tell someone where you're going. If you get lost, it [2]*is* / *will be* easier to find you.

You [3]*must* / *must not* take a map. If you [4]*don't* / *won't* follow a map, you'll probably get lost.

You [5]*shouldn't* / *must not* eat mushrooms. Some are very dangerous – if you [6]*eat* / *will eat* them, you can get extremely sick.

You [7]*should* / *shouldn't* run away from a bear. If you stay calm and walk away slowly, you [8]*will be* / *are* OK.

Self-Assessment

I can talk about accidents and injuries.

I can talk about parts of the body.

I can use *should/shouldn't* and *must/must not*.

I can use the zero conditional and first conditional.

LEARN TO ... GIVE USEFUL OPINIONS ABOUT YOUR PARTNER'S ENGLISH

Be polite when you give opinions about your partner's English. You can help each other improve.

1 **Read the advice about how to give useful opinions. Complete the advice with *should* or *shouldn't*.**

What you [1] ________ do to help your partner improve their English

You [2] ________ …

a say what you think in a mean way.
b talk about your partner's personality.
c say that something is better or worse than it is.

You [3] ________ …

d say what you think, but also be nice.
e say positive things.
f give ideas for how your partner can improve.

2 **Match 1–6 with the advice (a–f) in Exercise 1.**

1 ☐ *Well done! You're a really interesting person.*

2 ☐ *That wasn't your best English, but I know you can do better.*

3 ☐ *That was the worst presentation ever!*

4 ☐ *You made some mistakes with the first conditional. Why don't you study the grammar from the unit again?*

5 ☐ *You used a lot of adjectives to describe things. That was really nice!*

6 ☐ *Your English was awful!*

3 **Invent a story about an accident. Use one word or phrase from each box, and think about the answers to the questions below.**

crocodile knife mirror scissors snake

break cut get bitten hit slip

- What were you doing when the accident happened?
- What happened?
- How did you feel?
- Did anybody help you?
- What happened then?
- What should people do to avoid a similar accident?

4 **Take turns telling your stories. While your partner is speaking, think about what they do well and how they can improve.**

SHAPE IT!

5 **Give three helpful opinions about your partner's English. Use the phrases in the box.**

I liked the way you …
Why don't you … ?
You made some mistakes with …
You used … That was nice!

7 Are you connected?

LEARNING OUTCOMES

I can ...

- understand texts about technology
- give instructions to explain how to use something
- write an article
- understand how to use the present perfect: affirmative and negative, *will/won't*, *may*, *might*, and infinitives of purpose
- talk about and describe technology and transportation
- use collocations, recognize opinions, use words that describe sounds, and make and use flashcards.

Start It!

1 Look at the photo. What type of car is it?

2 Before you watch, what technology have you used today?

3 Who planned the first programmable computer? Watch and check.

4 Which technology would be most difficult to live without?

Watch video 7.1

p85

Grammar in Action 7.2

p87

Grammar in Action 7.3

p88

Everyday English 7.4

p90

Globetrotters 7.5

VOCABULARY
Communication and Technology

7.01 **1 Match the words in the box with 1–11 in the picture. Listen, check, and repeat.**

app	☐	emoji	☐	software	☐
chip	☐	message	☐	upload	1
device	☐	screen	☐	video chat	☐
download	☐	social media	☐		

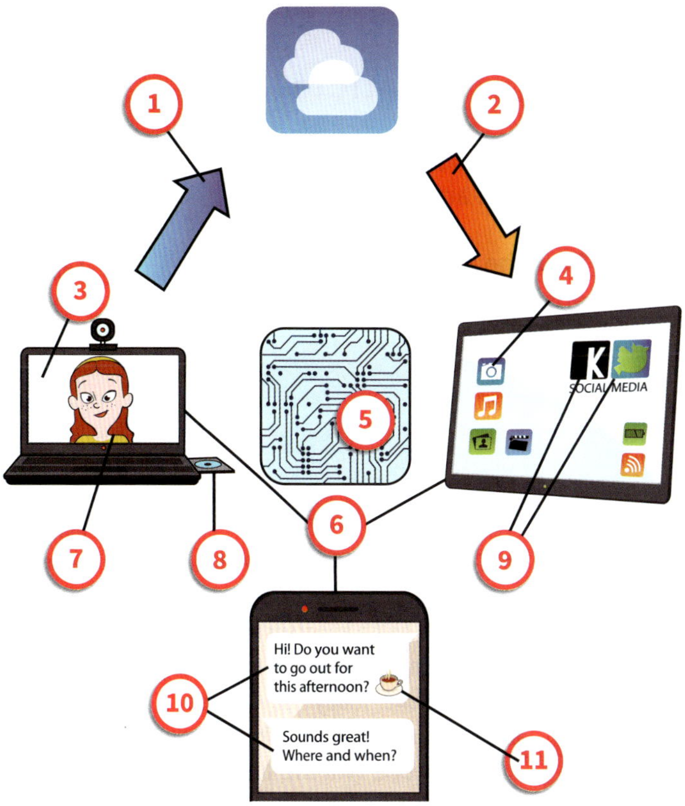

7.02 **2 Complete the sentences with words from Exercise 1. Then listen and check.**

1 My phone fell out of my pocket this morning and the *screen* broke.
2 I can't do a ______________ with you right now. I don't have a camera on my laptop.
3 Most of my friends ____________ photos to ______________ sites like Instagram.
4 Look at this ________ – it's great for practicing new English words. Why don't you __________ it, too?

Pronunciation p142

LEARN TO LEARN
Collocations

Some words are often used together – we call these collocations. Learn them as phrases.

3 Complete these collocations with words from Exercise 1. There is sometimes more than one possible answer.

1 ____________ software
2 use a messaging ____________
3 electronic ____________
4 send a ____________
5 computer ____________
6 ____________ photos

4 Take turns starting and finishing the collocations you made in Exercise 3.

Send a ...

Send a message?

Use It!

5 Use words from Exercise 1 to write three sentences about you or people you know.

1 *My brother has a lot of apps on his phone.*
2 ______________________
3 ______________________
4 ______________________

6 Compare your sentences.

I spend about three hours a day in front of a screen.

I only spend about two hours.

Explore It!

Is the sentence *T* (true) or *F* (false)?
People with nomophobia feel scared when they don't have their phone with them. ☐
Find another interesting fact about technology. Then write a question for your partner to answer.

READING

A Magazine Article

1 Look at the photos. What do you think the article is about?

7.06 2 Read the article and check your answer.

Smartphones and Us

Noah Smith investigates how smartphones have changed our lives.

In 1994, the IBM Simon arrived. It was a small computer that made calls! OK, it weighed half a kilogram and it didn't have a camera, but it was technically a smartphone. Today's devices are smaller, faster, and more fun. Nearly 3 billion people own one, and they have transformed our lives.

Communication

Smartphone technology has given us many ways to communicate, but the most popular is messaging. Users of one very well-known app, for example, send 60 billion messages every day!

And then there's video. Once, video calls were science fiction – they still are for my grandparents – but for my generation, video chats have become completely normal.

Entertainment

Gaming apps let us play our favorite games anywhere, anytime on our phones – and that's usually the real reason why my sister hasn't done her homework! She isn't alone. About 200 million people in the U.S.A. play online games, and globally the industry is worth billions of dollars. Personally, I'd rather listen to my favorite bands. Smartphones are great for that, too!

Sharing

Smartphones haven't made us nicer people, but together with social media, they've made it easier for us to have hundreds of "friends." Around 2.5 billion of us have created social media profiles. We post status updates, upload our photos, and share videos. Many of us have shared our whole lives online. Which reminds me – I haven't updated my status today!

3 Read the article again. Write what the numbers refer to.

1 half a kilogram ______
2 nearly 3 billion ______
3 60 billion ______
4 about 200 million ______
5 2.5 billion ______

4 EXAM Circle the correct answers.

1 What couldn't computers do before 1994?
A make calls B send emails C save documents

2 What was unusual about the IBM Simon compared to modern devices?
A It was smaller and faster.
B It had an excellent camera.
C It weighed half a kilogram.

3 What is the most popular form of smartphone communication?
A phone calls B messages C video chats

4 What does Noah's sister enjoy doing?
A playing games B sharing photos
C listening to music

7.07 5 Complete the words for the numbers. Then listen and check.

1 1,000,000,000,000 = one trillion
2 1,000,000,000 = one ______
3 1,000,000 = one ______
4 1,000 = one ______
5 100 = one ______

Voice It!

6 Do you agree with the statements below? Discuss with your partner, using the phrases in the box.

I strongly agree. I agree. I'm not sure. I disagree. I strongly disagree.

1 People use their smartphones too much.
2 Children under ten shouldn't have a smartphone.
3 There should be no smartphones in schools.
4 I couldn't live without a smartphone.

Finished? p124 Ex. 1

Watch video 7.2
Name two things Sophia has learned.
What's the best thing that the vlog has given her?

GRAMMAR IN ACTION

Present Perfect: Affirmative and Negative

	I/You/We/They	*He/She/It*
+	Smartphones [1] ________ **transformed** our lives.	Technology [3] ________ **given** us many ways to communicate.
–	Smartphones [2] ________ **made** us nicer people.	My sister [4] ________ **done** her homework.

1 **Complete the examples in the chart above with the correct form of *have* (*not*). Use the article on page 84 to help you.**

2 **Complete the sentences with the present perfect form of the verbs in parentheses.**

1 Smartphones have changed our lives. (change)
2 They ________ easier to carry. (become)
3 Smartphone technology ________ more interesting. (become)
4 Smartphones ________ it possible to communicate with more people. (make)
5 Noah ________ his online status. (not update)

7.08 **3** **Complete the conversation with the present perfect form of the verbs. Then listen and check.**

ask find leave look ~~lose~~
not charge not hear not see put

JACK What's wrong, Kim?
KIM I [1] 've lost my phone. Do you know where it is?
JACK No, I don't. I [2] ________ it ring, either. Maybe it's in your coat pocket.
KIM I [3] ________ in all my pockets. It's not there.
JACK Maybe you [4] ________ it in Mom's car.
KIM No, I don't think so. I used it this afternoon, but I can't remember where I left it.
JACK Maybe Mom [5] ________ it somewhere.
KIM No, I [6] ________ her and she says she [7] ________ it. Jack, can you call me?
JACK I think so. I [8] ________ my phone, but I think it has enough power left. Hang on … OK, I'm calling you …
KIM Here, look! I [9] ________ it. It was in my bag all the time.

4 **Answer the questions with present perfect sentences. Use the words in the boxes.**

break buy forget

password screen tablets

1

2

3

1 Why can't Orla use her laptop?
____
2 Why are Elena and Ruby so happy?
____
3 Why is Andrey upset?
____

Use It!

5 **Write three sentences about what you have or haven't done today. Use the ideas in the box.**

chat / on social media check / my emails
upload / a photo watch / TV

1 I've watched TV.
2 ________
3 ________
4 ________

6 **Tell your partner about the things you've done.**

I haven't uploaded a photo, but I've played my favorite computer game.

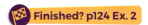

Finished? p124 Ex. 2

VOCABULARY AND LISTENING

Getting Around

7.09 **1 Complete the phrases with the verbs in the box. Listen, check, and repeat.**

catch/take	get into	get off	get on	get out of	go by	~~go on~~

1 

2 

3 

go on foot

_______ a train

_______ tram

4 

5 

6 

7 

_______ a plane

_______ a car

_______ a taxi

_______ a bus

Get It Right!

We use **take** and **catch** with planes and with public transportation. But we can't say ~~catch a taxi~~.

We **get on** and **off** public transportation or a bike. But we **get into** and **out of** a car.

We use **go by** with all transportation. But we say **go on foot**, not ~~go by foot~~.

2 Complete the sentences with verbs from Exercise 1.

1 I'm getting off this bus at the next stop.

2 My dad has _______ a taxi to the airport.

3 Yesterday we _______ to the island _______ ferry.

4 I bought my ticket from the driver when I _______ the bus.

5 Don't forget to turn off the lights before you _______ the car.

Use It!

3 Tell your partner about two different ways to get to these places from your home.

your school	a town in your country	New York

To get to school, I can go on foot to the bus stop and then catch a bus. Or I can go by bike.

A Radio Interview

4 Look at the forms of transportation in Exercise 5. Will we use them in the future? Discuss with a partner.

7.10 **5 Listen to the radio interview. Put the forms of transportation in the order you hear them (1–3).**

flying cars ☐

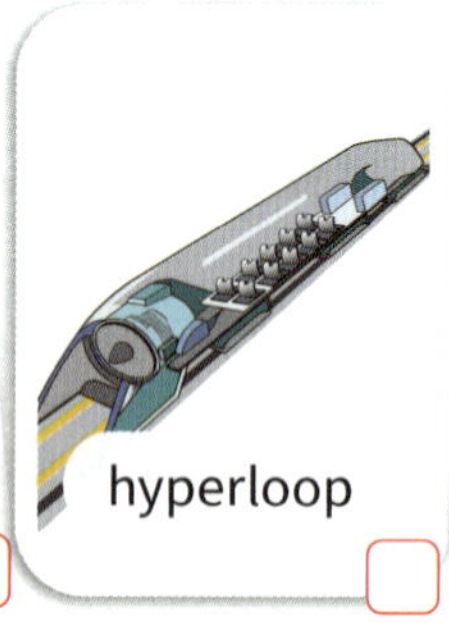

hyperloop ☐

jetpacks ☐

LEARN TO LEARN

Recognizing Opinions

It's important to understand the difference between facts and opinions. When people give an opinion, they often begin with phrases like these:

In my view … *In my opinion …* *I (don't) think …*

7.10 **6 Listen again. Which of these opinions does the professor have?**

1 Flying cars aren't the answer to traffic jams. ✓

2 There will be a lot of flying cars soon. ☐

3 People won't use jetpacks to get to work. ☐

4 The hyperloop is just science fiction. ☐

5 The hyperloop will change our lives. ☐

Watch video 7.3
What won't James be in ten years' time? How will he make the vlog look better?

GRAMMAR IN ACTION
Will/Won't, May, and *Might*

	Certain Predictions	Uncertain Predictions
+	It [1] ________ really **change** our lives.	We **may have** jetpacks one day just for fun. We **might see** hyperloops between big cities.
–	We [2] ________ **see** a lot of flying cars.	They [3] ________ **not be** useful for getting to work. We **might not need** to wait much longer.

1 **Complete the examples in the chart above.**

2 **Are these predictions *C* (certain) or *U* (uncertain)?**

1 Cars might be less noisy. U
2 Every family will have a flying car. ___
3 Fifty years from now, children may go to school by jetpack. ___
4 Jetpacks won't be very useful for most people. ___
5 Everyone will travel by hyperloop. ___
6 Some people might not want to travel on a hyperloop. ___

7.11 **3** **Listen to Danielle talking about transportation in the future. Which of the predictions in Exercise 2 does she make?**

____

Use It!

4 **Complete the sentences about the future with *will/won't* or *may/might* (*not*). Then compare your opinions in pairs.**

1 People ________ have their own airplanes.
2 People ________ go to work by bike.
3 We ________ need smartphones.
4 We ________ use paper.
5 There ________ be books and magazines.

Infinitives of Purpose

***To* + Infinitive**
A lot of us catch a bus [1] ________ (go) to work.
[2] ________ (solve) the problem, we should invent flying cars.
It takes a lot of energy [3] ________ (lift) a person off the ground.

5 **Complete the examples in the chart above with the correct form of the words in parentheses.**

6 **Match 1–5 with a–e.**

1 Can I borrow your phone
2 Is there a printer
3 You can use my laptop
4 Why don't we stop
5 To get there sooner,

a to have lunch?
b to check your emails.
c to make a call?
d we decided to fly.
e to print these photos?

Use It!

7 **Complete the sentences with your own ideas and tell your partner.**

1 I went to ________ to ________
____
2 I bought a ________ to ________
____
3 I took a ________ to ________
____

I went to Chicago to visit my cousin last summer.

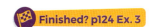

Finished? p124 Ex. 3

SPEAKING
Giving Instructions

7.12 **1 Listen to the conversation. What is Tom explaining to his dad?**

a How to take a photo
b How to record a video

TOM So, Dad, before [1] you start, switch the camera to video mode. Have you done that?
DAD Like this?
TOM Yes, that's right. It needs to be in video mode to record a video. Now, look at this little screen.
DAD I can't see anything.
TOM Ah. Remember [2] ______________ put your hand in front of the camera!
DAD Is this better?
TOM Not quite. Look, you need to keep your fingers here. That's it. Now, do you see this button?
DAD This one?
TOM No, not that one. This one here. It's [3] ______________ that it's turned on if you want to record sound. Oh, and [4] ______________ sure that the light is red. That means you're recording. Got it?
DAD Yes, I think so. Thanks, Tom!

7.12 **2 Complete the conversation with the phrases from the *Useful Language* box. Then listen and check.**

Useful Language

Before you start, …
It's really important that …
Make sure that …
Remember (not) to …

3 Look at the *Everyday English* box. Find and underline the phrases in the conversation.

Watch video 7.4
Everyday English

Got it? Like this?
Not quite. That's it.

4 Match the phrases in the *Everyday English* box with their meanings.

1 That's right. ______________
2 Do you understand? ______________
3 This way? ______________
4 Not exactly. ______________

PLAN

5 Work in pairs. Plan some instructions for using an electronic device. Write your ideas below.

What you are teaching people to do:

____

The steps that are needed to use the device:

1 ______________
2 ______________
3 ______________
4 ______________

SPEAK

6 Work in pairs. Practice a conversation giving instructions for your device. Remember to use infinitives of purpose, vocabulary from this unit, and phrases from the *Useful Language* and *Everyday English* boxes.

CHECK

7 Work with another pair. Listen to their conversation and complete the notes.

What are the instructions for?

____

Are the instructions clear? ______________

WRITING
An Article

1 **What are the students in the photo doing? What technology do you use at school?**

2 **Read the article. Underline the modern technology words it mentions.**

School Technology

1 Teaching has changed a lot. For instance, in the past, teachers used blackboards, and children wrote everything with pen and paper. What's more, the only technology in classrooms was a TV or perhaps a cassette player.

2 Today, in contrast, teachers use a lot of technology. For example, most classrooms have Wi-Fi. In addition, teachers use interactive whiteboards, and children use tablets to do exercises or play games. With technology such as video chat, classes can work with students in another country. This makes learning easier and more fun.

3 Some people think that robots might teach students one day. However, I don't think that will happen. Teachers help us learn things, but they take care of us, too. Robots can't do that. The technology may change over time, but the best teachers will always be real people.

3 **Read the article again. Are the sentences *T* (true) or *F* (false)?**

1 In the past, there was a lot of technology in the classroom. ___

2 It's normal now for classrooms to be connected to the Internet. ___

3 Today, students chat with their classmates using video chat. ___

4 Robots will replace teachers. ___

Useful Language

Giving examples:

For instance, For example, such as

Adding more information:

In addition, What's more,

4 **Read the phrases in the *Useful Language* box. Then circle the correct words.**

1 Tablets are often cheaper than laptops. *What's more, / For example,* they're easier to carry.

2 The first cell phones could only make calls. *In addition, / For instance,* they were huge.

3 In the future, schools might use technology *such as / what's more* 3-D printing.

PLAN

5 **Plan an article about technology in the home. Think about cooking, cleaning, and entertainment. Take notes for three paragraphs.**

1 Technology at home in the past: ___

2 Technology at home today: ___

3 Predictions for the future: ___

WRITE

6 **Write your article. Remember to include three paragraphs, past and present tenses, predictions with *will/won't* and *may/might* (*not*), and phrases from the *Useful Language* box.**

CHECK

7 **Do you ...**

- describe technology in the past?
- describe technology in the present?
- make certain and uncertain predictions for the future?

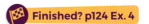

Finished? p124 Ex. 4

AROUND THE WORLD

READING
An Article

1 Look at the photos on page 91. Where do you think this is? What is happening in each photo?

7.13 2 Read the article. Match photos a–e with paragraphs 1–5.

3 Answer the questions.

1 Where does Seo-yun keep her smartphone at night? Next to her bed.

2 What are her two ways of getting to school?

______

3 How does Seo-yun pay for her bus journey?

______

4 What are the other passengers doing on the bus?

______

Globetrotters

Watch video 7.5
Hello, Robots!

- What things do you use robots for?
- What is an android?
- What do you think the future of robots will be?

Voice It!

4 Discuss the questions.

1 How does Seo-yun's family use technology to connect with the world?

2 How does technology improve human connection?

3 What are its negative effects?

One Morning in the High-Tech Capital of the World

1 [c] 6:30 a.m.

An alarm buzzes and Seo-yun's phone wakes her up for another day in Seoul, the world's "tech capital." In the bathroom, she tells the voice-activated shower to start. Water gushes from the shower, but it's too cold. "Warmer, please!" Seo-yun calls out.

2 [ ] 7:20 a.m.

In the kitchen, Dad makes breakfast. While they wait, Seo-yun and her sister, Ji-woo, watch cartoons on the "family hub" – a huge tablet screen built into the fridge door. They hear a "ping" from Seo-yun's phone – one of her friends has sent a message. Will she go to school on foot or take the bus? Seo-yun asks the family's voice-activated device to check for rain while she checks her travel app to see what the traffic is like.

3 [ ] 8:00 a.m.

Seo-yun has decided to take the bus. There's a beep as she swipes her phone over a sensor when she gets on, and then she takes a seat. On the way, she reads an online comic, and she puts in earphones to enjoy all the bangs, crashes, and other sound effects without disturbing other passengers. She doesn't need to worry, though. They're all glued to their screens, too!

4 [ ] 8:10 a.m.

Seo-yun's mom has taken the KTX bullet train to meet colleagues in Busan. The train roars between the two cities at nearly 300 kph. During the journey, she has a video chat with her boss. The journey may soon be much quicker. The government wants to build a new kind of train line called a hyperloop, with trains that zoom along at 1,000 kph.

5 [ ] 8:20 a.m.

Ji-woo has arrived at school, and the teacher's robot helper, iRobi, comes to Ji-woo with a whir of electric wheels. iRobi marks her attendance and uses face recognition to check her mood. "Excited?" asks iRobi. Of course. Today Ji-woo might have a gymnastics class with Genibo, the school's robot dog. That's education – Korean style!

LEARN TO LEARN

Words that Describe Sounds

There are many English words that sound similar to the sounds they describe.

5 Find words in the article for these sounds.

1 three sounds that a smartphone makes (paras 1, 2, and 3) buzzes ________ ________
2 the sound of water coming out fast (para. 1) ________
3 two loud sounds when one thing hits another (para. 3) ________ ________
4 the sound of a machine working quietly (para. 5) ________

6 Work in pairs. Say the words in the box and discuss what sounds you think they describe. Then use a dictionary to check.

crack	hiccup	hiss	meow	pop	splash	woof

Explore It!

Guess the correct answer.

South Korea has the world's fastest …

a internet speeds. b trains. c ferries.

Find another interesting fact about South Korea. Then write a question for your partner to answer.

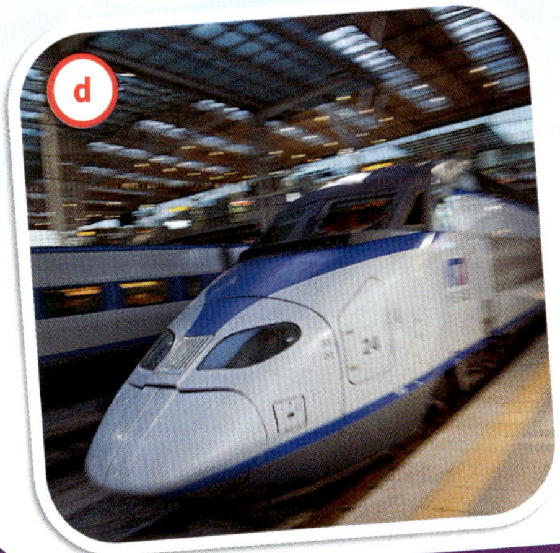

SHAPE IT!

CULTURE PROJECT

A 3-D Room Plan

A room plan shows the design of a room and the furniture inside it. Make a plan of a room with modern technology.

Teacher's Resource Bank

7 REVIEW

VOCABULARY

1 **Complete the crossword.**

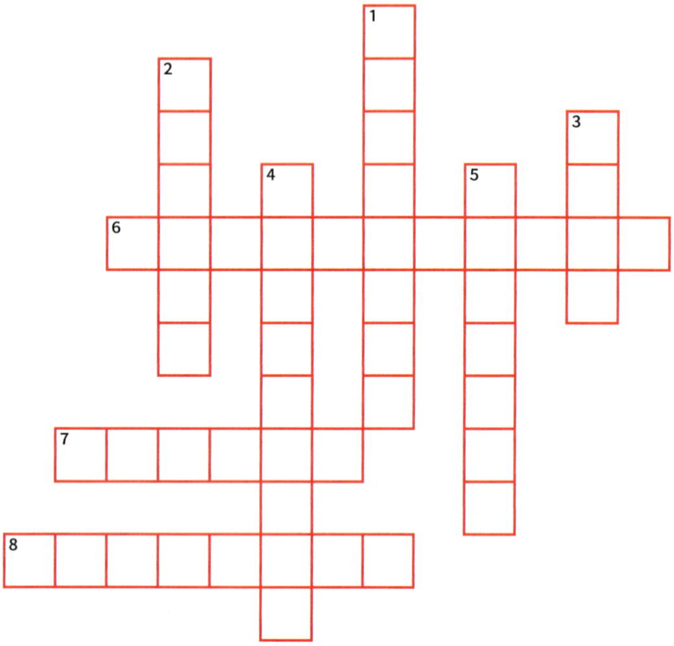

Across

6 *Facebook* and *Instagram* are examples of this.

7 A general word for an electronic gadget.

8 All the programs that tell a computer what to do.

Down

1 Take a file, photo, video, etc. from the Internet and put it onto your device.

2 Put a file from your device onto the Internet.

3 The "brain" inside your computer or phone.

4 This is when you see and talk to someone using your computer or phone.

5 A short text that you send to someone.

2 **Circle the correct words.**

1 Eva *caught* / *went by* the bus outside the bank.

2 Jo traveled from Boston to New York *on* / *by* train.

3 Nina went to the library *by* / *on* foot.

4 Zehra got *off* / *out* the tram at the last stop.

5 Luke *took* / *caught* a taxi from home and got *out* / *off* at the airport.

GRAMMAR IN ACTION

3 **Complete the sentences with the present perfect form of the verbs in parentheses.**

1 How annoying! My phone is on silent and I just realized that I ____________ five calls. (miss)

2 You don't need to call a taxi. I ____________ one with this app. (book)

3 I don't know what Dina's brother looks like. She ____________ any photos of him. (not share)

4 I ____________ their new album. I heard it isn't very good. (not download)

4 **Circle the correct answers.**

1 The bus … leave at 10:02 exactly. It's never late.
a may b will c won't

2 They … be able to do it, but they're trying.
a can't b might c may not

3 Hamza bought some tools … his bike.
a fix b to fix c for fix

4 We don't have enough ink … the photos.
a to print b for to print c for print

Self-Assessment

I can talk about communication and technology.

I can talk about getting around.

I can use the present perfect to make affirmative and negative sentences and questions.

I can use *will*/*won't*, *may*, and *might* to make predictions.

I can use *to* + infinitive to talk about purpose.

LEARN TO … MAKE AND USE FLASHCARDS

You can use flashcards to learn collocations and phrases with prepositions.

1 Match the front and back of the flashcards.

1 use a messaging ______

2 get into / ______ a car

3 ______ addition

4 ______ / download photos

5 ______ instance

a upload

b app

c for

d get out of

e in

2 Match the flashcards in Exercise 1 with the different types of flashcard a–c below.

a a phrase with the preposition missing ☐ ☐

b a collocation with one word missing ☐

c opposite collocations with one of them missing ☐ ☐

3 Choose five collocations or phrases with prepositions from Unit 7. Use them to make the different types of flashcards in Exercise 2.

SHAPE IT!

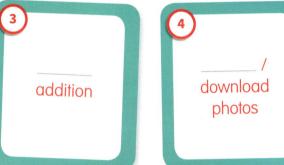

4 Show the front of your flashcards from Exercise 3 to your partner. Can they guess what is on the back of each flashcard?

______ device

Mobile … Voice-activated …

No, it begins with the letter "e."

Electronic device?

Yes! That's right!

5 Discuss the questions with your partner.

Which are …

1 easier to make: flashcards with phrases with prepositions or flashcards with collocations?

2 easier to remember with flashcards: phrases with prepositions or collocations?

8 What is success?

LEARNING OUTCOMES

I can ...

- understand comments on a web page and a talk about a young inventor
- answer questions in a job interview
- write a competition entry
- understand how to use present perfect for experience, and reflexive and indefinite pronouns
- talk about exceptional jobs and qualities, and achievements
- form people words take notes, and make a vocabulary plan
- manage my time and create a timeline

Start It!

1 Look at the photo. What did the girl and her mother do?
2 Before you watch, think of three great human achievements.
3 Why do people say fire is a great human achievement? Watch and check.
4 Think of three personal achievements for you.

Watch video 8.1

p97

Grammar in Action 8.2

p99

Grammar in Action 8.3

p100

Everyday English 8.4

VOCABULARY
Exceptional Jobs and Qualities

8.01 **1 Match the jobs with the photos. Listen, check, and repeat.**

athlete	☐	inventor	☐
businessman/ businesswoman	☐	mathematician	☐
composer	☐	scientist	☐
engineer	1	writer	☐

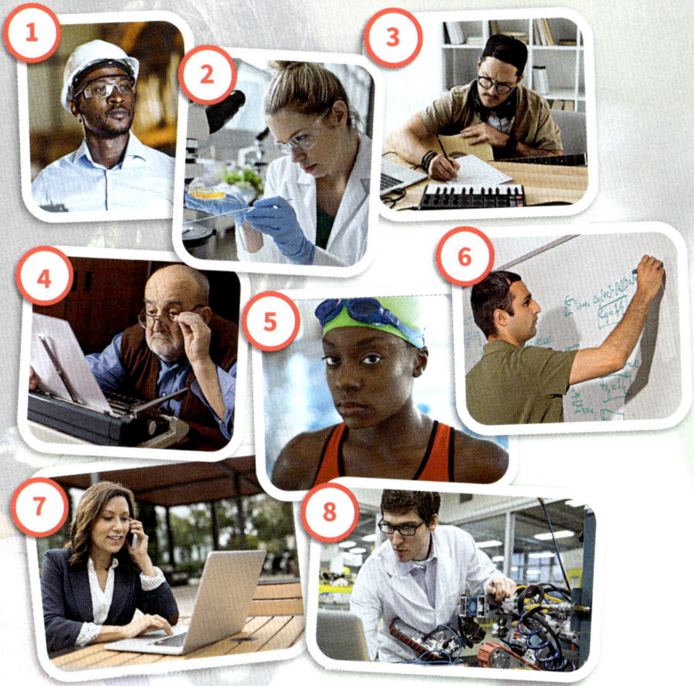

8.02 **2 Circle the correct words. Then listen and check.**

1 Athletes like runners and swimmers have incredible *creativity* / *strength*.
2 The scientist Albert Einstein was famous for his great *intelligence* / *strength*.
3 At just four years old, Mozart showed a lot of *skill* / *determination* as a composer.
4 J. K. Rowling's *creativity* / *intelligence* as a writer made her famous around the world.
5 Ada Lovelace was an English mathematician. Her *talent* / *creativity* for math helped to make the modern computer possible.
6 The inventor Thomas Edison worked with a lot of *determination* / *talent* over many years to make his light bulb work.

LEARN TO LEARN
Word Formation: People Words

To form nouns to describe people, we often add extra letters to a verb or a noun. We sometimes need to change other letters.

3 Complete the chart with words from Exercise 1.

Verb / Noun	Suffix	People Word
invent	-or	1 inventor
compose write	-er	2 ______ 3 ______
mathematics	-ian	4 ______
science	-ist	5 ______
business	-man -woman	6 ______ 7 ______

4 Test your partner. Ask who … ?

Who writes music? *A composer.*

Use It!

5 Choose three jobs from Exercise 1. Take notes about the special qualities the jobs need.

1 ______
2 ______
3 ______

6 Discuss your ideas.

I think a writer needs a lot of talent and creativity.

Explore It!

Guess the correct answer.

How old was Louis Braille when he invented his famous alphabet for the blind?

a 10 **b** 15 **c** 25

Find another interesting fact about an amazing achievement. Then write a question for your partner to answer.

READING
Online Comments

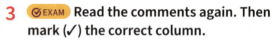

1 **Look at the photos and discuss the questions.**

1 Are the people successful?

2 What do you need to be successful in these areas?

8.03 **2** **Read the online comments. In which area is each person successful?**

Teenagers Taking the World by Storm

Yesterday's article about teenagers' achievements has made a big impression. We've never had so many comments!

1 Krtin Nithiyanandam is only 17, but the intelligence and creativity of this British teen are amazing. He hasn't been to college, but he's done laboratory research into Alzheimer's disease and is the inventor of a new test for it. He's worked with Cambridge University scientists and has won awards. Genius!

smartypants **11 m ago**

2 Have you ever heard of Mikaila Ulmer? This Texas kid has won one of the U.S.A.'s most famous game shows, has made a fortune, and has even met the president. She started a lemonade business and entered a TV competition for entrepreneurs. She won and made a deal worth millions of dollars. I haven't tried her lemonade, but it's called BeeSweet. Mikaila gives money to charities that protect bees, and she's even written a book. For a 13-year-old businesswoman, she's doing pretty well!

Marion_T **56 m ago**

3 We've heard about some incredible prodigies, but how about Alma Deutscher? She's an incredible 12-year-old musician from England. Home-schooled, Alma started playing the piano at two and showed talent even then. She's given concerts all over the world, and she's also a composer. She's composed pieces for whole orchestras and has even written an opera. I'm doing my best to learn the violin, so when I saw Alma on television, I was amazed. With all that skill, I wonder … has she ever played a wrong note? I doubt it!

Bowfrog **1h 10 m ago**

3 EXAM **Read the comments again. Then mark (✓) the correct column.**

Who …	Krtin	Mikaila	Alma
1 is only 12 years old?			✓
2 is 17 years old?			
3 invented a medical test?			
4 sold lemonade?			
5 plays the piano?			
6 helps protect bees?			

4 **Find and underline phrases in the comments with *do* or *make*. Complete the chart with two more examples for each.**

Do	*Make*
laboratory research	a big impression

Voice It!

5 **Discuss the questions.**

1 Who do you think has had the most effect on people's lives: Krtin, Mikaila, or Alma? Why?

2 Do you know of another young person who has achieved a lot?

Finished? p125 Ex. 1

Watch video 8.2
Has Joann ever lost an art competition?
Which countries has Joann been to?

GRAMMAR IN ACTION
Present Perfect for Experience

	I/We/You/They	*He/She/It*
+	We**'ve heard** about some incredible prodigies.	He**'s worked** with Cambridge University scientists.
–	I **haven't tried** her lemonade. We**'ve** [1] never **had** so many comments.	He **hasn't been** to college.
?	**Have** you [2] ______ **heard** of Mikaila Ulmer? Yes, I **have**. / No, I **haven't**.	**Has** she [3] ______ **played** a wrong note? Yes, she **has**. / No, she **hasn't**.

Pronunciation p142

1 **Complete the examples in the chart above with *ever* or *never*. Use the online comments on page 96 to help you.**

Get It Right!

We use an affirmative verb with **never**.

I've never played golf. **NOT** ~~*I haven't never played golf.*~~

8.06 **2** **Maya Flynn is cycling around the world for charity. Complete the interview with the present perfect form of the verbs. Then listen and check.**

PAUL How far [1] have you cycled (you / cycle), Maya?
MAYA [2] ______ (I / ride) 15,000 km so far. I have another 12,000 to go!
PAUL How many countries [3] ______ (you / cross)?
MAYA [4] ______ (I / be) to three continents so far, and [5] ______ (I / visit) 12 countries.
PAUL [6] ______ (you / have) any funny experiences along the way?
MAYA Well, an emu chased me in the Australian outback. [7] ______ (I / never experience) that before!
PAUL No, not many people have! And how [8] ______ ______ (your bicycle / be)?
MAYA [9] ______ (it / not have) any problems at all. It's a great bike.
PAUL So how much money [10] ______ (you / make)?
MAYA [11] ______ (I / not reach) my target, but [12] ______ (I / make) $30,000 so far.
PAUL That's amazing! Good luck with the rest of your journey.

3 **Write questions and short answers about the people in the online comments on page 96.**

1 Krtin / work / in a laboratory?
Has Krtin worked in a laboratory?
Yes, he has.

2 Mikaila and Alma / be / to college?
______
______

3 Marion_T / try / BeeSweet lemonade?
______
______

4 Bowfrog / hear / Alma play?
______
______

Use It!

4 **Use the words in the box and write questions with the present perfect and *ever* in your notebooks.**

be on TV climb a mountain perform in a concert raise money for charity win a competition win a race

5 **Ask and answer your questions.**

Have you ever won a competition?

Yes, I have. I won an art competition in elementary school.

Finished? p125 Ex. 2

VOCABULARY AND LISTENING

Phrasal Verbs: Achievement

8.07 **1 Listen and repeat the verbs in the box. Complete the sentences with the correct form of the verbs. Then match them with the pictures.**

~~come up with~~	give up	
keep up with	look up to	set up
show off	take part in	work out

1 The professor was so happy when he finally came up with the answer! [g]

2 Marcus loves to __________ charity races. [ ]

3 Martha is nearly at the top. She isn't going to __________ now! [ ]

4 The others can't __________ Grandma. [ ]

5 My brother __________ his own business when he was ten. [ ]

6 Thalia really __________ her mom. She wants to be just like her one day. [ ]

7 The math problem is hard to __________. [ ]

8 Aiden likes __________ on the court! [ ]

a 

e 

b 

f 

c 

g 

d 

h 

Use It!

2 Use phrasal verbs from Exercise 1 to write three examples from your own life. Compare with a partner.

1 __________

2 __________

3 __________

I wasn't very good at the piano, but I didn't give up.

A Talk

3 Discuss the questions.

1 What is the girl doing? 2 What is difficult for her?

8.08 **4 Listen to a talk. Were your ideas right?**

LEARN TO LEARN

Taking Notes

Write key words when you listen. Then use your notes to remember the ideas that you heard.

8.08 **5 Listen again and take notes for each heading.**

Personal details

1 Ann Makosinski – 20 – Canadian (parents Polish/Filipino)

Her flashlight – how it works

2 __________

Why she thought of the idea

3 __________

Her achievements

4 __________

Her E-Drink mug – how it works

5 __________

6 Explain how Ann's inventions work. Use your notes from Exercise 5.

Watch video 8.3
What skill should everyone learn?
Who does the vlogger say that everyone should know?

GRAMMAR IN ACTION

Reflexive Pronouns

Singular	I → [1]myself	you → yourself	he → himself	she → [4]______	it → itself
Plural	we → [2]______	you → [3]______	they → themselves		

1 **Complete the examples in the chart above.**

2 **Complete the sentences about the talk on page 98 with reflexive pronouns.**

1 Ann taught herself the science she needed.
2 Ann's flashlight switches ______ off.
3 Ann made the flashlight ______ .
4 Her inventions don't need batteries. They power ______ in other ways.
5 If we believe in ______ , we can achieve anything.

8.09 **3** **Match 1–6 with a–f. Then listen and check.**

1 I surprised c
2 John and I introduced ___
3 Jane, make sure that you take care of ___
4 Mike has taught ___
5 You and Vicky should make ___
6 Stan and Ollie prepared ___

a ourselves to the new neighbors.
b themselves well for the match.
c myself when I did so well on my exams.
d yourselves some sandwiches for lunch.
e himself Spanish and French.
f yourself while I'm away.

Use It!

4 **Discuss the questions.**

1 Have you taught yourself a skill? What?
2 How do you reward yourself when you've done something good?
3 Where do you imagine yourself ten years from now?

I taught myself to swim when I was eight.

Indefinite Pronouns

People	Things	Places
someone (somebody)	[1]______	somewhere
everyone (everybody)	everything	[3]______
no one (nobody)	[2]______	nowhere
anyone (anybody)	anything	[4]______

Ann Makosinski is **someone** I really look up to.
Anything is possible.
No one has thought of these ideas before.

5 **Complete the columns in the chart above.**

8.10 **6** **Circle the correct words in the article. Then listen and check.**

TEENAGER SAILS INTO RECORD BOOKS

Dutch teenager Laura Dekker has become the youngest person ever to sail solo around the world. Laura is only 16 years old. [1]*No one* / *Anyone* so young has achieved this before. Sailing is [2]*something* / *nothing* her whole family is crazy about, and Laura learned [3]*anything* / *everything* she knows about it from her parents. By the time she was 13, there wasn't [4]*anywhere* / *nowhere* she couldn't sail by herself. [5]*Everyone* / *Someone* has a dream, and Laura's achievement shows that [6]*something* / *nothing* is impossible if you want it enough.

Use It!

7 **Complete the sentences. Then compare with your partner.**

Everyone in my family likes ______
I don't know anyone who has ______
Something I really want to do is ______
______ is somewhere I want to visit one day.

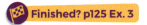

Finished? p125 Ex. 3

SPEAKING
An Interview

8.11 **1 Listen to the conversation. What does Angie want to do?**

a learn to cook very well

b organize a team

JO So, Angie, why do you want to join our training program?

ANGIE Well, [1] I'm passionate about food. I've taught myself a lot about it, but the training will give me the chance to learn new skills.

JO So have you ever worked in a kitchen?

ANGIE Yes, [2] ______ working in a restaurant. My grandparents run a restaurant, and I help them on weekends.

JO Oh, really? And what skills have you developed?

ANGIE [3] ______ cooking. But the main thing is [4] ______ ______ be a good team player.

JO That's interesting. Tell me more.

ANGIE Well, I also help the wait staff, you know. We take orders from customers and that kind of thing.

8.11 **2 Complete the conversation with the phrases from the *Useful Language* box. Then listen and check.**

Useful Language

I've learned the basics of …

I'm passionate about …

I've had plenty of experience …

I've learned how to …

3 Look at the *Everyday English* box. Find and <u>underline</u> the phrases in the conversation.

Watch video 8.4
Everyday English

Tell me more.	that kind of thing
the main thing is	you know

4 Match the *Everyday English* phrases with their uses.

You want to …

1 get more information. ______

2 refer to similar examples. ______

3 say your most important point. ______

4 check the person understands. ______

PLAN

5 Work with a partner. In your notebook, take notes on questions to ask in a job interview for one of these jobs.

computer programmer fashion designer gardener photographer zookeeper

SPEAK

6 Practice the interview with your partner. Remember to use the present perfect to talk about experiences, vocabulary from this unit, and phrases from the *Useful Language* and *Everyday English* boxes.

CHECK

7 Work with another pair. Listen to their interview and complete the notes.

What questions did the interviewer ask?

______

______

What experience does the interviewee have?

______

Should the person get the job? ______

WRITING
A Competition Entry

1 **Read the advertisement. What sort of competition is this? What is the prize?**

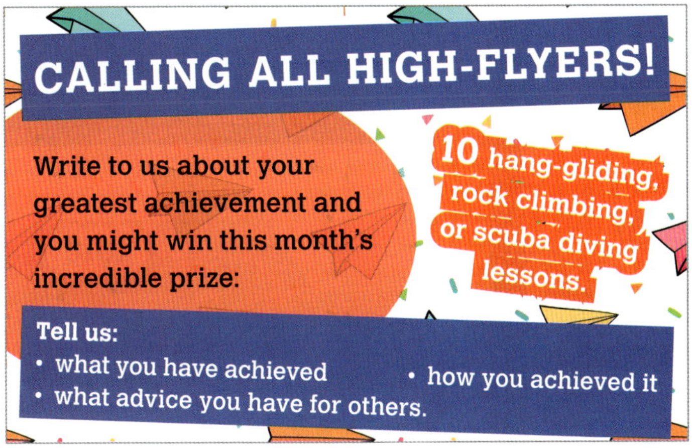
CALLING ALL HIGH-FLYERS!
Write to us about your greatest achievement and you might win this month's incredible prize:
10 hang-gliding, rock climbing, or scuba diving lessons.
Tell us:
• what you have achieved
• how you achieved it
• what advice you have for others.

2 **Read Ajani's competition entry. What has he achieved?**

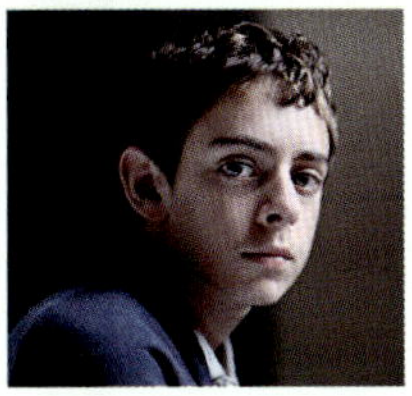

My name is Ajani. My family came to the UK from Afghanistan when I was seven.

My greatest achievement is learning English. When I first arrived, I couldn't understand anyone. At school, I couldn't read or write, and everything was very difficult. However, after a lot of effort, I've managed to learn English. I've even won a national story-writing competition.

How did I do it? First of all, I had a wonderful teacher named Mrs. Connor. She helped me to develop my writing skills. But I also taught myself. I've read plenty of books in English, I've watched a lot of lessons on the Internet, and I've practiced speaking with friends.

If you want to learn a language, my advice to you is to believe in yourself and never give up.

3 **Read Ajani's entry again. Are the sentences *T* (true) or *F* (false)?**

1 Ajani is not from England. ___
2 He came to the UK by himself. ___
3 He still doesn't speak much English. ___
4 He speaks English when he's with friends. ___
5 He thinks you need determination to succeed. ___

Useful Language

after a lot of effort	My advice to you is …
How did I do it?	my greatest achievement

4 **Rewrite the sentences using the phrases in the *Useful Language* box. You might need to write two sentences.**

1 I think you should get a teacher. ___
2 The team worked hard and won the prize. ___
3 Do you want to know how I learned to fly a plane? ___
4 Learning French was the best thing I have done. ___

PLAN

5 **Plan your own competition entry. In your notebook, take notes for four paragraphs about one of your achievements.**

1 Introduce yourself.
2 Explain the achievement.
3 Explain how you achieved it.
4 Give advice for other people.

WRITE

6 **Write your competition entry. Remember to include the present perfect, reflexive pronouns, vocabulary from this unit, and phrases from the *Useful Language* box.**

CHECK

7 **Do you …**

- have four paragraphs?
- explain your achievement clearly?
- give useful advice?

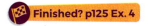

Finished? p125 Ex. 4

TECHNOLOGY PROJECT

A Timeline

1 **Read texts 1–6 on the timeline quickly. Then match them with the pictures (A–F).**

1 C 2 ☐ 3 ☐ 4 ☐ 5 ☐ 6 ☐

2 **For each question, choose the correct inventor. Some questions have more than one answer.**

Which inventor or inventors …

1 worked with a brother? d, f
2 studied how birds fly? ______
3 had an accident? ______
4 wasn't European? ______
5 didn't fly the machine himself? ______
6 designed an aircraft with an engine? ______

a Eilmer of Malmesbury
b Leonardo da Vinci
c Denis Bolor
d Joseph-Michel Montgolfier
e Jules Giffard
f Orville Wright

How to Manage Your Time

3 **Look at some ideas to think about before you start a project. Mark (✓) the ideas connected to planning your time.**

a Decide on a topic for the project. ☐
b Think about all the tasks you need to do in the time available. ☐
c Prioritize tasks – decide what's most and least important. ☐
d Include some extra time. ☐
e Decide who will do what. ☐
f Set long-term deadlines. ☐
g Set short-term deadlines. ☐
h Review your project regularly to see if you are keeping to your deadlines. ☐

8.12 **4** **Listen to two students planning a project. Which ideas in Exercise 3 do they talk about?**

____ ____ ____ ____ ____

1

Eilmer of Malmesbury, England, has had a great idea. He ties himself to a pair of wings and jumps off the top of a tower. Eilmer flies for 200 meters. No one has ever flown so far. However, Eilmer hasn't thought about the landing! He hurts himself badly, but also gets himself a place in the history books.

1010

4

French businessman Joseph-Michel Montgolfier and his brother, Jacques-Étienne, have invented the world's first hot-air balloon. Now they make a second flight with passengers. But they don't put themselves on board. The three lucky passengers are a hen, a duck, and a sheep!

1783

5

French engineer Jules Giffard connects a steam engine to a huge balloon. It's the first "airship." People have never seen anything like it before. It's the first aircraft that someone can steer. However, the first time Giffard sets off in his airship, it flies around in circles. He can't steer it against the strong Paris winds!

1852

HIGH (AND NOT SO HIGH) ACHIEVERS

THE EARLY HISTORY OF FLIGHT

2 The brilliant Italian scientist and inventor Leonardo da Vinci has looked into how birds fly. Using his discoveries, he designs the world's first flying machine – the Ornithopter. But he has the intelligence not to try it himself! Later, other people try out similar designs, but no one gets very far.

1485

3 Frenchman Denis Bolor has come up with his own flying machine that uses wings with springs. Poor Bolor tries to show off his idea and kills himself when the springs break.

1536

6 It's 10:35 a.m. on December 17. American engineer Orville Wright has lifted himself into the air. He's flying the Wright Flyer, a motor-powered airplane he designed with his brother Wilbur. Orville keeps the Flyer in the air for 12 seconds and travels 37 meters. It isn't a long-distance flight, but it has changed the world forever.

1903

A

B
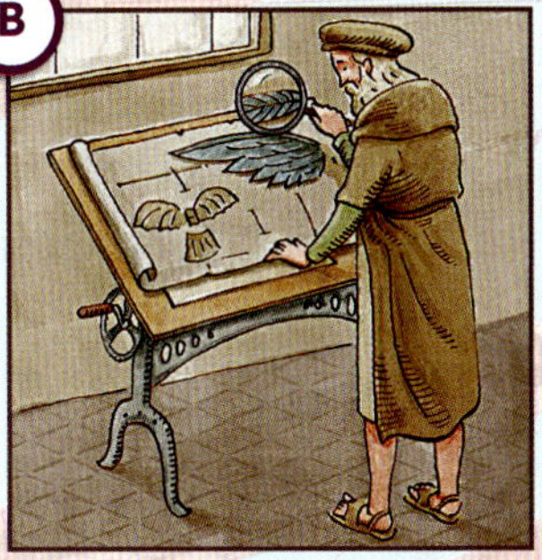

C

D
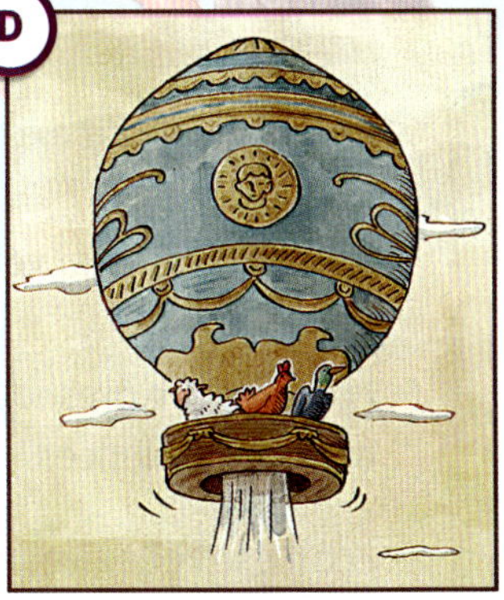

E
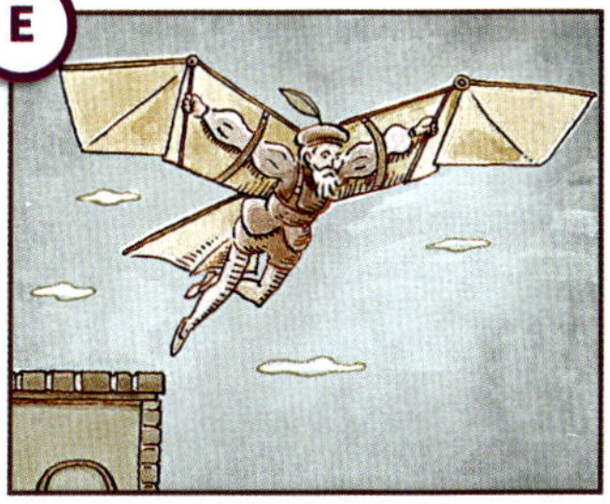

F
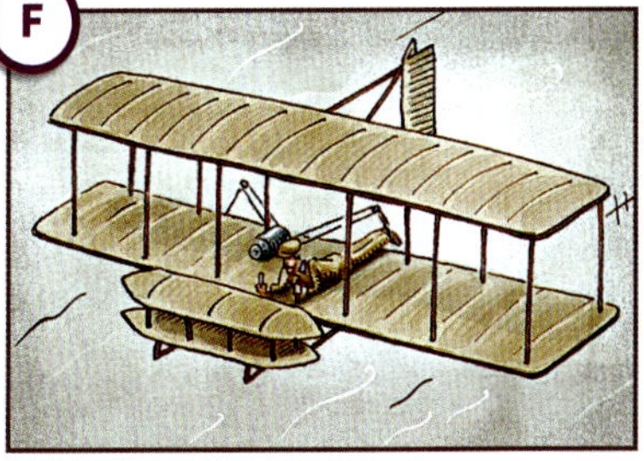

PLAN

5 Work in groups. Plan a timeline. Choose one of the inventions in the box or choose your own. Then complete the steps below.

the Internet	the bicycle
the computer	the skyscraper

- Decide what tasks you need to do to complete your timeline and how long each will take.
- Set long-term and short-term deadlines and include some extra time.
- Decide who will do each task.
- Research the information you need.
- Find or make pictures for your timeline.

PRESENT

6 Display your timeline on the classroom wall. Remember to include important dates, people and events, interesting pictures, and the tips in *How to Manage Your Time*.

CHECK

7 Look at your classmates' timelines. Which ones have interesting facts? Discuss in your group.

8 REVIEW

VOCABULARY

1 Complete the sentences with the words for jobs and qualities.

1. She's going to succeed. She's got plenty of d__________.
2. You need a lot of s__________ to be a concert pianist.
3. C__________ is important if you want to be a good designer.
4. I don't have enough s__________ in my arms to do rock climbing.
5. Nick has written some brilliant songs. I think he'll be a professional c__________.
6. I am terrible at math. I could never be a m__________!
7. I could be an i__________. I have a lot of ideas for new machines.

2 Complete the sentences with words from both boxes. Use the correct form of the verbs. Use some words more than once.

come	give	keep	set	work

off	out	up	with

1. I did ballet for three years, but I __________ because I wasn't good at it.
2. Mira is running too fast for me. I can't __________ her.
3. We'll need to arrive early to __________ our cookie table at the market.
4. Do you know the answer? I can't __________ it __________.
5. Amol has __________ a brilliant idea for our team project.

GRAMMAR IN ACTION

3 Complete the questions with *ever* and the verbs in the box. Then write the short answers.

have	ride	see	try	visit

1 **A** __________ you __________ a snake?
B __________. I saw one in our yard.

2 **A** __________ your brother __________ an accident in his car?
B __________. He's a very careful driver.

3 **A** __________ your parents __________ the U.S.A.?
B __________. They went there six years ago.

4 **A** __________ you __________ to invent something?
B __________, but it wasn't successful!

5 **A** __________ Fiona __________ a horse?
B __________. Unfortunately, she fell off!

4 Circle the correct words.

1. Dan set up a business *themselves / himself.*
2. We built our house *myself / ourselves.*
3. You won't achieve *anything / anywhere* if you don't try.
4. This computer has taught *itself / myself* to play chess.
5. Is there *no one / anyone* who knows Patrick's address?

Self-Assessment

I can talk about exceptional jobs and qualities.

I can use phrasal verbs to talk about achievement.

I can use the present perfect to talk about experiences.

I can use reflexive pronouns.

I can use indefinite pronouns.

LEARN TO ... MAKE A VOCABULARY STUDY PLAN

You can learn vocabulary better by studying it more than once. A study plan can help you do this.

1 Do the quiz. Circle your answers and find out your score.

Do you need a vocabulary study plan? FIND OUT!

Do you ...

1. write new vocabulary in your notebook?
   always / *sometimes* / *never*
2. use flashcards to learn vocabulary?
   always / *sometimes* / *never*
3. look at your vocabulary notes when you do your homework?
   always / *sometimes* / *never*
4. study your vocabulary notes before a test?
   always / *sometimes* / *never*
5. study your vocabulary notes more than three times a week?
   always / *sometimes* / *never*

Results

always = 2 points sometimes = 1 point never = 0 point

8–10: Well done! You study vocabulary well, but why not try a new study plan?

4–7: Not bad, but a study plan can help you.

0–3: Oh, no! You really need a study plan!

2 Ask your partner the quiz questions. Underline their answers.

3 Compare scores with your partner. Do you both agree with what it says about you?

4 Match 1–3 with a–c. Which sentence surprises you most? Discuss with your partner.

1. We remember vocabulary better when we study it once and ___
2. When you use flashcards to learn vocabulary, ___
3. It's necessary to see, hear, or say a word ___

a. 17 times before we remember it well.
b. then a few days later (but not the next day).
c. you remember it better.

5 Make a list of eight words from this unit that you want to learn. Make flashcards.

___ ___ ___
___ ___ ___
___ ___

SHAPE IT!

6 Follow steps 1–4 to make a 10-day vocabulary study plan.

1. Write the dates on the plan, starting with tomorrow's date.
2. On the shaded days, test yourself with your flashcards from Exercise 5.
3. When you finish studying each day, write "Yes!" in the "Done?" box.
4. On day 11, answer the question and circle "a lot" or "a little."

Day	1	2	3	4	5	6	7	8	9	10	11
Date											How much has the plan helped me learn vocabulary? *a lot* / *a little*
Done?											

9 How do you express yourself?

LEARNING OUTCOMES

I can ...

- understand texts about music
- make polite refusals
- write a review
- understand how to use *going to*, *will*, the present continuous for the future, and the simple present for the future
- talk about and describe musical instruments and genres, and dance styles
- recognize stress patterns, distinguish between speakers, use referencing, and practice your English during vacation

Start It!

1 Look at the photo. What do you think the man is doing?
2 Before you watch, how does music make you feel?
3 How do people who can't hear enjoy music? Watch and check.
4 What instruments do you play or do you want to play?

Watch video 9.1

p109

Grammar in Action 9.2

p111

Grammar in Action 9.3

p112

Everyday English 9.4

p114

Globetrotters 9.5

VOCABULARY
Musical Instruments and Genres

9.01 **1** **Match the words in the boxes with the genres (1–6) and musical instruments (7–14) in the pictures. Listen, check, and repeat.**

classical ☐	hip-hop ☐	reggae ☐
folk 1	jazz ☐	rock ☐

bass ☐	microphone ☐
drums ☐	saxophone ☐
guitar ☐	trumpet ☐
keyboard ☐	violin ☐

2 **How many other musical instruments and genres can you think of?**

Get It Right!

We say **play football**, **tennis**, **golf**, etc.

And we also say **play the piano**, **the guitar**, **the trumpet**, etc.

LEARN TO LEARN
Stress Patterns

It's important to learn which syllable is stressed when you learn a new word.

9.02 **3** **Complete the chart with the words in Exercise 1. Then listen and check. Can you add one more word to some groups?**

O	folk,
Oo	
oO	
Ooo	classical,
ooO	

4 **Take turns clapping the rhythm of a word from Exercise 1. Your partner guesses the word.**

Use It!

5 **Discuss the questions.**

1 What kind of music do you like listening to?

2 Can you or your friends or family play a musical instrument? Which one?

3 Which instruments do you like the sound of?

Explore It!

Guess the correct answer.

Chicago rapper Twista is one of the fastest rappers in the world. What's the fastest he can rap?

a 10 syllables per second

b 20 syllables per second

c 30 syllables per second

Find another interesting fact about music. Then write a question for your partner to answer.

READING
An Events Guide

1 **Look at the photos of four musicians. What kind of music do you think they play?**

9.03 **2** **Read the events guide. Match musicians 1–4 with the genres that they are going to perform.**

blues	☐	pop	☐
country	☐	raga	☐

3 **Match concerts A–D with these features. Sometimes there is more than one concert.**

1 __A__ has only one performer
2 ____ includes an electronic instrument
3 ____ is free for some people
4 ____ has more than two performers
5 ____ includes a violin
6 ____ starts before eight o'clock
7 ____ is cheaper for college students
8 ____ starts the latest

4 **Find adjectives in the guide that mean …**

1 alone __solo__
2 very excited ____
3 famous ____
4 very unusual ____
5 surprising ____
6 talented ____

Voice It!

5 **Put the concerts in the events guide in order from most interesting to least interesting. Explain your choices to your partner.**

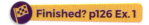

Finished? p126 Ex. 1

WATERSIDE ARTS CENTER

What's on at the Waterside

A Tuesday 8 p.m.
Bunny Scraggs
$8.00, $3.00 (student discount)

We think this show will surprise reggae fans. The Dubster Brothers' bassist also plays blues piano, and he's going to share that talent tonight. In this solo performance, Bunny's going to play and sing his favorite blues classics. However, if you want to hear some of the Dubster Brothers' hits, we're sure Bunny won't disappoint!

B Thursday 7 p.m.
Janet Glyndebourne and the Donuts
$5, no charge for under 16s

We're thrilled to welcome Janet Glyndebourne to Waterside. However, the well-known opera star isn't going to sing Mozart. Instead, she's going to join Kim Green on synthesizer and Bod on percussion, and they're going to play a concert of pure pop. We're sure it will be a great evening!

C Saturday 7:30 p.m.
Dr Jay and the Rodeo Band
$10.00, $4.00 (student discount)

For one night only, hip-hop artist Dr. Jay is going to lead country favorites the Rodeo Band (Helen Smith on banjo and vocals, Liam Jones on double bass, Lucy-Anne Flynn on violin). Are you really going to miss this unique event? We're sure you won't want to!

D Sunday 9:30 p.m.
Angus Beardsley Plays Raga
$15.00, $7.00

Rock legends Axel Heads have announced that they aren't going to tour again. Their fans will miss them, but we have some unexpected news! The band's bass player, Angus "The Beard" Beardsley, is also a gifted violinist. On Saturday he's going to team up with sitar player Jagjit Rakha to perform Indian raga. But is "The Beard" going to sing in Hindi, too? Come and find out!

Watch video 9.2
Which music festival is Fiona going to? What music is Evita going to listen to?

GRAMMAR IN ACTION

Going To

	I/He/She/It	You/We/They
+	He [1]*'s going to* **share** that talent tonight.	They [3] ________ **play** a concert of pure pop.
–	Janet **isn't going to sing** Mozart.	Axel Heads [4] ________ **tour** again.
?	[2] ______ "The Beard" ________ **sing** in Hindi?	**Are** you really **going to miss** this unique event?

1 **Complete the examples in the chart above with the correct form of *going to*. Use the events guide on page 108 to help you.**

2 **Complete the sentences about the events guide with the correct form of *going to*.**

1 The concerts *aren't going to start* (not start) before 7 p.m.
2 Two concerts ________ (take) place on the weekend.
3 Bunny Scraggs ________ (play) blues piano.
4 Janet Glyndebourne ________ (not perform) classical music.

9.04 **3** **Complete the conversation with the correct form of *going to*. Then listen and check.**

AMY Hi, Josh. [1] *Are you going to go* (you / go) out tomorrow evening?
JOSH No, [2] ________ (I / stay) at home and watch a movie. What about you?
AMY Yeah. Dr. Jay is at the Waterside. [3] ________ (I / not miss) that.
JOSH Wow! Really?
AMY Yeah, really. [4] ________ (I / buy) my ticket this morning.
JOSH Hmm. Sounds interesting. [5] ________ (Aneta / join) you?
AMY No! [6] ________ (she / not come). She can't stand Dr. Jay. Why don't you come?
JOSH OK, you've convinced me. But how [7] ________ (we / get) there? [8] ________ (we / not walk), are we?
AMY [9] ________ (my dad / give) us a ride.

Will and *Going To*

Get It Right!

We often use **will** for predictions and **going to** for intentions.

*We're sure it **will** be a great evening.*
*Bunny **is going to** play his favorite blues classics.*

4 **Decide if these sentences are *P* (predictions) or *I* (intentions). Then complete the sentences and check your answers on page 108.**

1 We think this show *will* surprise reggae fans. *P*
2 We're sure Bunny ________ disappoint! ____
3 She ________ join Kim Green. ____
4 Dr. Jay ________ lead the Rodeo Band. ____

5 **Complete Lia's message to Max. Use the verbs in the box with *going to* or *will*.**

be	buy	fail	~~go~~	like	not be able	play

Hey Max. [1] *Are* you and Mo *going to go* to Jo's party? I think it [2] ________ fun. Jo's brother has a band, and they [3] ________ at the party. I'm sure you [4] ________ them. [5] ______ you ________ tickets for the Z Men concert? I probably [6] ________ to go. We have a test that week, and I [7] ________ it if I don't study.

Use It!

6 **Tell your partner about your intentions and predictions for the weekend.**

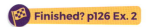

Finished? p126 Ex. 2

VOCABULARY AND LISTENING

Dance Styles

9.05 **1 Match the words in the box with the photos. Listen, check, and repeat.**

ballet dancing	☐	modern dance	☐
ballroom dancing	1	salsa dancing	☐
breakdancing	☐	swing	☐
disco dancing	☐	tap dancing	☐
folk dance	☐	Zumba	☐

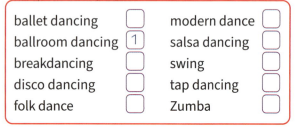

1

2

3

4

5

6

7

8

9

10

Use It!

2 Discuss the dance styles in Exercise 1.

1 What type of music accompanies the styles?
2 What do people usually wear for these styles?
3 Which dance style do you think looks best? Why?

A Discussion

9.06 **3 Listen to a conversation between four students. What are they talking about?**

a a show they have seen
b a show they are planning

LEARN TO LEARN

Distinguishing Between Speakers

When you listen to a group of people speaking, but you cannot see them, it can be difficult to understand who says what. For each person, consider these things:

- Are they male or female?
- Are they old or young?
- Do they say any names?

9.06 **4 EXAM Listen again and match the people with the tasks. There are two extra tasks.**

1 Imogen ____
2 Marta ____
3 Adam ____
4 Jack ____

a recording the show
b meeting the dancers
c writing the program
d organizing the music
e selling tickets
f putting out the seats

Voice It!

5 Discuss the questions.

1 Have you ever helped organize a school show or a similar event?
2 What do you think is the most difficult part of organizing a show?

GRAMMAR IN ACTION

Present Continuous for Future

Watch video 9.3
What is Paulo doing on Saturday night? What time does the movie begin?

Present Continuous for Future Plans
I [1] ________ **writing** the program.
I [2] ________ **not doing** anything on Friday afternoon.
[3] ________ you **recording** the show, Adam?

Pronunciation p142

1 **Complete the examples in the chart above.**

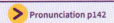

9.06 **2** **Listen again to the conversation between Imogen and her friends on page 110. Correct the sentences.**

1 The teachers are having a party on Friday afternoon.
They aren't having a party. They're having a meeting.

2 Ten dance groups are performing.
____
____

3 Jack is recording the show on his phone.
____
____

9.08 **3** **Complete Lilia's post with the present continuous form of the verbs in the box. Then listen and check.**

bring come leave meet not do perform play ~~return~~

Thank you, New Haven! You were a fabulous audience last night! We [1] *'re returning* in April, so I hope we'll see some of you again. Later today, we [2] ________ for Hartford. We [3] ________ a new play there called *The Bell*, and I [4] ________ a girl who has the power to see the future. Hey, Hartford! If you [5] ________ anything on Friday night, come along. Guess who [6] ________ to see us on our first night – Jennifer Lawrence! She [7] ________ some friends, and we [8] ________ them backstage after the performance. Wow!

Simple Present for Future

Simple Present for Scheduled Events
It [1] ________ (begin) at seven-thirty.
The doors [2] ________ (open) until seven o'clock.
What time [3] ________ the show ________ (start)?

4 **Complete the examples in the chart above with the correct form of the verbs in parentheses.**

5 **Complete sentences 1–4 using the simple present for the future.**

DANCE-FEST

Barnsley Dance Festival, Saturday, June 21

12:30–2:00: African Beat Workshop
Learn traditional African dances.

3:00–4:00: The Langley Dance School
Watch the world's favorite ballet, *Swan Lake*.

6:15–7:00: Tarantella Talk
Gianna Romano gives a talk about one of Italy's most famous dances.

7:30–9:00: The Bronx River Combo
See this New York street dance group doing hip-hop, krumping, and more.

end last ~~start~~ take

1 The festival *starts* at lunchtime.
2 African Beat ________ place first.
3 The ballet ________ for more than an hour.
4 The Bronx River Combo's performance ________ until 9 p.m.

Use It!

6 **Ask and answer the questions about each event at Dance-Fest.**

1 What time does it start and end?
2 What is happening in the event?

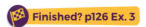

Finished? p126 Ex. 3

SPEAKING
Making Polite Refusals

9.09 **1** **Listen to the conversation. What event is Harry going to? Why can't Jess go?**

HARRY Hi, Jess. I'm going to book tickets for the jazz festival on Saturday. [1] Do you feel like coming along?

JESS [2] __________ my cousin Helen's visiting me, and I'll be with her all day long.

HARRY [3] __________ join us if she wants.

JESS That's really nice of you, Harry, but Helen can't stand jazz!

HARRY Oh, that's too bad. Look, they're playing for two nights. What are you up to on Friday? [4] __________ come then instead?

JESS Hmm. What time does it start?

HARRY 7:30.

JESS Oh, that's no good either, Harry. I have a guitar lesson and it starts at 7:15.

HARRY OK. Never mind, Jess. Maybe another time.

JESS Sure. [5] __________. I'm sure it'll be a great concert.

9.09 **2** **Complete the conversation with phrases from the *Useful Language* box. Then listen and check.**

Useful Language

Do you feel like ...?	I'd love to, but ...
(She's) welcome to ...	Thanks for asking, though
Would you like to ...?	

3 **Look at the *Everyday English* box. Find and underline the phrases in the conversation.**

Watch video 9.4
Everyday English

all day long Never mind. That's no good.
That's too bad. What are you up to?

4 **Match the phrases in the *Everyday English* box with their meanings.**

1 That isn't convenient. __________
2 It doesn't matter. __________
3 for the whole day __________
4 That's sad. __________
5 What plans do you have? __________

PLAN

5 **Work with a partner. Think of an event to go to and reasons why one of you can't go.**

SPEAK

6 **In pairs, practice a converstion making polite refusals. Remember to use *going to*, *will*, the simple present and present continuous, vocabulary from this unit, and phrases from the *Useful Language* and *Everyday English* boxes.**

CHECK

7 **Work with another pair. Listen to their conversation and complete the notes.**

What event do they talk about?

____

Why can't one of them go?

____

____

WRITING
A Review

1 **Read the review quickly. Which dance styles can you see in this show?**

"Hiplet" – A New Dance Experience!

Crash Dance Crew is a dance group from London. Their show, *City Dreams*, tells the story of three teenagers who have come to the city to make a new life for themselves. The show is a unique mix of hip-hop and ballet called hiplet. Three musicians on keyboards, vocals, and turntable play a mix of rap and electro funk.

It's an action-packed story, but there are some very funny moments, too. The costumes are colorful, and I was impressed by the music. However, the highlight of the show is the dancing. The mix of styles works well. On the downside, tickets are expensive and there's no student discount.

Crash Dance Crew play at the Miami Olympia Theater next week. After that, they're touring other cities in the U.S.A. All in all, if you love dance, this superb show is a must-see.

2 **Read the review again and correct these sentences.**

1 The performers are from Miami.
The performers are from London.

2 An orchestra plays the music for the show.

3 The writer liked the music most.

4 Tickets are cheaper for students.

5 The show is only happening in Miami.

3 **In a review, it's a good idea to use lots of adjectives. Find and underline all the adjectives in the dance show review. Discuss with a partner what they describe.**

4 **Find and underline the *Useful Language* phrases in the review. Then match them with phrases a–e.**

Useful Language

[1]All in all ☐
[2]If you love (dance), this (show) is a must-see. ☐
[3]I was impressed by … ☐
[4]On the downside ☐
[5]The highlight of the show is … ☐

a The best part is
b I loved
c It's disappointing that
d In summary
e Fans of (dance) will love this

PLAN

5 **Plan a review of a concert or show you have seen. Take notes for three paragraphs in your notebook.**

1 A general description of the show
2 Details about the dancing, music, costumes, etc. and your opinions of them
3 A summary of your opinion of the show

WRITE

6 **Write your review. Remember to give your opinions and to include adjectives, the simple present to describe the show, and phrases from the *Useful Language* box.**

CHECK

7 **Do you …**

- use three paragraphs?
- say what you liked and didn't like?
- summarize your opinions at the end?

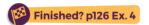

Finished? p126 Ex. 4

AROUND THE WORLD

Globetrotters

Watch video 9.5
The Schuhplattler

- Which dances from other countries do you know?
- Where is the *Schuhplattler* dance from?

READING
A Travel Article

1 **Look at the photo of the dance on page 115. Discuss the questions.**

1. What do you know about this dance?
2. What more would you like to know about it?

9.10 **2** **Read the article. Does it mention any of your ideas from Exercise 1?**

3 **Read the article again and answer the questions in your notebook.**

1. How long does the Festival de Jerez last? Two weeks
2. Who goes to the festival?
3. What can you do at the festival?
4. What traditions does flamenco come from?
5. When did performers start using guitars?
6. What mistake do people often make about flamenco?
7. What part of a flamenco performance can the audience take part in?

Voice It!

4 **Discuss the questions.**

1. Folk dance is a form of cultural expression. Is folk dance an important part of your culture?
2. How is cultural expression important for a community?

Festival de Jerez:
A Flamenco Heaven

by Dan Philips

Every year, the Spanish city of Jerez puts on a festival of flamenco dance that lasts for two wonderful weeks. For me and flamenco fans around the world, [1]it's the highlight of the year. People from over 30 different countries will show up here, all crazy about flamenco.

Every day, there are performances of flamenco. [2]Some take place in the beautiful Villamarta Theater, but most happen in the small flamenco clubs all around Jerez, known as *peñas*. And if you're interested in taking it up yourself, the greatest flamenco teachers from around the world are going to give classes.

The festival begins on February 23 and ends on March 10.
Don't miss out!

SOME HISTORY

Flamenco is typically Spanish, but it has a long international history. Over five centuries ago, the Roma came to Europe from India and brought their traditional music. [3]Their traditions mixed with local traditions from the south of Spain and [4]those of Jewish and North African immigrants, and the result was flamenco.

The 19th century was the "golden age" of flamenco. The first flamenco schools opened [5]then, in Seville, Cádiz, and Jerez. Performers began to use guitars, and dance became more important. Flamenco became the art we know today.

A GUIDE FOR BEGINNERS

Instruments: The two most important of [6]these are the guitar and the castanets, but you might see performances with trumpets, violins, or even a whole orchestra.

Songs: People often think that flamenco is only dancing. In fact, the songs, called *cante*, are the real heart of it. The words are often by Spain's most famous poets.

Dance: *Zapateado* is the dance that flamenco dancers do. They stamp their feet and click their castanets in fast, complicated rhythms. Nobody nods off during a flamenco concert!

Jaleo: This is the hand-clapping and shouting that make flamenco so exciting. The clapping, called *palmas*, is much more difficult than it looks. But anyone can join in the shouting, so don't be shy!

LEARN TO LEARN

Referencing

Writers often use words such as *this* and *that* to refer back to something they have already mentioned in the text.

5 What do underlined words 1–6 in the article refer to?

1 the festival
2 ______
3 ______
4 ______
5 ______
6 ______

6 Find and underline six phrasal verbs in the article with the verbs below. Complete the sentences using the correct form.

join ~~miss~~ nod put show take

1 Buy tickets early so you don't miss out.
2 My mom ______ flamenco guitar last year.
3 They ______ the biggest concerts in the Villamarta Theater.
4 This music is so boring – it's making me ______.
5 We ______ late and couldn't get into the concert.
6 Would you like to ______ the dance with us?

Explore It!

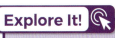

Guess the correct answer.

Jerez is also home to a world-famous … school.

a rock climbing b horseback riding
c film

Find three more interesting facts about Spanish traditions. Choose your favorite fact and write a question for your partner to answer.

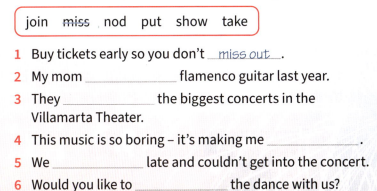

SHAPE IT!

CULTURE PROJECT

A Webpage

A webpage gives important information in an attractive, organized way. Design a webpage about a festival.

Teacher's Resource Bank

9 REVIEW

VOCABULARY

1 Write the names of the musical instruments.

1  __________

2 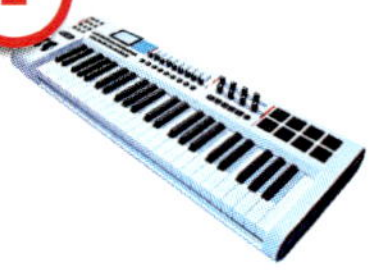 __________

3  __________

4  __________

5  __________

6  __________

2 Complete the dance styles.

1 F__________ dances are old, traditional dances.
2 Couples usually wear formal clothes for b__________ dancing.
3 You can hear a dancer's steps when they're t__________ dancing.
4 B__________ dancing is a street dance that often goes with hip-hop music.
5 People need to train for years to become professional b__________ dancers.

GRAMMAR IN ACTION

3 Complete the sentences with the verbs in the box. Use the correct form of *going to* or *will*.

be	enjoy	learn	meet	not be	not visit	show	tour

1 My favorite band __________ the U.S.A., but they probably __________ my town.
2 Erin thinks we __________ able to learn these dance steps, but we __________ her that we can.
3 James has decided he __________ the piano, and I think he __________ it.
4 I __________ Rosie at the salsa class, but I'm sure she __________ late, as usual!

4 Complete the sentences with the simple present or present continuous form of the verbs.

1 Adriana __________ (bring) her guitar to the party on Saturday.
2 We need to hurry. The show __________ (start) in five minutes.
3 Sara and Jeb __________ (not come) to the theater tomorrow. They have too much homework.
4 There's a bus that __________ (get) to the concert hall at 7:15.
5 The concert __________ (not end) until 11 o'clock. That's pretty late.
6 What __________ you __________ (do) tomorrow night? Do you want to come to my concert?

Self-Assessment

I can talk about musical instruments and genres.

I can talk about dance styles.

I can use *will* and *going to* to talk about predictions and intentions.

I can use the present continuous and the simple present to talk about future plans and scheduled events.

LEARN TO LEARN

LEARN TO ... PRACTICE YOUR ENGLISH DURING VACATION

It's important to practice English during vacation, especially when the vacation is long.

1 **Read the conversation between Egor and Polina. Then circle the correct answers.**

EGOR Two months without English classes!

POLINA But if we don't practice, we'll forget everything.

EGOR I don't want that! We've learned a lot this year.

POLINA Well, why don't we make a list of things we can do in English during the vacation?

EGOR That's a great idea!

1 They're speaking ... the school year.
   a during   b at the end of
2 They don't want to ... their English.
   a forget   b use
3 They're going to ...
   a ask for help.   b think of ways to practice.

2 **Egor and Polina begin their list. What do ideas 1–6 practice? Write *S* (speaking), *L* (listening), *R* (reading), or *W* (writing).**

Things to Do in English over the Summer

1 Podcasts (easy ones on English online) L
2 Keep a scrapbook of places we visit. ___ , ___
3 Change the language of our phone apps to English. ___
4 Pay attention to station and airport announcements in English when we travel. ___
5 Send messages to each other in English! ___ , ___
6 Help a tourist who speaks English. ___ , ___
7 ______
8 ______
9 ______
10 ______

3 **Work in pairs. Think of four more ways to practice English during vacation – one for speaking, listening, reading, and writing. Write them in Egor and Polina's list (7–10).**

SHAPE IT!

4 **Make a plan for practicing English during vacation.**

1 Choose four of the ten ideas from the list and write them under "Ideas" in the chart.
2 Decide when or how often you are going to do these things. Complete the chart.

	Ideas	When? / How Often?
Speaking	Record a voice message for my aunt in English.	Once a week.
Listening	Listen to airport announcements.	When I fly to see my cousin.
Speaking		
Listening		
Reading		
Writing		

5 **Tell your partner what you're going to do. Are there any things you can do together?**

For speaking, I'm going to record a voice message for my aunt once a week.

Why don't you record one for me, too? Then I can send you one back!

Great idea! That will help our listening as well!

1 FINISHED?

A B C D E F G H I J K L M
N O P Q R S T U V W X Y Z

1 What do they like watching? Use the code and write the TV shows.

1 Miriam — sports shows
2 Ahmed — ______
3 Lidia and Ryan — ______
4 Mya's parents — ______
5 Sara's brother — ______

2 Write sentences about four more differences.

In A, Emma is talking on her phone. In B, she's listening to music.

1 ______
2 ______
3 ______
4 ______

3 Read the clues and write the adverbs.

1 The director is shouting at the actors. Usually he's very quiet! How is he speaking? loudly
2 I'm reading this book and it's taking me a long time. How am I reading? ______
3 My teacher says I'm a good student! How am I doing? ______
4 I'm very busy. I want to do all my homework before lunchtime. How am I working? ______
5 I always understand my science teacher. How does she explain things? ______

4 Complete the puzzle and find the mystery word.

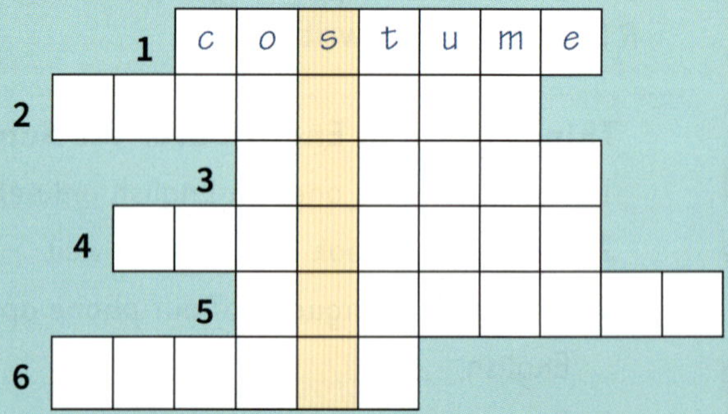

1 c o s t u m e
2
3
4
5
6

1

2 FINISHED?

1 Circle eight weather words.

P	E	T	V	W	A	R	M	C
S	H	O	C	E	G	H	K	L
N	D	H	O	T	O	I	R	O
O	F	E	L	O	L	C	U	U
W	I	N	D	Y	P	Y	I	D
Y	P	P	O	S	U	N	N	Y

2 Put the letters in order to find eight simple past verbs. Then write the infinitive form of the verbs.

1 hottguh thought–think
2 tea ______
3 masw ______
4 rakdn ______
5 aderh ______
6 koto ______

3 Find four sentences in the grid by connecting the words. You can move in any direction: →←↑↓↖↗↙↘.

There →	weren't ↓	There	were	a	kitchen
were	any	in	a	some	There
There	students	sofa	the	was	children
wasn't	in	wallet.	classroom.	a	in
the	any	room.	the	nice	the
a	living	money	in	park.	some

4 Look at the box for one minute. Then cover it and write all the useful objects you can remember.

fork, ______

3 FINISHED?

1 Circle the letters and write the adjectives of feeling.

1

w	x	c
s	o	d
y	r	e
e	r	i

worried

2

e	o	l
r	n	s
l	e	r
y	s	v

______

3

u	s	u
n	e	o
t	r	v
i	d	e

______

4

e	d	r
y	i	f
r	g	a
o	n	s

______

5

e	l	u
u	s	p
m	e	r
t	b	a

______

2 Look at the picture for one minute. Then close your book and write sentences about what the people were doing at 7 a.m.

Tilly and Milly were sitting up in their beds.

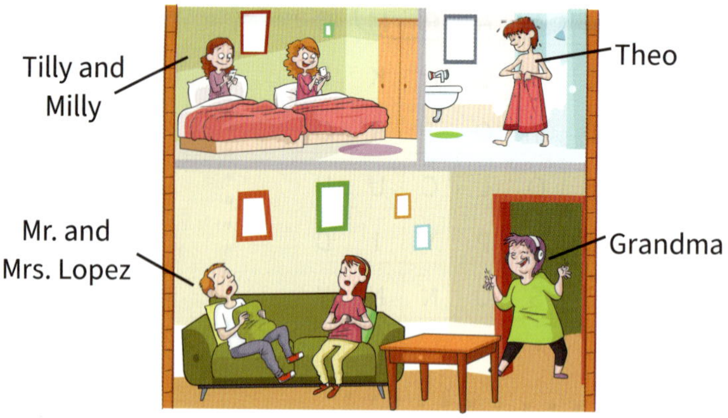

3 Find all the words in the same color to make five questions. Then write and answer the questions in your notebook.

What were you doing at 10 p.m. last night? I was ...

What	Did you go	selfies	at 10 p.m.
Were you	two days ago	were you sitting	yesterday
shopping	were you doing	with friends	for an exam
How many	last Saturday	did you take	in your last class
Who	studying	next to	last night

4 Complete 1–8 with prepositions of movement. Then put the letters in circles in order to find out what ice cream Milo had (9).

Milo went [1] *o u t o f* his house. He walked [2] ___ ___ ___ ◯ the street, and he walked [3] ◯ ___ ___ ___ the bus stop. Then he went [4] ◯ ___ ___ ___ ___ ___ the road. He walked [5] ◯ ___ the steps, and he went [6] ___ ___ ◯ ___ the bridge. Then he went [7] ___ ___ ___ ___ the steps on the other side and [8] ___ ___ ◯ ___ the park. Finally, he stopped to buy some [9] ___ ___ ___ ___ ___ ___ ___ butter ice cream!

4 FINISHED?

1 Circle ten money verbs.

A	O	S	E	L	L	C	N	J	D
W	C	O	F	R	E	A	S	V	O
B	O	R	R	O	W	Y	P	Y	C
S	S	Y	G	W	R	P	E	U	H
C	T	E	H	E	A	R	N	I	A
P	L	P	N	H	N	T	D	S	N
D	S	A	V	E	W	M	R	N	G
N	V	Y	D	P	L	E	N	D	E

2 Read the information and complete the chart about famous shopping malls.

- The West Edmonton Mall is 27 years older than the Dubai Mall.
- The West Edmonton Mall is 12,000 m² smaller than the Dubai Mall.
- The Dubai Mall is the biggest. It has 870 more stores/departments than Harrods.
- The Dubai Mall is the most popular. It has 39 million more shoppers per year than Harrods.

	West Edmonton Mall, Canada	Dubai Mall, UAE	Harrods, UK
Opened	1 1981	2008	1849
Size	490,000 m^2	2 ______	20,000 m^2
Shoppers per year	32 million	54 million	4 ______
Stores or departments	more than 800	3 ______	330

3 What's the problem? Write sentences with *too*, *too much*, *too many*, and (*not*) *enough*.

1

2
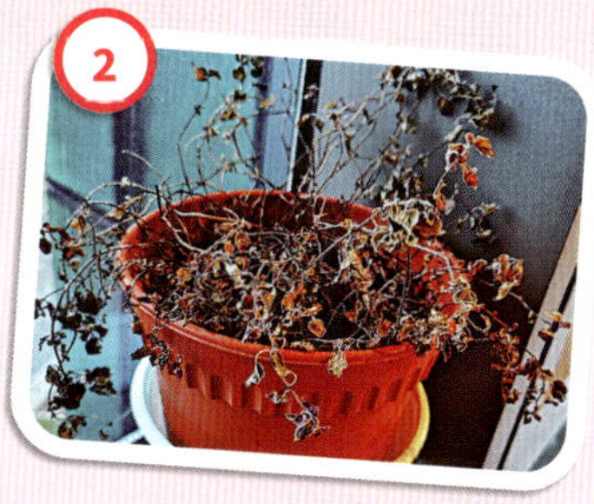

There are too many people.

______

3

4

______

______

4 What are these people's jobs? What are they doing in the photos? Write sentences.

They're firefighters. They're putting out a fire.

______

______

______

5 FINISHED?

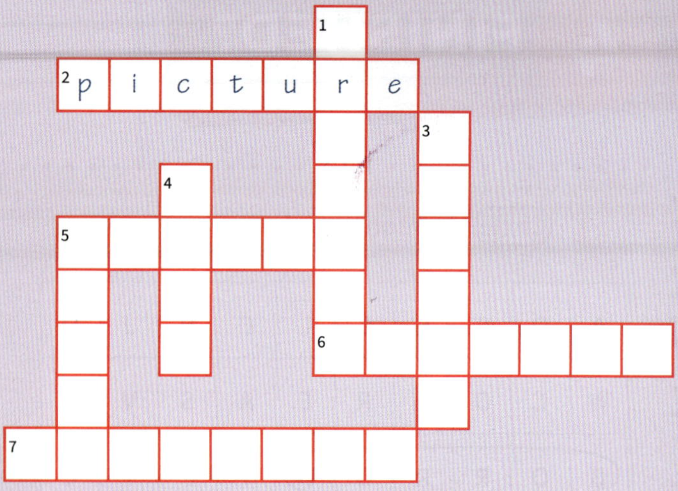

1 Read the clues and complete the crossword.

Across

2 There's a nice picture of a mountain on the wall.
5 It's best to put milk and cheese in the ________.
6 My room is full of ________ with books on them.
7 Grandpa is relaxing in his favorite ________.

Down

1 I put the keys in the chest of ________.
3 I need to vacuum the ________ because there is dirt on it!
4 I don't have a dishwasher. I wash the dishes in the ________.
5 Please don't leave your dirty clothes all over the ________.

2 Complete the clues with *as … as* or *enough* and the adjectives in parentheses. Then think of answers for the clues.

1 I'm as tall as (tall) a wardrobe and wide enough (wide) for lots of books. What am I? a bookcase
2 I'm ________________ (comfortable) a sofa, but I'm not ________________ (large) for two people. What am I? ________
3 I'm ________________ (soft) a blanket, but I'm ________________ (big) to cover the room. What am I? ________
4 I'm ________________ (long and wide) the floor, but you aren't ________________ (tall) to touch me. What am I? ________

3 Find four more phrases in the chart. Are they things you have to do or don't have to do? Write four sentences.

drink	a lot of	water
eat	TV shows	at school
watch	hard	every night
work	enough	chocolate
sleep	for eight hours	for five hours

I have to drink enough water.
1 ________________
2 ________________
3 ________________
4 ________________

4 Look at the pictures. Then find and circle six household chores.

redoingtheironingoaloadingthedishwasheringdoingthedishespermakingyourbedladcleaningthebathroomnonavacuumingthestairsin

6 FINISHED?

1 **Six accidents happened at the campsite yesterday. Complete the words. Then use the letters in circles to find the boy's name.**

1 A boy got s t u n g by some bees.
2 His father ___ ___ ___ his head on a tree.
3 His friend ___ ___ ___ ___ ___ ___ ___ over a ball.
4 His little sister ___ ___ ___ ___ off her bike.
5 His cousin ___ ___ ___ ___ ___ ___ ___ ___ his ankle.
6 His big sister ___ ___ ___ ___ ___ ___ her hair.

The boy's name is ___ ___ ___ ___ ___ ___ .

2 **Read the rules and write the places.**

1 You must pay before you get on. You shouldn't talk to the driver. If someone old gets on, you should give them your seat. a bus

2 You must not use your phone and you shouldn't talk to your friends during the show. If you want something to eat or drink, you should buy it before you go in. ______________

3 You must not take big bottles of liquid. You must take your computer and tablet out of your bag. You shouldn't arrive late, in case it takes a long time. ______________

4 You must not make a fire. You should look out for dangerous animals, and you shouldn't eat any plants that you don't know. You shouldn't leave any trash. ______________

3 **Write the answer to these riddles.**

1 If you're very rich, you need this. If you're very poor, you have this. If you eat or drink this, you won't live long. What is it? nothing

2 If there are three apples and you take away two, how many will you have? ______________

3 If Mary's mother's children are named April and May, what is her other child named? ______________

4 If I get wet, you'll get dry. What am I? ______________

5 If you don't break this, you won't be able to use it. What is it? ______________

4 **Write the parts of the body you can see in these photos.**

1 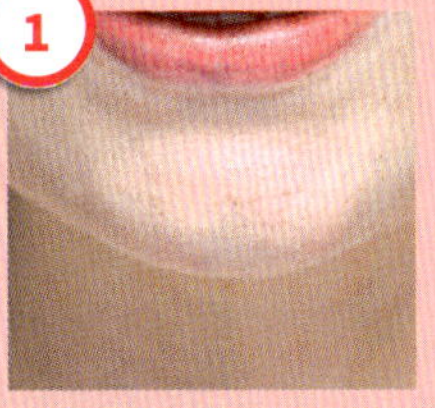
chin

2 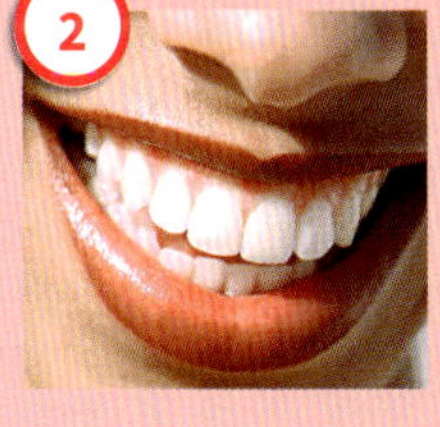
____

3 
____

4 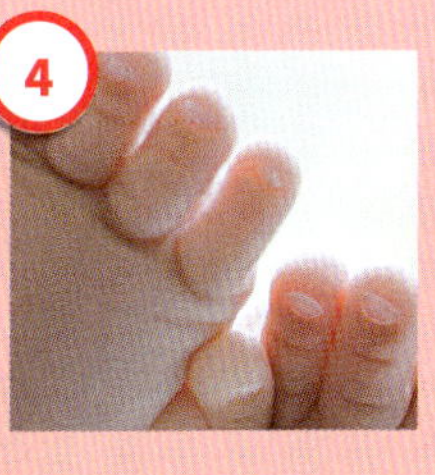
____

5 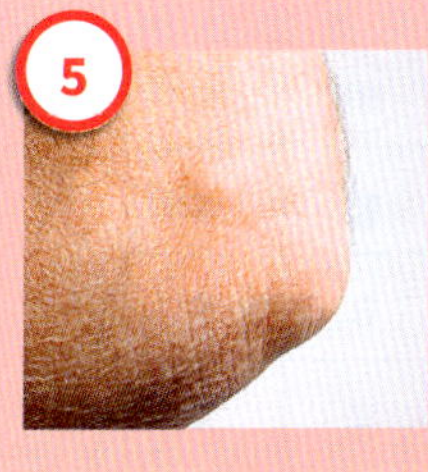
____

6 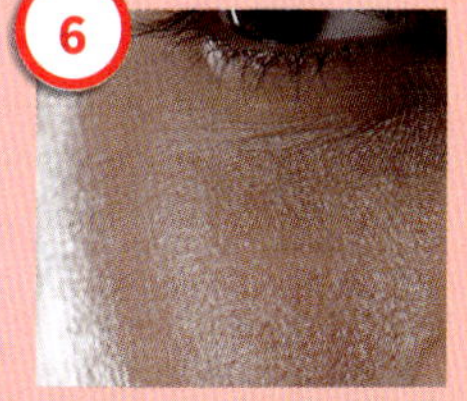
____

7 FINISHED?

1 Circle the letters and write the technology words.

1

y	v	b
e	r	a
s	o	w
h	f	t

software

2

d	o	b
f	w	f
l	n	l
d	a	o

3

t	d	e
a	e	v
s	c	i
j	e	p

4

h	d	a
n	u	o
l	p	l
w	v	q

5

h	m	e
e	g	s
n	a	s
e	g	p

2 Put the letters in order to complete sentences 1–4. Then put the blue letters in order to complete sentence 5.

1 

2 

3 

4 

1 Someone has taken her laptop. (ntkae)

2 He hasn't __________ his phone. (cgehard)

3 They've __________ their tablet. (tols)

4 She's __________ the screen on her phone. (sdehmas)

5 No one __________ __________ a good day!

3 In your opinion, will we have these things in the future? Write sentences using *will/won't*, *might*, or *may* and the infinitive.

1 *flying cars – take us on vacation* — We might have flying cars to take us on vacation.

2 *3-D printers – make furniture at home* __________

3 *hoverboards – get around town* __________

4 *hologram teachers – teach us at home* __________

5 *translator headsets – understand and speak any language* __________

4 Circle seven types of transportation and four transportation verbs in the train.

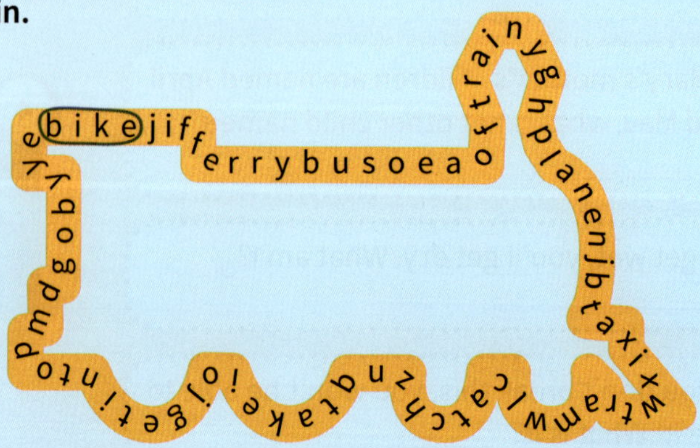

8 FINISHED?

3  4  5 

1 Who needs the things in the pictures? Write the jobs in the puzzle. What's the mystery word?

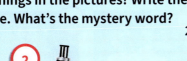

2 

1 

6 

7 

1 w r i t e r
2
v
3
4
5
6
7

2 Use the code to complete the questions. Then write the answers.

A	B	C	D	E	F	G	H	I	J	K	L	M
✦	♥	☛	◗	➾	✇	❍	✳	★	☎	♣	✎	✪
N	**O**	**P**	**Q**	**R**	**S**	**T**	**U**	**V**	**W**	**X**	**Y**	**Z**
➽	❖	✖	✤	❁	✈	❄	✠	✉	●	✂	✆	➤

1 ✉★✈★❄➾◗ ❄✳➾ ✠♣

Have you ever visited the UK?

____

2 ●❁★❄❄➾➽ ✦ ♥❖❖♣

Have you ever ______________________?

____

3 ✈➾➾➽ ✦➽ ➾✎➾✖✳✦➽❄

Have you ever ______________________?

____

4 ✪➾❄ ✦➽✆❖➽➾ ✇✦✪❖✠✈

Have you ever ______________________?

____

3 Circle six reflexive pronouns and eight indefinite pronouns.

l	y	o	u	r	s	e	l	f	s	w	i	e	x	c
t	k	o	s	o	m	e	o	n	e	b	v	i	v	q
o	e	s	e	v	e	r	y	o	n	e	v	s	a	v
m	y	s	e	l	f	a	e	c	r	d	e	j	b	q
t	s	h	u	o	e	y	n	a	v	r	e	v	m	n
h	m	e	n	u	o	t	g	y	e	t	t	q	e	o
e	p	r	a	r	t	w	o	h	t	e	h	r	y	t
m	w	s	n	s	z	k	w	w	a	h	e	g	r	h
s	f	e	y	e	s	o	m	e	t	h	i	n	g	i
e	m	l	w	l	n	a	w	i	w	g	w	n	u	n
l	c	f	h	v	d	e	l	y	t	w	i	e	g	g
v	o	h	e	e	z	e	r	r	p	s	s	v	s	h
e	o	j	r	s	v	e	k	y	g	y	e	u	m	f
s	s	g	e	v	v	d	p	b	b	x	n	l	b	g
e	h	t	h	e	h	i	m	s	e	l	f	h	f	t

4 Put the letters in the inventor's machine in order to complete the phrasal verbs.

1 look up to
2 take ________ in
3 come up ________
4 ________ out
5 ________ up
6 ________ up
7 ________ up with
8 ________ off

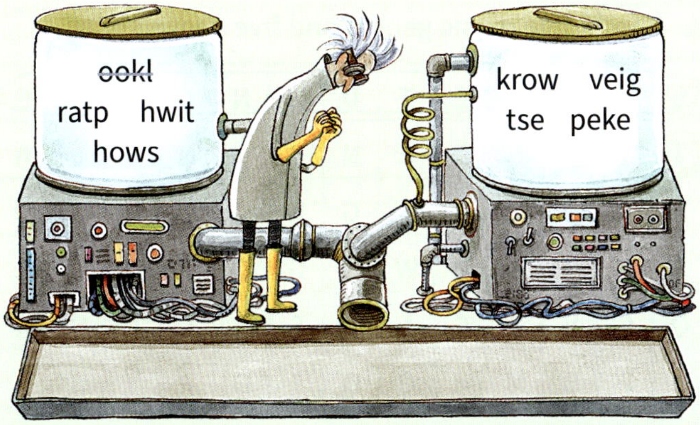

9 FINISHED?

1 Look at the photos. Write the missing instruments and the genre of music you think they are playing.

1 

saxophone

jazz

2 

3 

4 

5 

2 Follow the lines and write sentences about what the people are and aren't going to do.

Danny / buy

Danny isn't going to buy a keyboard. He's going to buy a guitar.

Chloe / play

Pablo / take up

Olivia and Leo / learn

3 Use the code. Write Sophie and Matt's secret plans for the weekend.

1  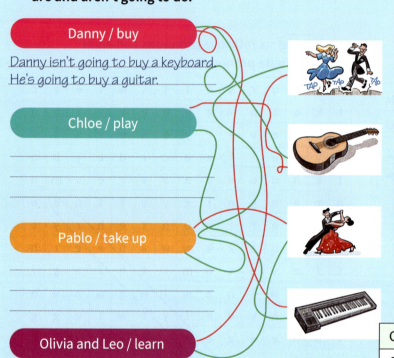

Sophie

K'o oggvkpi oa htkgpfu qp Ucvwtfca gxgpkpi, cpf yg'tg iqkpi vq ugg c oqxkg cv vjg vjgcvgt.

I'm meeting my friends on Saturday

2 

Matt

Dgp cpf K ctg iqkpi vq c tqem eqpegtv kp Ejkeciq. Qwt vtckp ngcxgu cv vjtgg q'enqem.

C	D	E	F	G	H	I	J	K	L	M	N	O
A	**B**	**C**	**D**	**E**	**F**	**G**	**H**	**I**	**J**	**K**	**L**	**M**
P	Q	R	S	T	U	V	W	X	Y	Z	A	B
N	**O**	**P**	**Q**	**R**	**S**	**T**	**U**	**V**	**W**	**X**	**Y**	**Z**

4 Circle five music genres and five dance styles.

B	A	L	L	E	T	D	A	N	C	I	N	G	E	O	D	O	G	J	W	A	E	M	U
J	T	A	P	D	A	N	C	I	N	G	L	A	C	I	S	S	A	L	C	B	J	N	Y
Z	A	G	U	R	U	G	N	I	C	N	A	D	K	A	E	R	B	V	Y	M	I	L	F
S	G	Z	E	O	W	O	G	Q	F	P	B	X	H	W	S	W	I	N	G	U	U	L	O
Q	G	V	Z	C	L	E	S	E	L	F	M	R	A	R	Z	T	J	Y	K	Z	F	F	L
K	P	B	M	K	G	Q	F	O	R	Y	B	S	X	I	V	B	K	S	O	N	C	O	K

STARTER VOCABULARY BANK

Free Time and Hobbies

chat online	listen to music	take photos
download songs	make cookies/videos	write a blog
go shopping	play an instrument	
go for a bike ride	read books/ magazines	
hang out with friends		

Sport

basketball	swimming
gymnastics	table tennis
hockey	track and field
rugby	volleyball
sailing	windsurfing

1 Correct the verbs in these sentences.

1 Do you want to ~~play~~ _____ swimming with us?
2 My mom often ~~makes~~ _____ shopping on Saturday.
3 We ~~go~~ _____ basketball at school.
4 I usually ~~do~~ _____ photos with my phone.
5 Does your brother ~~play~~ _____ track and field?

Personal Possessions

bus pass

camera

headphones

keys

laptop

money

passport

phone

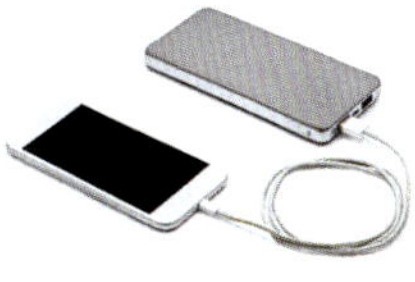
portable charger

tablet

2 Are the sentences *T* (true) or *F* (false)?

1 You need a passport to make cookies. ___
2 You use a camera to download songs. ___
3 You can use headphones to listen to music. ___
4 You use a portable charger to write a blog. ___
5 You can use your laptop to chat online. ___
6 You can use your phone to read books. ___

LEARN TO LEARN

Making Vocabulary Flashcards

Make vocabulary flashcards to help you learn new words. Draw a picture on one side and write the word on the other.

3 Use the flashcards you made in class. Take turns picking up a flashcard, looking at the picture, and naming the thing. Ask your partner questions about the things they have.

Bus pass. Do you have a bus pass? *Yes, I do.* *Where is it?* *It's ...*

1 VOCABULARY BANK

TV Shows

cartoon

comedy

cooking show

documentary

drama

game show

reality show

soap opera

sports show

streaming series

talk show

the news

1 Complete the chart so it is true for you. Discuss with your partner.

	Name of Show	Type of Show
I love		
I like		
I don't mind		
I hate		

*I love **MasterChef Junior**. It's a **cooking show**.*

Me too! I watch it every week.

*I like **Futurama**. It's a **cartoon**.*

I hate it. It's boring, but my brother watches it.

Making Movies

actor	(digital) camera	director	makeup artist	set
camera operator	costume	lights	script	sound engineer

2 Who or what are these people talking about? Write the correct making movies words.

1 She can make a 30-year-old actor look like an old man. ______
2 The actors look amazing when they wear these! ______
3 The conversations between the girl and her mother are very realistic. ______
4 He's so good at his job. You can hear every noise the animals make. ______
5 She sometimes tells the actors to speak louder. ______

LEARN TO LEARN

Look, Cover, Remember

Use the look, cover, remember technique to help you learn new vocabulary.

3 Look at the words for making movies for one minute. Then close your book. Write the words you can remember in your notebook. Compare with a partner.

2 VOCABULARY BANK

The Weather

cloudy

cold

dry

foggy

hot

icy

rainy

snowy

stormy

sunny

warm

wet

windy

1 Complete the puzzle and find the mystery word.

	1						
		2					
		3					
4							
		5					

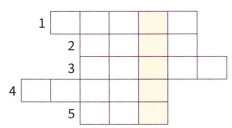

1 We can go skiing when it's ________.
2 Water that falls from the sky is ________.
3 We can go to the beach when the weather is ________.
4 A gray or white thing in the sky is a ________.
5 A place is ________ when it doesn't rain.
The mystery word is ________.

Useful Objects

blanket, bowl, comb, cup, fork, hairbrush, knife, lamp, mirror, pillow, plate, scissors, spoon, toothbrush

2 Circle the correct word.

1 I used a *spoon* / *knife* / *fork* to cut the meat.
2 He put his head on the *pillow* / *lamp* / *blanket*.
3 Can you put these cookies on a *bowl* / *cup* / *plate*, please?
4 I need to brush my teeth. Where's my *comb* / *hairbrush* / *toothbrush*?
5 Anna looked at her hair in the *mirror* / *lamp* / *scissors*.

LEARN TO LEARN

Connecting Words with Places

When you learn new words, think of places where you can use them. This will help you remember them.

3 Write the useful objects you can usually find in these places.

1 bedroom: ________
2 kitchen: ________
3 bathroom: ________

3 VOCABULARY BANK

Adjectives of Feeling

afraid

angry

bored

embarrassed

excited

lonely

nervous

surprised

tired

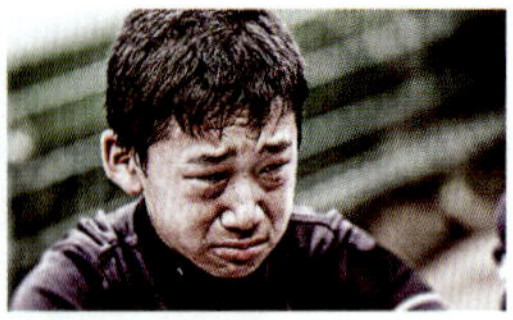
upset

worried

1 Write the correct adjective to describe how these people are feeling.

1 Dad wants to go to bed. He really needs to sleep. ________
2 I don't like this club because we do the same things every week. ________
3 Sasha is crying because she lost her phone. ________
4 All his friends go to a different school. ________
5 Did you really see Katie this morning? I thought she was in New York! ________

Prepositions of Movement

across	between	into	out of	past	under
along	down	off	over	through	up

2 Match 1–5 with a–e.

1 Mom was angry when she found dirty clothes under
2 Polly was afraid to walk through
3 I was very excited when I took the present out of
4 Chloe was embarrassed when she fell off
5 Dad was worried because the children had to go across

a her bike.
b its box.
c my brother's bed.
d a busy street.
e the woods.

LEARN TO LEARN

Practice New Words in Context

Try to practice new words in sentences you often use. This will help you remember them.

3 Choose four prepositions and write four sentences that are true for you. Then tell your partner.

1 ________
2 ________
3 ________
4 ________

My bus goes past the swimming pool on the way to school.

4 VOCABULARY BANK

Money Verbs

borrow	cost	lend	pay	sell
change	earn	owe	save	spend

1 Complete the sentences with the money verbs. Sometimes there is more than one possible answer. Ask and answer with a partner.

1 Who ________ for your phone?
2 Do you usually ________ all your pocket money?
3 Do you do any jobs to ________ money?
4 Do you ever ________ money from your friends?
5 How much does a good laptop ________ ?

Caring Jobs

caregiver

firefighter

garbage collector

lawyer

lifeguard

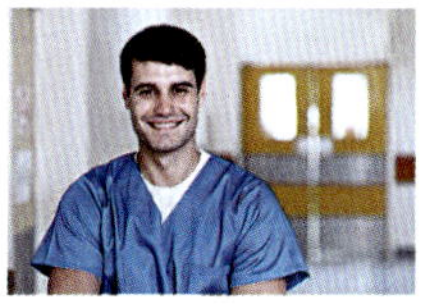
nurse

paramedic

police officer

preschool teacher

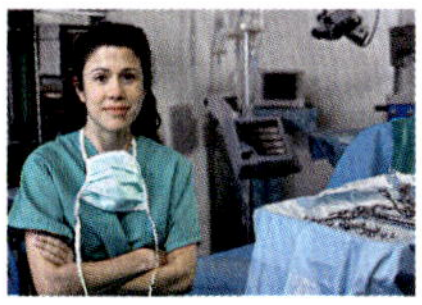
surgeon

vet

volunteer

2 Are the sentences *T* (true) or *F* (false)?

1 Caregivers help old and sick people. ____
2 Paramedics usually take care of animals. ____
3 Lifeguards often work at big soccer matches. ____
4 Nurses often work in hospitals. ____
5 Lawyers are people who work, but don't earn money. ____

LEARN TO LEARN

Stress Patterns

Knowing the stress pattern of a word can help you pronounce it and understand it when people say it.

3 Circle the correct stress pattern for each word.

1 firefighter	ooO	Ooo	oOo
2 paramedic	ooOo	Oooo	oOoo
3 police officer	oO ooo	oo Ooo	oo ooO
4 volunteer	ooO	oOo	Ooo
5 garbage collector	oo Ooo	oO ooo	Oo ooo

5 VOCABULARY BANK

Furniture

armchair

bookcase

carpet

ceiling

chest of drawers

cupboard

desk

floor

fridge

picture

shelves

sink

wardrobe

1 **Circle eight items of furniture.**

sinkwerpicturemokfloorcdcupboardaltceilingquicarpetbifbookcasepumwardrobeas

Household Chores

do the dishes	dust (the furniture)	mop the floor
do the ironing	load/empty the dishwasher	sweep the floor
do the laundry	make the bed	vacuum (the carpet)

2 **Cover the list of household chores. Circle the correct words.**

1 Could you do the *bed* / *carpet* / *dishes*, please?

2 Ben helped me load the *dishwasher* / *cupboards* / *bookcase*.

3 I make my *ironing* / *bed* / *washing* every morning.

4 We really need to dust the *furniture* / *bed* / *kitchen*.

5 She usually vacuums the *fridge* / *carpet* / *cupboard* once a week.

LEARN TO LEARN

Using Spidergrams

Creating spidergrams can help you to remember new words that are related.

3 **Complete the spidergram with verbs for household chores. Some chores can go with more than one room.**

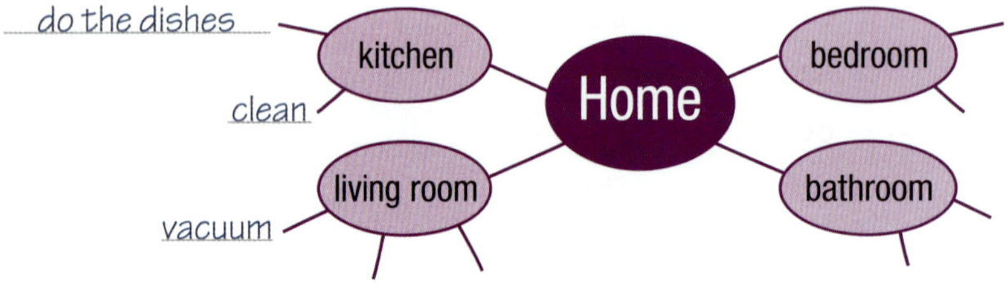

6 VOCABULARY BANK

Accidents and Injuries

break (your leg)	cut (your finger)	get stung (by a bee)	slip
bruise (your leg)	fall off (your horse)	hit (your head)	sprain (your ankle)
burn (your hand)	get bitten (by a mosquito)	scratch (your arm)	trip over (a chair)

1 Put the words in the correct order to make sentences.

1 his / my / dad / stove / burned / hand / the / on

____

2 broke / horse / fell / her / and / her / leg / off / Lena

____

3 Sara / tripped / sprained / and / ankle / her

____

4 hit / his / cupboard / on / a / Dan / door / head

____

5 neck / my / I / stung / on / by / a / got / bee

____

Parts of the Body

cheek

chest

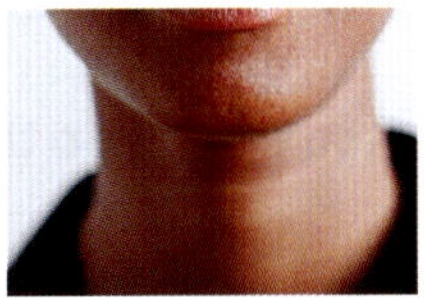
chin

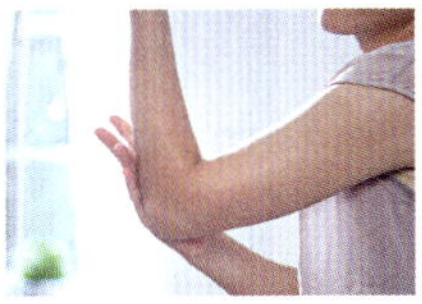
elbow

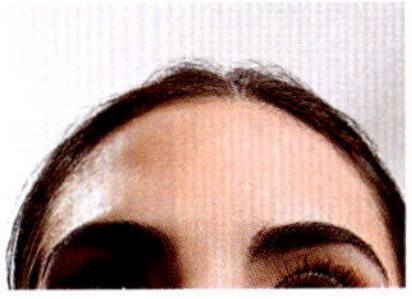
forehead

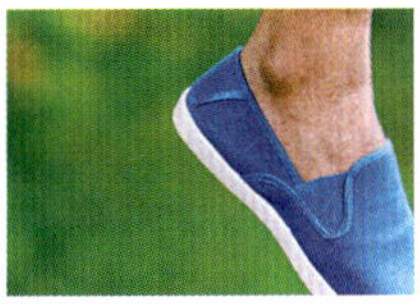
heel

knee

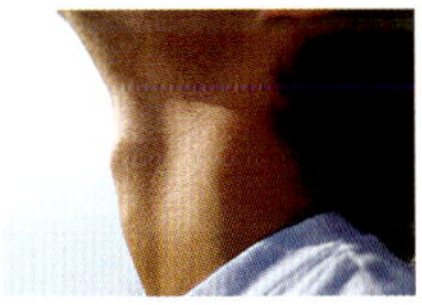
neck

shoulder

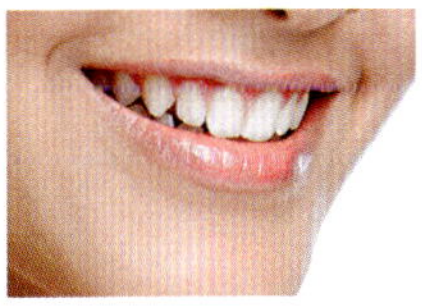
teeth

toe

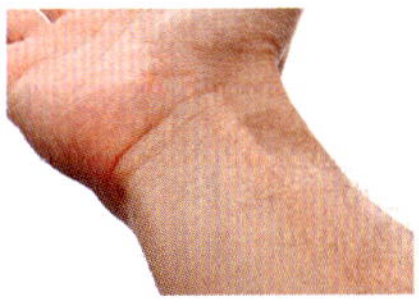
wrist

2 Underline the incorrect word.

1 You can break your *cheek* / *toe* / *wrist*.
2 You can sprain your *wrist* / *ankle* / *forehead*.
3 You can get bitten on your *elbow* / *teeth* / *shoulder*.
4 Your *neck* / *chin* / *forehead* is part of your face.
5 Your *heel* / *toe* / *knee* is part of your foot.
6 Your *shoulder* / *wrist* / *chest* is part of your arm.

LEARN TO LEARN

Making a Picture Dictionary

Drawing and labeling pictures helps you remember new vocabulary.

3 Close your book. Draw a person in your notebook. Label the parts of the body. Then check to see if you have remembered all the words.

7 VOCABULARY BANK

Communication and Technology

app	device	emoji	screen	software	video chat
chip	download	message	social media	upload	

1 Match 1–5 with a–e.

1 I sent Julia a message
2 Ibrahim downloaded an app
3 I'm going to upload
4 Bella had a long video chat
5 She added an emoji

a with her cousin.
b the photos from our trip.
c because she left her keys at my house.
d to show she was joking.
e to help him learn English words.

Getting Around

catch/take (a plane)

get into / take (a taxi)

get off (a bus)

get on (a train)

get out of (a car)

go by (tram)

go on foot

2 Look at the photos of people getting around. How often do you do these things? Complete the chart. Then compare with a partner.

Every day	
Often	
Sometimes	
Never	

LEARN TO LEARN

Collocations

Some words are often used together – we call these collocations. Learn them as phrases.

3 Underline and correct a mistake in each sentence. There is sometimes more than one possible answer.

1 You should get out of the bus near the museum.
____

2 Dad goes to work on train.
____

3 We got on a taxi and went to the airport.
____

4 They went by a plane to Japan.
____

5 Get in the train at Portland station.
____

8 VOCABULARY BANK

Exceptional Jobs and Qualities

athlete

businessman/
businesswoman

composer

engineer

inventor

mathematician

scientist

writer

creativity
determination
intelligence
skill
strength
talent

1 **Choose two exceptional jobs you think you would be good at and two you think you would be bad at. Write the qualities each job needs. Compare with a partner.**

1 ______________________________
2 ______________________________
3 ______________________________
4 ______________________________

Phrasal Verbs: Achievement

come up with	keep up with	set up	take part in
give up	look up to	show off	work out

2 **Complete the sentences with the phrasal verbs.**

1 Jack ______________ his older brother, who is an amazing mathematician.
2 My math homework was very difficult, and in the end I had to ______________ .
3 Yesterday my sister ______________ a great idea for earning money.
4 Sophia walks very quickly. I can't ______________ her.
5 My grandfather ______________ this business in 1960.

LEARN TO LEARN

Personalizing Vocabulary

When you learn new words, use them in sentences to talk about your life. This will help you remember them.

3 **Choose three of the phrasal verbs for achievement and write sentences about people you know. Compare with a partner.**

1 ______________________________
2 ______________________________
3 ______________________________

My cousin is a businesswoman, and she set up a business with her friend.

I took part in my school play last year.

9 VOCABULARY BANK

Musical Instruments and Genres

classical	jazz
folk	reggae
hip-hop	rock

bass	keyboard	trumpet
drums	microphone	violin
guitar	saxophone	

1 What am I? Write the musical instrument.

1 I'm round and you hit me with sticks. ______
2 I make the singer sound louder. ______
3 I have black and white parts that you press with your fingers. ______
4 I'm not big, but I'm very loud. You blow air into me. ______
5 I have four strings. You hold me against your neck. ______

Dance Styles

ballet dancing

ballroom dancing

breakdancing

disco dancing

folk dance

modern dance

salsa dancing

swing

tap dancing

Zumba

2 Are the sentences *T* (true) or *F* (false)?

1 You do ballroom dancing with a partner. ___
2 Breakdancing is a slow type of dance. ___
3 Folk music is often used for disco dancing. ___
4 You need special shoes for ballet dancing. ___
5 Tap dancing makes a noise on the floor. ___

LEARN TO LEARN

Visualizing

Thinking of an image to go with new words can help you remember their meaning. The more unusual the image, the better!

3 Think of a strange or funny image for each of the dance styles. Tell your partner your ideas. Whose ideas are the most unusual?

1 **Look at the title and picture and discuss the questions.**

1 Have you heard of El Dorado?
2 What and where do you think it is?

2.12 **2** **Read the text. Check your answers to Exercise 1.**

3 **Complete the sentences with years.**

1 1520s – Spanish conquistadors first heard about the Muisca people.
2 ______ – Sir Walter Raleigh failed to find El Dorado.
3 ______ – They searched Lake Guatavita for gold.
4 ______ – They first went to look for "El Dorado."
5 ______ – Alexander von Humboldt proved the site at Lake Parime did not exist.

4 **Why did the Europeans want to explore and control the Americas? Discuss with a partner.**

5 **Match the words in bold with the definitions.**

1 a long search for something that may not exist or is difficult to find ______
2 a small flat boat, often made of wood ______
3 a traditional story ______
4 a fight during a war, usually to take control of a place ______

Explore It!

Guess the correct answer.

People once believed there was gold worth … in Lake Guatavita.

a $1 million b $50 million c $300 million

Find another interesting fact about a legend. Then write a question for your partner to answer.

The Legend of El Dorado

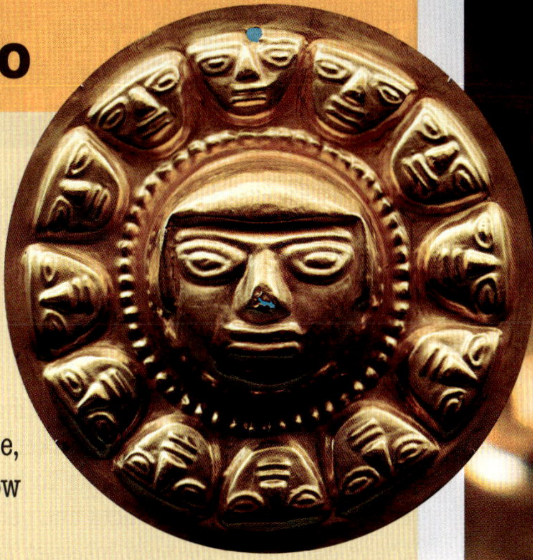

In the 1500s, Europeans were discovering and trying to take control of the Americas. In the 1520s, Spanish conquistadors heard about the Muisca people, who lived in what is now Colombia.

The stories suggested that the Muisca had a huge amount of gold. When they chose a new chief, they covered him in gold and sailed him on a **raft** into the middle of Lake Guatavita. The chief put all the gold into the lake as a gift for the gods.

In 1537, the Spanish decided to look for the chief, who they named "El Dorado," but without success. Then in 1545, they looked for gold in Lake Guatavita. They discovered a few objects, and they became sure that there was a whole city of gold somewhere in the Amazon jungle. People started to refer to the golden city as El Dorado.

Many people looked for El Dorado over the centuries. These included the British explorer Sir Walter Raleigh. In 1617, on his second expedition to South America, he fought a **battle** with the Spanish on the Orinoco River, as both the British and the Spanish searched for El Dorado. The British king was unhappy about this conflict and executed Raleigh on his return.

The **myth** of El Dorado continued to grow. Maps in the seventeenth and eighteenth centuries even showed the city next to a legendary lake, Lake Parime. But nobody ever found it, and in 1803 the German explorer Alexander von Humboldt disproved the existence of this site.

After hundreds of failed expeditions, people finally realized that El Dorado never existed. The phrase "looking for El Dorado" means to go on a hopeless **quest**.

4 SOCIAL STUDIES

The Best Things in Life Are (Almost) Free

There is no doubt that money is **essential** to daily life. People earn money to buy food, pay the **bills**, or save for something special like a vacation or a present. Life becomes extremely difficult for people when there isn't enough money for their basic needs.

However, many people spend too much money on items they do not need. Marketing and advertising **encourage** people to buy an enormous range of products and services, and these days, with 24-hour internet access, it is easier than ever to spend money at the touch of a button.

How American teenagers spend their money, according to a recent survey

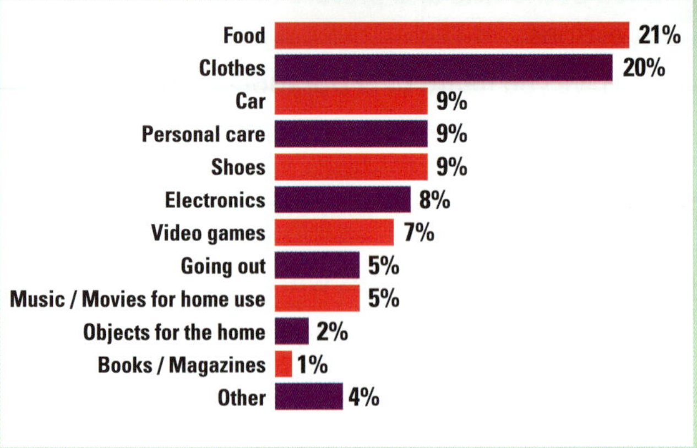

Some people believe that consuming so much is unhealthy, and we should make an effort to find interests that do not cost anything at all. If you want to do this, there are a number of options, and a good way to start is by looking at local websites. There are many free events for local communities, and you just need to select an activity that interests you. You could choose from music, dance, sports, art, tourism, walking, and many, many more.

Of course, you need access to a computer or phone to check a website. That costs money, but if it helps you to save money in the long run, then it is a good **investment**. Why not take a look today? It may be the first step in reducing your spending and starting a new low-cost life.

1 Discuss the questions.

1 Why do we need money?

2 What kinds of things can we do in our free time without money?

4.12 **2 Read the article. Are your ideas from Exercise 1 mentioned?**

3 Are the sentences *T* (true) or *F* (false)?

1 People need money for their basic needs. T

2 Teenagers don't need vacations or presents. ___

3 U.S. teenagers spend less than a quarter of their money on clothes. ___

4 We can use technology to find free events. ___

5 If you want to save money, you sometimes have to spend a little first. ___

4 Complete the sentences with the words in bold.

1 I bought a cheap phone to save money, but it was a bad ____________ because it broke and I had to buy a new one.

2 That video game isn't an ____________ item. I think you should save your money.

3 Please don't ____________ Ben to buy any more sneakers. He already has plenty of pairs.

4 Lisa has almost no money left each month after she pays the ____________.

Explore It!

Guess the correct answer.

The average U.S. household spends more money on … than on food.

a transportation b entertainment c healthcare

Find another interesting fact about spending in your country. Then write a question for your partner to answer.

SMALL BUT DEADLY

Imagine you are trekking through a rainforest. You're amazed at the rich variety of wildlife, although you're nervous about meeting a jaguar or a boa constrictor. Suddenly, you see something bright and yellow on a plant. You move closer and realize that it is a tiny frog. "Frogs aren't dangerous," you think, and you hold out your hand …

Stop! The animal in front of you is *Phyllobates terribilis*, or the golden poison frog. It is the most poisonous land animal in the world.

The golden poison frog is an amphibian that lives in the rainforests of Colombia. It is only about 5 cm long and weighs less than 25 grams. It is a **carnivore**, and it eats ants, beetles, and centipedes that only live in the rainforest. Scientists believe this specific diet produces the poison that the frogs secrete from their backs. If a human touches a golden poison frog, it can cause **swelling**, nausea, paralysis, or even death.

Incredibly, these frogs may also be good for humans. Scientists are investigating how they can use frog poisons in medicines to treat heart conditions. However, **deforestation** and pollution mean the golden poison frog is in danger. If we do not protect the tropical rainforests, this beautiful but **deadly** animal will soon disappear.

So, if you see one of these creatures in the jungle, keep your distance and leave it alone. Then you will both stay safe.

1 **Look at the title and photo. What information can you guess about this frog?**

6.13 **2** **Read the article. Were your ideas correct?**

3 **Complete the fact file about the golden poison frog.**

SCIENTIFIC NAME:	1	*Phyllobates terribilis*
TYPE OF ANIMAL:	2	
SIZE:	3	
WEIGHT:	4	
DIET:	5	
HOME:	6	

4 **Complete the sentences.**

1 The golden poison frog can hurt people if ______

______

2 It can help people because ______

______

5 **Complete the sentences with the words in bold.**

1 This snake has a ______ bite. It can kill you.

2 There was ______ on his toe where he was stung. His toe was bigger than usual.

3 Because of ______, a lot of animals have lost their homes.

4 An animal that eats meat (for example, a cat) is a ______.

Explore It!

Guess the correct answer.

The golden poison frog has enough poison to kill …

a a cat. **b** 20,000 mice. **c** an elephant.

Find another interesting fact about a dangerous animal. Then write a question for your partner to answer.

8 TECHNOLOGY

1 **Look at the photos. Do you know what the invention is and who invented it?**

8.13 **2** **Read the article. Check your answers to Exercise 1.**

3 **Put the events in order.**

a [1] Farnsworth entered invention competitions.
b [ ] He went to college.
c [ ] He had an idea while he was working on his family's farm.
d [ ] Businesses took up his ideas.
e [ ] He produced the first version of a fully electronic television.
f [ ] He had to get a job.

4 **Imagine you're going to spend 24 hours without looking at any type of screen. How can you spend your time? Discuss your ideas with a partner.**

5 **Match the words in bold with the definitions.**

1 plants that farmers grow ______
2 change slowly over a long time ______
3 stop doing something before you have completely finished ______
4 first example of an invention ______

Explore It!

Guess the correct statement.

a After his invention, Philo Farnsworth had a television in every room of his house.
b Philo Farnsworth became one of the first television news presenters.
c Philo Farnsworth didn't like television and didn't allow his family to watch it.

Find another interesting fact about television. Then write a question for your partner to answer.

Philo Farnsworth:
A Big Influence on the Small Screen

The television is probably the world's most popular form of entertainment. On average, people around the world watch three hours of television per day, and in Europe and North America, it is closer to four hours. But who is responsible for this amazing invention?

It isn't an easy question to answer because, over the years, different people developed different types of televisions. One of these was Philo Farnsworth, a farmer's son from Utah in the U.S.A. He built the first all-electronic TV set. This young man's creativity and determination made a big difference in the development of the small screen.

Farnsworth was always interested in inventions. As a young teenager, he took part in invention competitions and made mechanical gadgets that helped with household chores. In 1921, at the age of 15, he came up with the basic idea for a totally electronic television. He was looking at the parallel lines of **crops** on his family's farm when he realized that he could separate images into parallel lines of light, which he could transform into television images.

Farnsworth was a brilliant student and started college, but he was forced to **drop out** and work after his father died. However, he continued to work on his invention. Finally, in 1928, he finalized his **prototype** TV. His invention continued to **evolve** and improve, and throughout his career, different companies produced different versions of it. The television continues to evolve quickly – today's flat-screen smart TVs will surely look old-fashioned to future generations.

PRONUNCIATION

UNIT 1

Contractions: *To Be*

1.04 **1 Listen and repeat.**

1. **I am** sitting in my bedroom. > **I'm** sitting in my bedroom.
2. **He is** taking a selfie. > **He's** taking a selfie.
3. **You are** walking on the moon. > **You're** walking on the moon.
4. **We are** listening to music. > **We're** listening to music.

1.05 **2 Listen and (circle) the option you hear. Practice saying the sentences.**

1. (*They are*) / *They're* listening to music.
2. *She is* / *She's* reading a blog.
3. *He is* / *He's* skiing in France.
4. *You are* / *You're* watching TV.
5. *It is* / *It's* eating.

UNIT 2

/t/, /d/, and /ɪd/

2.03 **1 Listen and repeat.**

1 /t/ walk**ed** 2 /d/ liv**ed** 3 /ɪd/ want**ed**

2 Write the verbs in the correct column.

~~agreed~~ arrived changed cooked decided helped looked survived traveled wanted

1 /t/ or /d/	2 /ɪd/
agreed,	

2.04 **3 Listen and check.**

UNIT 3

Word Stress in Adjectives

1 How many syllables do these adjectives have?

afraid	2	angry		bored	
nervous		excited		lonely	
upset		surprised		tired	

3.02 **2 Listen and check.**

3 Match the words in Exercise 1 with their stress patterns. Complete the chart.

1 oO	2 Oo	3 oOo	4 O
afraid			

3.03 **4 Listen and repeat the sentences.**

1. Sam's afraid of dogs.
2. My best friend is very upset.
3. I'm worried about exams.
4. I studied all night and I'm very tired.
5. I feel embarrassed when I forget someone's name.

UNIT 4

-er Ending Sounds

4.06 **1 Listen and repeat.**

/ər/ garbage collect**or** preshool teach**er** fitt**er** bett**er**

4.07 **2 Listen and repeat the sentences.**

1. My sister's a firefighter.
2. The teacher is happier than the actor.
3. Life is better when you're healthier.

UNIT 5

Have: /f/ vs /v/

5.08 **1 Listen and (circle) the option you hear: /f/ or /v/.**

1. Jenny and Peter **have** to make their beds every day. (/f/) / /v/
2. I **have** a new bed. /f/ / /v/
3. George and Helen **have** to make dinner every Saturday. /f/ / /v/
4. Tom doesn't **have** to help in the house. /f/ / /v/
5. Do you **have** an extra pencil? /f/ / /v/
6. Sam and Dan don't **have** to do much. /f/ / /v/

5.09 **2 Listen and repeat the sentences.**

1 I **have** to do the gardening this weekend.
2 My brothers **have** a really big wardrobe.
3 We don't **have** to go to school on Monday.
4 We **have** a bookcase in the living room.
5 Does Jake **have** to do the dishes?

UNIT 6

/ʌ/ and /ʊ/

6.04 **1 Listen and repeat.**

1 /ʌ/ must must not
2 /ʊ/ should cook full

2 Write the words in the correct column.

~~brother~~ could cousin cut foot put stung

1 /ʌ/	2 /ʊ/
brother,	

6.05 **3 Listen, check, and repeat.**

6.06 **4 Listen and repeat the sentences.**

1 She cut her foot, but she couldn't call her cousin.
2 I must put some books in the cupboard.

UNIT 7

The Letter *i*

7.03 **1 Listen and repeat.**

1 /ɪ/ chip film kick
2 /aɪ/ like online hi

2 Write the words in the correct column.

bike device ~~Internet~~ online printer video Wi-Fi will write

1 /ɪ/	2 /aɪ/
Internet,	

7.04 **3 Listen, check, and repeat.**

7.05 **4 Listen and repeat the sentences.**

1 James can't get Wi-Fi, so he doesn't have Internet.
2 I can watch videos online on my new device.

UNIT 8

Intonation in Questions

8.04 **1 Listen and repeat.**

1 Was Mozart a scientist?
2 Where do you live?
3 Have you cycled 100 kilometers?
4 What did you do last night?

2 Circle the question endings where Nick's voice goes up. Underline the endings where it goes down.

NICK How long have you been a teacher?
MR. K Well, Nick. It's been 20 years now.
NICK Really? That's a long time! Do you like it?
MR. K Yes, but some days are harder than others.
NICK What do you like best about it?
MR. K The best thing is seeing students improve.
NICK That's great. Do you think you'll be a teacher for the next 20 years?
MR. K Well, I hope so!

8.05 **3 Listen, check, and repeat.**

UNIT 9

Sentence Stress

1 How many syllables do these sentences have? Then underline the words you think are stressed.

1 We're going to play jazz. [6]
2 We'll buy a new guitar. [ ]
3 Is Jake playing the drums? [ ]
4 We're going to a free concert. [ ]

9.07 **2 Listen, check, and repeat.**

3 Clap the rhythm of these sentences.

1 She often sings in a band.
2 Is the piano your favorite instrument?
3 The concert starts at eight o'clock.
4 Adam is organizing the music.

IRREGULAR VERBS

Infinitive	Past Simple	Past Participle
be	was/were	been
beat	beat	beaten
become	became	become
begin	began	begun
break	broke	broken
bring	brought	brought
build	built	built
burn	burned	burned
buy	bought	bought
catch	caught	caught
choose	chose	chosen
come	came	come
cost	cost	cost
cut	cut	cut
do	did	done
draw	drew	drawn
drink	drank	drunk
drive	drove	driven
eat	ate	eaten
fall	fell	fallen
feed	fed	fed
feel	felt	felt
fight	fought	fought
find	found	found
fly	flew	flown
forget	forgot	forgotten
get	got	gotten
give	gave	given
go	went	gone
grow	grew	grown
hang	hung	hung
have	had	had
hear	heard	heard
hide	hid	hidden
hit	hit	hit
hold	held	held
keep	kept	kept

Infinitive	Past Simple	Past Participle
know	knew	known
leave	left	left
lend	lent	lent
lose	lost	lost
make	made	made
meet	met	met
pay	paid	paid
put	put	put
read	read	read
ride	rode	ridden
ring	rang	rung
run	ran	run
say	said	said
see	saw	seen
sell	sold	sold
send	sent	sent
set	set	set
show	showed	shown
shut	shut	shut
sing	sang	sung
sit	sat	sat
sleep	slept	slept
speak	spoke	spoken
spend	spent	spent
stand	stood	stood
swim	swam	swum
take	took	taken
teach	taught	taught
tell	told	told
think	thought	thought
throw	threw	thrown
understand	understood	understood
wake	woke	woken
wear	wore	worn
win	won	won
write	wrote	written

ACKNOWLEDGEMENTS

The authors and publishers acknowledge the following sources of copyright material and are grateful for the permissions granted. While every effort has been made, it has not always been possible to identify the sources of all the material used, or to trace all copyright holders. If any omissions are brought to our notice, we will be happy to include the appropriate acknowledgements on reprinting and in the next update to the digital edition, as applicable.

Key: **CLIL** = Content and Language Integrated Learning, **F** = Finished, **SU** = Starter Unit, **U** = Unit, **VB** = Vocabulary Bank

Text

U4: Text about Mark Boyle. Copyright © Mark Boyle. Reproduced with kind permission of Jessica Woollard.

Photography

The following photographs are sourced from Getty Images:

SU: Photo and Co/DigitalVision; bubaone/DigitalVision Vectors; TongSur/DigitalVision Vectors; appleuzr/DigitalVision Vectors; cnythzl/DigitalVision Vectors; VOISIN/PHANIE/Passage; Image Source/DigitalVision; Image Source/Image Source; Fgorgun/iStock/Getty Images Plus; MachineHeadz/iStock/Getty Images Plus; luismmolina/E+; Ian Dikhtiar/EyeEm; SensorSpot/E+; pbombaert/Moment; ABBPhoto/iStock/Getty Images Plus; momokey/iStock/Getty Images Plus; Frederick Bass; Creative Crop/DigitalVision; Richard Newstead/Moment; Terri Lee-Shield Photography/iStock/Getty Images Plus; Nathan Stirk/Getty Images Sport; **U1:** JGI/Tom Grill; moodboard - Mike Watson/Brand X Pictures; Devon Strong/Stone/Getty Images Plus; Roberto Westbrook; vm/E+; WLDavies/E+; ARTPUPPY/DigitalVision Vectors; Daviles/iStock/Getty Images Plus; Cliff Lipson/CBS Photo Archive/CBS; Newton Daly/DigitalVision; Jasmin Merdan/Moment; ullstein bild Dtl./ullstein bild; dmbaker/iStock/Getty Images Plus; Westend61; LajosRepasi/iStock/Getty Images Plus; ildarss/iStock/Getty Images Plus; Kcris Ramos/Moment Unreleased; George Konig/Hulton Archive; Mims/RooM; Juanmonino/iStock/Getty Images Plus; J Carter Rinaldi/FilmMagic; portishead1/E+; The Asahi Shimbun; liangpv/DigitalVision Vectors; Nigel Killeen/Moment; NurPhoto; Wibowo Rusli/iStock/Getty Images Plus; Nicola Katie/E+; 4x6/DigitalVision Vectors; A-Digit/DigitalVision Vectors; davidf/E+; mocoo/iStock/Getty Images Plus; **U2:** Hisham Ibrahim/Photodisc; Frantois Marclay/Moment; Mitchell Funk/iStock/Getty Images Plus; Westend61; Tim Graham/Getty Images News; Pacific Press/LightRocket; AnnaFrajtova/iStock/Getty Images Plus; Archive Holdings Inc./Archive Photos; bradwieland/iStock/Getty Images Plus; DEA PICTURE LIBRARY/De Agostini; Shalom Ormsby Images Inc/DigitalVision; Juanmonino/E+; jiduha/iStock/Getty Images Plus; Bettmann; Print Collector/Hulton Archive; Charly_Morlock/iStock/Getty Images Plus; Fotosearch/Archive Photos; stellalevi/E+; mocoo/iStock/Getty Images Plus; Steve Mason/Photodisc; James Mahan/iStock/Getty Images Plus; **U3:** Image_Source_/iStock/Getty Images Plus; Jose Luis Pelaez Inc/DigitalVision; Neustockimages/E+; Betsie Van Der Meer/DigitalVision; Steve Debenport/E+; Shinyfamily/iStock/Getty Images Plus; gawrav/E+; Rob Lewine; GK Hart/Vikki Hart/Stone; ozgurdonmaz/iStock/Getty Images Plus; songdech17/iStock/Getty Images Plus; Zelma Brezinska/EyeEm/EyeEm; HEX; KidStock/Blend Images; ersinkisacik/E+; Truitt Rogers/Photolibrary/Getty Images Plus; T2 Images/Cultura; tomertu/iStock/Getty Images Plus; DNY59/E+; Sergiy1975/iStock/Getty Images Plus; Alberto E. Rodriguez/Getty Images Entertainment; mocoo/iStock/Getty Images Plus; Maica/iStock/Getty Images Plus; **U4:** Fuse/Corbis; jessicaphoto/iStock Unreleased; mtreasure/iStock/Getty Images Plus; Laetizia Haessig/EyeEm; GCShutter/E+; heshphoto/Image Source; Chuvashov Maxim/Image Source; RUSS ROHDE/iStock/Getty Images Plus; Oliver Helbig/EyeEm/EyeEm; Matt Cardy/Getty Images News; Sally Anscombe/Moment; John Gress/Corbis Historical; John Wood Photography/iStock/Getty Images Plus; RichLegg/E+; Bill Stormont/iStock/Getty Images Plus; Asanka Brendon Ratnayake/iStock/Getty Images Plus; kali9/E+; Wavebreakmedia/iStock/Getty Images Plus; Thamrongpat Theerathammakorn/EyeEm; fotostorm/iStock/Getty Images Plus; Razvan/iStock/Getty Images Plus; Gregory Shamus/Getty Images Sport; Alexander Puell/Moment/Getty Images Plus; Agata Kryn/EyeEm; RoschetzkyIstockPhoto/iStock/Getty Images Plus; dolgachov/iStock/Getty Images Plus; ColorBlind Images/The Image Bank/Getty Images Plus; mocoo/iStock/Getty Images Plus; Sladic/iStock/Getty Images Plus; **U5:** David Santiago Garcia/Aurora; Martine Roch/Moment; Cristiano Gala/iStock/Getty Images Plus; Ryan McVay/DigitalVision; Martin Poole/DigitalVision; Sporrer/Rupp/Cultura; Mark Hunt; Martin Konopka/EyeEm; urbazon/E+; Jonathan Gelber; CasarsaGuru/E+; Comstock/Stockbyte; PhotoAlto/Jerome Gorin/PhotoAlto Agency RF Collections; Jose Luis Pelaez Inc/DigitalVision; Grosshans Grosshans/EyeEm; KatarzynaBialasiewicz/iStock/Getty Images Plus; Alvis Upitis/Photographer's Choice RF; ra-photos/E+; Paul Almasy/Corbis Historical; Johner Images/Brand X Pictures; Klaus Mellenthin/Westend61; ihorga/iStock/Getty Images Plus; Yvette Cardozo/Photolibrary; Himsyah Inchakep/EyeEm; mocoo/iStock/Getty Images Plus; Richard Newstead/Moment; Cavan Images; andresr/E+; mocoo/iStock/Getty Images Plus; **U6:** Barcroft Media/Barcroft Media; Viktoria Rodriguez/EyeEm; maerzkind/iStock/Getty Images Plus; Gordon Scammell/LOOP IMAGES/Corbis Documentary; James Gritz/Photodisc; T. Eidenweil/imageBROKER; vandervelden/iStock/Getty Images Plus; micheldenijs/Getty Images/iStockphoto; Fotofeeling/Westend61; Robert Niedring/MITO images; Hill Street Studios/DigitalVision; Westend61; moodboard/Getty Images Plus; Jef Wodniack/iStock/Getty Images Plus; Anton Petrus/Moment; Pavliha/E+; SteveMcsweeny/iStock/Getty Images Plus; Frans Lemmens/Corbis Unreleased; JuhaHuiskonen/E+; David Fettes/iStock/Getty Images Plus; mocoo/iStock/Getty Images Plus; ONOKY - Brooke Auchincloss; **U7:** metamorworks/iStock/Getty Images Plus; PhotoAlto/Frederic Cirou/PhotoAlto Agency RF Collections; Dan Hallman/iStock/Getty Images Plus; Maskot/Maskot; AntonioFrancois/iStock/Getty Images Plus; Liam Norris/iStock/Getty Images Plus; VLIET/iStock Unreleased; Johner Images; Mike Harrington/DigitalVision; uniquely india; Javier Pierini/Stockbyte; THEPALMER/E+; Donald Iain Smith; SolStock/E+; dmbaker/iStock/Getty Images Plus; Bedrin-Alexander/iStock/Getty Images Plus; Maskot; fstop123/iStock/Getty Images Plus; Mongkol Chuewong/Moment; Steve Vidler/SuperStock; LeoPatrizi/E+; Wavebreakmedia Ltd/Lightwavemedia; SeanPavonePhoto/iStock/Getty Images Plus; Junior Gonzalez; monsitj/iStock/Getty Images Plus; mocoo/iStock/Getty Images Plus; **U8:** Caiaimage/Sam Edwards; Halfpoint Images/Moment; Hero Images/Hero Images; LightFieldStudios/iStock/Getty Images Plus; Jovo Marjanovic/EyeEm/EyeEm; Ariel Skelley/DigitalVision; FangXiaNuo/E+; Diverse Images/Universal Images Group; Hill Street Studios/DigitalVision; Westend61/Brand X Pictures; Morjachka/iStock/Getty Images Plus; Kristine Joy Tropicales/Moment Open; South China Morning Post; digitalskillet/iStock/Getty Images Plus; Bloom Productions/iStock/Getty Images Plus; Gary Bennett/EyeEm/EyeEm; Denis Goujon/EyeEm/EyeEm; mocoo/iStock/Getty Images Plus; **U9:** Guylain Doyle/Lonely Planet Images/Getty Images Plus; Bennett Raglin/BET/Getty Images Entertainment; D-Keine/E+; HEX; Lane Oatey/Blue Jean Images; Claudiad/E+; Nigel Roddis/Getty Images News; suteishi/E+; George Shelley/Corbis; Tim Graham/The Image Bank/Getty Images Plus; Stephanie Nantel/Moment; jonya/E+; Peathegee Inc; Kike Calvo/Universal Images Group; FatCamera/iStock/Getty Images Plus; StephanHoerold/E+; Hill Street Studios/Blend Images; Tony Anderson/The Image Bank; drbimages/iStock/Getty Images Plus; Jon Feingersh Photography Inc/DigitalVision; Urilux/E+; harrastaja/E+; 8213erika/iStock/Getty Images Plus; Elizabeth Fernandez/Moment; Education Images/Universal Images Group; Neil Farrin/AWL Images; Christian Jakubaszek/Getty Images Entertainment; Prisma Bildagentur/Universal Images Group; Lebedinski/iStock/Getty Images Plus; carlosbezz/iStock/Getty Images Plus; J-Elgaard/iStock/Getty Images Plus; sihuo0860371/iStock/Getty Images Plus; Jonathan Kitchen/Photographer's Choice RF; RapidEye/E+; mocoo/iStock/Getty Images Plus; Valeriy_G/iStock/Getty Images Plus. **CLIL2:** Alfredo Maiquez/Lonely Planet Images/Getty Images PlusAdam Woolfitt/roberthardingclaffra/iStock/Getty Images Plus; **CLIL4:** JGI/Jamie Grill; **CLIL6:** Bjorn Holland/Photodisc; Malven/E+; Doug88888/Moment Open; Anakrubah/iStock/Getty Images Plus; **CLIL8:** Bettmann; Underwood Archives/Archive Photos; robbin0919/iStock/Getty Images Plus; **F4:** Francisco Goncalves/Moment Open; Nor Hashikin Rohani/EyeEm; The Good Brigade/DigitalVision; Mike Kemp; Glowimages; Ariel Skelley/DigitalVision; Hero Images; UpperCut Images; **F6:** PhotoAlto/Milena Boniek/PhotoAlto Agency RF Collections; Ken Reid/iStock/Getty Images Plus; mediaphotos/iStock/Getty Images Plus; fotostorm/iStock/Getty Images Plus; BananaStock/BananaStock; uniquely india; **F8:** Manita Charoenpru/EyeEm/EyeEm; Dorling Kindersley/Dorling Kindersley; alle12/E+; Selektor/iStock/Getty Images Plus; mbbirdy/E+; richcano/E+; krisanapong detraphiphat/Moment; **F9:** Ryan McVay/Photodisc; Arthur Baensch/Corbis/Getty Images Plus; moodboard/iStock/Getty Images Plus; skynesher/E+; shironosov/iStock/Getty Images Plus; ddukang/iStock/Getty Images Plus; grandriver/E+; **VB1:** yogysic/DigitalVision Vectors; simonkr/E+; Kondo Photography/Cultura; Thomas Barwick/DigitalVision; amygdala_imagery/iStock Unreleased; GoodLifeStudio/E+; Michael Cogliantry/The Image Bank/Getty Images Plus; scyther5/iStock/Getty Images Plus; GoodLifeStudio/E+; Caspar Benson; Caiaimage/Chris Ryan; Tashi-Delek/E+; **VB2:** Tobias Ackeborn/Moment; Westend61; cinoby/E+; Bobby Sanderson/EyeEm; Ian Spanier/Image Source; JianGang Wang/iStock Unreleased; Matt Mawson/Moment; Alex Potemkin/E+; Australian Land, City, People Scape Photographer/Moment; Maskot; Johner Images - Fridh, Conny/Brand X Pictures; Douglas Sacha/Moment Open; Maya Karkalicheva/Moment; **VB3:** eelnosiva/iStock/Getty Images Plus; Westend61; J-Elgaard/E+; laflor/E+; andresr/E+; Image

Source; AaronAmat/iStock/Getty Images Plus; Wavebreakmedia/iStock/Getty Images Plus; GoodLifeStudio/iStock/Getty Images Plus; Shoji Fujita/DigitalVision; Slonov/E+; **VB4:** damircudic/E+; Chris Ryan/OJO Images; Ken Seet/Corbis/VCG; shapecharge/iStock/Getty Images Plus; Tashi-Delek/E+; kali9/E+; PeopleImages/E+; Sean Justice/Stockbyte; skynesher/E+; Hero Images; **VB5:** PaulMaguire/iStock/Getty Images Plus; Connel_Design/iStock/Getty Images Plus; Thomas Hauser/EyeEm; RonFullHD/iStock/Getty Images Plus; Serg_Velusceac/iStock/Getty Images Plus; Tuayai/iStock/Getty Images Plus; Brian Klutch/DigitalVision; cla78/iStock/Getty Images Plus; JazzIRT/E+; Antenna; Image Source; JoeGough/iStock/Getty Images Plus; Csondy/E+; **VB6:** PhotoAlto/Frederic Cirou; blackred/iStock/Getty Images Plus; Westend61; Praiwan Wasanruk/iStock/Getty Images Plus; Image Source; smerindo_schultzpax/Moment; Michael Interisano/Perspectives/Getty Images Plus; PhotoAlto/Ale Ventura; Squaredpixels/iStock/Getty Images Plus; ImagesBazaar; Kenny Williamson/Moment; eugenesergeev/iStock/Getty Images Plus; **VB7:** Erik Isakson; damircudic/E+; BrankoPhoto/E+; Ronnie Kaufman/DigitalVision; Caiaimage/Chris Ryan; IpekMorel/iStock Editorial/Getty Images Plus; Westend61; **VB8:** Yuri_Arcurs/E+; AJ_Watt/E+; oonal/E+; Hill Street Studios/DigitalVision; kali9/E+; Luis Diaz Devesa/Moment; **VB9:** Erik Isakson/Corbis; Ayakovlev/iStock/Getty Images Plus; Homer Sykes/The Image Bank/Getty Images Plus; BraunS/E+; GoodLifeStudio/E+; Niyaz_Tavkaev/iStock/Getty Images Plus; joshblake/E+; FatCamera/E+.

The following photographs are sourced from other libraries/sources.s

SU: Currency Images are courtesy of the Bureau of Engraving and Printing.

Icons: Prithvi/Noun Project; Agni/Noun Project; mikicon/Noun Project; Baboon designs US/Noun Project; Tanguy Keryhuel; FR/Noun Project; Icons Bazaar/Noun Project; Adrien Coquet, FR/Noun Project; Vectors Market/Noun Project; TukTuk Design/Noun Project; iconsphere, ID/Noun Project; i cons, US/Noun Project; kim Eriksson/Noun Project; Delwar Hossain, BD/Noun Project; Kirby Wu, TW/Noun Project; Magicon, HU/Noun Project; Baboon designs, US/Noun Project.

U1–7: Carboxylase/Shutterstock.

Illustration

U1: Oliver Flores; **U2:** Jose Rubio; Mark Duffin, **U3:** Oliver Flores; Antonio Cuesta; Oliver Flores; **U5:** Jose Rubio; Antonio Cuesta; **U6:** Oliver Flores; Alex Herrerias; **U7:** Antonio Cuesta; Alex Herrerias; Jose Rubio; **U8:** Jose Rubio; Oliver Flores; **U9:** Oliver Flores; **F1:** Alex Herrerias; **F2:** Jose Rubio; **F3:** Antonio Cuesta; **F5:** Jose Rubio; **F6:** Alex Herrerias; **F7:** Alex Herrerias; **F8:** Oliver Flores; **F9:** Alex Herrerias.

The following illustrations are sourced from other sources:

U5: Illustration based on the image, *Nautilus House*. Copyright © Arquitectura Orgánica. Reproduced with kind permission; Illustration based on the image, *The PAS House*. Copyright © PAS House – skatestudyhouse.com. Reproduced with kind permission; Illustration based on the image, *The Keret House*. Copyright © Polish Modern Art Foundation/Bartek Warzecha. Reproduced with kind permission.

Video Clips

The following stills are sourced from Getty Images.

U1: Daily Herald Archive/SSPL/Hulton Archive; MicrovOne/iStock/Getty Images Plus; **U2:** Merlinus74/Creatas Video+; **U3:** OmniMovi Ltd/Corbis Video; simonkr/Creatas Video; **U4:** The Lighthouse Film Co, Inc./Lighthouse Films; **U5:** junlongyang/Moment/Getty Images Plus; Fondation GoodPlanet/Yann Arthus-Bertrand; **U6:** konstantynov/Creatas Video+; **U7:** Alexandrea Day/Getty Images Editorial Footage; Sky News/Film Image Partner; **U8:** Silverwell Films/Archive Films: Editorial; **U9:** kali9/Creatas Video; Do Diligence Inc./Image Bank Film.

Cover Design and Illustrations: Collaborate Agency

Video Production: Lucentum Digital

Audio Recordings: Eastern Sky Studios

Typesetting: Aphik, S.A. de C.V.

Contributing Authors: Daniel Vincent, Liz Walter, and Kate Woodford

Versioner: Suzanne Harris

American English Consultant: Multimodal Media

Freelance Editors: Sue Costello, Meredith Levy, Jacqueline French, and Cara Norris-Ramirez

The authors and editors would like to thank all the teachers and consultants who have contributed to the development of the course, in particular:

Mexico: Ana Belem Duran; Nelly Marina Elizalde; Julio Andrés Franco Del Campo; Nimbe García Haro; Raoul Josset Paquette; Adriana Maldonado Torres; Ana Edith Ramos Ramírez

Brazil: Beatriz Affonso; Alessandra Bautista; Ana Carolina De Luca; Esdras Fattobene; Maria Claudia Ferreira; Itana Lins; Maria Helena Meyer; Valéria Moraes Novoa; Odinéia Morandi; Regina Pedroso De Araujo; Andrea Perina; Simone Rodrigues; Jacqueline Saback; Clice Sales; Silvia Teles

Turkey: Belgün Akçelik; Peggy Alptekin; Hayri Arslan; Ayşe Aylin Kündüroğlu; Nihan Çalışkan; Selin Dinçkal Erkenci; Bengü Özbek; Saliha Şimşek

SHAPE IT! 2

COMBO

WORKBOOK

Annie Cornford

CAMBRIDGE
UNIVERSITY PRESS

CONTENTS

STARTER

Welcome!

VOCABULARY AND READING

Free Time and Hobbies

1 ☆ Match six of the phrases in the box with the photos.

1 chat online ~~2 download songs and listen to music~~ 3 go shopping 4 go for a bike ride 5 hang out with friends 6 make cookies 7 make videos 8 play an instrument 9 read books 10 read magazines 11 take photos 12 write a blog

a 
2

b 

c 

d 

e 

f 

Sports

2 ☆ Put the letters in the correct order to make sports words. The first letter is given.

1 b e a t l n n e t s i — table tennis
2 b r g y u — r ______
3 k t a r c n d a e i l f d — t ______
4 i s a g i l n — s ______
5 c e h o k y — h ______
6 n m a y s g t s c i — g ______
7 b y v l e l a l o l — v ______
8 s a a b b l l t e k — b ______
9 w s i g m i m n — s ______
10 s w n f i u r n g d i — w ______

A Blog Post

3 ☆ Read Pablo's blog post. What is his best friend's favorite activity? ______

Home News Blog Lifestyle

My Friends and Their Hobbies

Hi there, Pablo here! Today my blog is about two of my friends and their hobbies.

Carla lives in an apartment in our building. We go to the same school, but we aren't in the same class. Carla loves riding her bike, so she usually cycles to school. I don't cycle when the weather's bad, but I like to ride my bike with her in the summer. Carla also plays hockey and does gymnastics – she's very athletic!

Nico is my best friend – he's Italian. He speaks Italian at home with his family, but he doesn't speak Italian with me. He plays volleyball on our school team on Wednesday afternoons and Saturday mornings. On Sundays, we often do his favorite free-time activity: making pizza! His dad's a chef in a pizzeria, so Nico knows a lot about pizza – and I like eating pizza a lot!

4 ☆☆ Read the blog again. Circle the correct options.

1 Carla and Pablo go / *don't go* to the same school.
2 Pablo *cycles* / *doesn't cycle* to school every day.
3 Carla's very *good* / *bad* at sports.
4 Pablo's best friend *speaks* / *doesn't speak* Italian.
5 Pablo likes *making* / *eating* pizza.

Explore It!

Guess the correct answer.

Marathon runners often lose height when they run a race. On average, a marathon runner is *1 cm* / *5 cm* / *10 cm* shorter at the end of a race.

Find another interesting fact about running. Write a question and send it to a classmate in an email, or ask them in the next class.

GRAMMAR IN ACTION AND VOCABULARY

Simple Present

1 ☆ **Complete the sentences with the simple present form of the verbs in the box.**

go	make	~~play~~	not see	write

1 Max *plays* computer games every day.
2 Lena's friend ______ to a different school.
3 We ______ our friends on Sunday evenings.
4 I ______ my blog two or three times a week.
5 Martha ______ videos of her pets.

2 ☆☆ **Write questions about Pablo's blog and answer them. Then check on page 4.**

1 when / Pablo / ride his bike with Carla ?
When does Pablo ride his bike with Carla?
Pablo rides his bike with Carla in the summer.
2 what sports / Carla / do ?
______
______
3 where / Nico's father / work ?
______
______
4 what / Nico / know a lot about ?
______
______

Adverbs of Frequency

3 ☆☆ **Put the words in the correct order to make sentences.**

1 computer / often / I / magazines / read / .
I often read computer magazines.
2 never / hockey / Iris / late / practice / is / for / .
______
3 takes / photos / great / always / Paul / .
______
4 sometimes / next / Molly / to / friend / sits / her / .
______
5 music / you / listen / Do / to / usually / loud / ?
______

Personal Possessions

4 ☆☆ **Find the ten personal possessions in the photos in the wordsearch. Mark (✓) the photos when you find the words.**

✓

T	N	O	H	M	C	H	S	A	L	J	N
A	Z	Q	S	O	I	B	C	D	S	G	H
B	U	R	R	N	O	A	L	H	S	S	J
L	Y	D	K	E	Y	S	H	E	F	C	H
E	F	M	W	Y	R	P	S	A	O	H	G
T	V	L	S	I	E	T	D	D	P	A	C
F	K	S	C	P	A	S	S	P	O	R	T
K	V	W	J	H	D	S	U	H	R	G	O
L	A	P	T	O	P	D	B	O	T	E	S
O	B	U	P	N	L	P	D	N	A	R	A
U	(C	A	M	E	R	A)	C	E	B	R	L
T	E	Y	N	J	A	N	W	S	L	E	G
D	S	K	L	H	Q	L	D	A	E	D	F
B	U	S	P	A	S	S	P	N	M	O	V

LISTENING AND GRAMMAR IN ACTION

A Conversation

S.01 **1** ☆ **Listen and circle the correct option.**

Hannah meets Mrs. Hayes at the *store / gym / bus stop*.

S.01 **2** ☆☆ **Listen again. Mark (✓) the activities that Hannah and Joe do.**

	Gymnastics Class	Running Club	Photography Club	Play Video Games
Hannah	✓			
Joe	✗			

S.01 **3** ☆☆ **Listen again. Are the sentences *T* (true) or *F* (false)?**

1 Mrs. Hayes likes doing sports on the weekend. F
2 Joe goes to a running club on Saturday evenings. ____
3 The gymnastics class is one and a half hours long. ____
4 The school's photography club is once a week. ____
5 Joe likes writing video games. ____
6 Hannah does her homework on the weekend. ____

Love, Like, Don't Mind, Hate + -ing

4 ☆☆ **Complete the sentences with the correct form of the verbs in the box.**

~~be~~ help play speak use write

1 Susie hates *being* late for class, so she always arrives early.
2 Harry doesn't mind ____________ soccer, but it's not his favorite sport.
3 I love ____________ English, so I often call my cousins in the U.S.A.
4 Do you like ____________ headphones when you listen to music?
5 Bella loves ____________ her blog. It's really good, and we all read it.
6 Good friends don't mind ____________ you when you have a problem.

To Have

5 ☆☆ **Complete the questions and short answers with the correct form of *to have*.**

1 A *Do* you *have* your own computer?
B Yes, *I do*.
2 A ____________ Jack ____________ his own keys?
B Yes, ____________.
3 A ____________ Enzo and Lou ____________ a French mother?
B No, ____________.
4 A ____________ I ____________ the right phone number for you?
B No, ____________.
5 A ____________ we ____________ any math homework today?
B Yes, ____________.
6 A ____________ your mom ____________ a new laptop?
B Yes, ____________.

6 ☆☆ **Circle the correct options to complete the email.**

Dear Leo,

I [1]*have* / *has* some exciting news. We [2]*have* / *don't have* new neighbors, and there's a girl named Jessica – she's my new friend. [3]*Do we have* / *We have* a lot in common? Yes, we [4]*don't* / *do*! She's my age and she [5]*has* / *have* long dark hair, just like me. She loves [6]*listen* / *listening* to music and singing, and she [7]*has* / *doesn't have* her own band – so cool! She [8]*don't have* / *doesn't have* any sisters or brothers, but I don't mind [9]*to share* / *sharing* my annoying little brothers with her! Jessica and I [10]*love* / *hate* hanging out together already!

See you soon!

Anita

WRITING

A Personal Profile

1 ★ **Read Bruna's profile of her brothers. When are they all free to hang out together?**

____

HOME ABOUT ME ARCHIVE FOLLOW

1 Hi! My name's Bruna, and this profile is about my two brothers. We're from São Paulo, in Brazil. My brothers are named Victor and Lucas. Victor's nine years old and Lucas is 12. I'm 14.

2 Lucas is crazy about soccer, like a lot of people in Brazil! He practices on Mondays, Wednesdays, Fridays, and Saturdays! He never minds getting home late because he just loves playing. Victor's favorite free-time activity is swimming. He has a great coach, and he gets up early for lessons with her in the pool at the gym.

3 Lucas and Victor also like playing table tennis, and we all love doing that together. We have a table tennis table in our garage, and we often play on Sundays when we're all free. I sometimes find Lucas annoying, but he's usually a lot of fun, and Victor is OK. Do you have brothers and sisters? What are they like?

2 ★★ **Read the profile again. Are the sentences *T* (true) or *F* (false)?**

1 Lucas and Victor have one sister. T
2 Lucas has soccer practice on the weekend. ____
3 Lucas never gets home late from practice. ____
4 Victor prefers table tennis to swimming. ____
5 Bruna doesn't play table tennis with her brothers. ____

3 ★★ **Read the profile again. Underline one example of …**

1 *'s* for possession
2 *'s* for *is*
3 commas in a list

4 ★★ **Rewrite the text with contractions, apostrophes, and commas in your notebook.**

My friend Mason has a big family. He has two brothers two sisters and 35 cousins. They all live on the same street! In Masons house, there are a lot of pets. They have two dogs three cats four rabbits and a parrot! They have a big house and a big yard, so there is lots of space!

PLAN

5 ★★ **Write a profile of a friend or a family member. Take notes for each paragraph.**

1 Their family and friends:

____

____

2 Their favorite free-time activity:
- what it is and where they do it
- how often they do it

____

____

3 Other free-time activities:
- what they like doing on their own or with friends
- when and where they do the activities

____

____

WRITE

6 ★★★ **Write your profile. Remember to include three paragraphs, the information in Exercise 5, the simple present, adverbs of frequency, *love*, etc. + *-ing*, and *to have*.**

CHECK

7 **Do you …**
- describe the family and friends of the person in your profile?
- explain their favorite free-time activity?
- say what else they like doing, and when?

1 What are you watching?

VOCABULARY

TV Shows

1 ☆ **Complete the words with the missing vowels.**

1 str *e a* m *i* ng s *e* r *i e* s
2 sp _ rts sh _ w
3 d _ c _ m _ nt _ ry
4 dr _ m _
5 g _ m _ sh _ w
6 t _ lk sh _ w
7 s _ _ p _ p _ r _
8 th _ n _ ws
9 c _ m _ dy
10 c _ _ k _ ng sh _ w
11 c _ rt _ _ n
12 r _ _ l _ ty sh _ w

2 ☆ **Circle the correct options.**

1 What is the first prize on the TV *drama* / *game show* this week?
2 Dan loves food, so he watches all the *sports* / *cooking* shows.
3 Adele is talking to some great guests on tonight's *soap opera* / *talk show*.
4 We always laugh a lot at the new *drama* / *comedy* on Channel 4 because it's really funny.
5 Sam watches *the news* / *a streaming series* to learn about world events.
6 Now they use computers to make *documentaries* / *cartoons*. They don't draw them by hand.

3 ☆ **Match the definitions with TV shows from Exercise 1.**

1 a show about a subject, like history or nature. *documentary*
2 information about real world events. ______
3 information about tennis, soccer, basketball, etc. ______
4 an animated story, usually for younger people. ______
5 a show on which you answer questions and win prizes. ______
6 a show about real people in their ordinary lives. ______

4 ☆☆ **Complete the text about Elena's family with the words in the box.**

comedies	cooking shows	~~dramas~~
soap operas	streaming series	talk shows

My parents enjoy watching TV [1] *dramas*, especially when they are true stories from history. They both like [2] ______ with famous chefs, too. My dad also enjoys [3] ______ on late-night TV. They make him laugh, but I don't think his favorite shows are funny at all! My mom watches [4] ______ with interesting celebrities talking about their latest movies, and I sometimes watch them with her. My grandma enjoys her favorite [5] ______ because she knows all the characters and is interested in their lives. I usually prefer [6] ______ to regular TV shows because I can watch them when I want to. I love that!

Explore It!

Guess the correct answer.

Blue Peter, the oldest children's TV show in the world, is about *40* / *60* / *80* years old.

Find another interesting fact about a TV show in your country. Write a question and send it to a classmate in an email, or ask them in the next class.

READING

Tweets

1 ☆ **Read the tweets. Which tweeter isn't very happy?**

____

2 ☆☆ **Read the tweets again and check the meaning of these words in a dictionary. Then complete the sentences.**

billion ~~competitor~~ fact live support

1 Amy's not a *competitor*. She's watching the event on TV today.

2 There's an interesting __________ about the number of people that watched the last Olympics.

3 More than 3 __________ people watch the World Cup Final on TV. That's more than 3,000 million people!

4 The game is __________ – all the action is happening now.

5 Which team on tonight's game show do you __________?

3 ☆☆ **Read the tweets again and answer the questions.**

1 At what time can people watch the UEFA Champions League Final live?
at eight o'clock

2 What doesn't Manny want to watch?
____

3 Where is Amy today?
____

4 What sport does Amy like playing?
____

5 What can people watch on Channel 1 at the moment?
____

6 Where is Antonio today?
____

4 ☆☆☆ **Answer the questions with your own ideas.**

1 Do you prefer playing sports or watching them on TV? Why?
____

2 Do you ever watch sports live? Which ones?
____

Channel 1 Sports @Channel1Sports
It's the day of the UEFA Champions League Final, and you can see it live on our sports show from eight o'clock tonight or later, on demand, from 11! More than 4 billion people watch soccer on TV. Are you one of them? Tweet us and tell us: Are you watching or playing sports right now?

Manny Ellis @MEllis
I want to watch basketball on TV today, but my sister's here with her friend. They're sitting in the living room and watching a really bad comedy show! So I'm in the kitchen watching the game on a tiny tablet!

Amy Mount @aMount
I'm at my friend's house, and we're waiting for the big final to begin on Channel 1. We love watching sports on TV. We often play soccer too, but today we're eating snacks and supporting our team.

Channel 1 Sports @Channel1Sports
Right now on Channel 1, we're showing a documentary about the history of the Olympics. Here's an interesting fact: Around 3.5 billion people watched the last Olympics! But what do you think – do more people watch the Olympics or the World Cup Final? Which other sports are good to watch on TV?

Antonio González @toni2020
I think cycling's a great sport to watch on TV, but today I'm standing on the side of the road watching the competitors in my country's famous three-week event: the *Vuelta a España*! They're doing a very long part of the race today: over 200 km in one day!

GRAMMAR IN ACTION

Present Continuous

1 ☆ **Circle the correct options.**

1 In my school, we *learning* / *'re learning* how to edit videos.
2 Leni *is making* / *is makeing* clothes for the school production.
3 Helena and Jack *are watch* / *are watching* their favorite show.
4 Who *is sitting* / *is siting* next to you in class today?
5 My brother *isn't eating* / *not eating* much at the moment.
6 *Are you waiting* / *You waiting* for the news to begin?

2 ☆ **Complete the sentences with the present continuous form of the verbs in parentheses.**

1 She *'s chatting* (chat) with her friends online.
2 He ______ (prepare) his history presentation.
3 We ______ (wait) for the school bus.
4 He ______ (make) a video about skateboarders.
5 They ______ (not cry); they ______ (laugh).
6 I ______ (not watch) anything; I ______ (work)!

3 ☆☆ **Put the words in the correct order to make questions. Then match them with the answers from Exercise 2.**

a those / crying / are / Why / boys / ?
Why are those boys crying? [5]
b on the computer / Anita / doing / What / is / ?
______ [ ]
c you / there / all / Why / standing / are / ?
______ [ ]
d park / doing / the / Miguel / What / is / at / ?
______ [ ]
e Why / late / working / is / tonight / Paul / ?
______ [ ]
f you / What / watching / are / on TV / ?
______ [ ]

4 ☆☆ **Write questions and short answers with the present continuous.**

1 you / cycle / to school? (✓)
Are you cycling to school? *Yes, I am.*
2 we / listen / to the instructor? (✗)
______ ______
3 she / wait / for the next episode? (✓)
______ ______
4 they / enjoy / the show? (✗)
______ ______
5 you / send / a message to a friend? (✗)
______ ______
6 I / help / you? (✓)
______ ______

5 ☆☆ **Complete the email with the correct present continuous form of the verbs in the box.**

learn	look forward to	~~not use~~		
prepare	take	use	work	write

Dear Uncle Dominic,

Mom tells me you have a new camera and that you want to give me your old one because you [1] *aren't using* it. Great! I hear it's better than the one I [2] ______ at the moment, so I [3] ______ this email to say thank you! [4] ______ you ______ lots of great photos now with your new camera?

I [5] ______ a presentation for my media studies class with a classmate this week. We [6] ______ a lot about taking black and white photos – it's interesting! We [7] ______ on a series of winter photos. So I [8] ______ the new camera very much!

Thanks again and see you soon.

Jo

VOCABULARY AND LISTENING

Making Movies

1 ☆ **Complete the crossword. Use the clues.**

Across

3 Please move those … . They're shining in my eyes.

5 I'm wearing a gorilla … , and I'm getting very hot!

8 A sound … knows when the actors are too quiet or too loud.

10 I'm hoping to be a camera … when I finish school.

Down

1 Marius is writing the … for his documentary project.

2 Where are they building the … for the new soap opera?

4 The best … in *The Hunger Games* is Josh Hutcherson.

6 A … artist named Lucy is making that young woman look older.

7 The … is just sitting in her chair and telling us what to do.

9 I can take great photos with my new digital … .

2 ☆ **Match 1–5 with a–e.**

1 She's a top makeup artist, [b]
2 You can take hundreds of photos [ ]
3 The sound engineer [ ]
4 Steven Spielberg [ ]
5 The studio goes dark [ ]

a is a famous movie director.
b and she can change actors' appearances.
c when the lights go out.
d is wearing big headphones.
e with a digital camera.

A Guided Tour

3 ☆☆ (1.01) **Listen to a girl on a tour of a soap opera set and answer the questions.**

1 In which city do they film the soap opera? ______
2 How many families are in the soap opera? ______
3 What is the street on the soap opera called? ______

4 ☆☆ (1.01) **Listen again and circle the correct answers.**

1 What is the name of the soap opera?
a *Best Friends* b *Teenlife* (c) *Time of Our Lives*

2 One of the main actors is named … .
a Adele Johnson b Tom Bridges c Lauren Thomas

3 The soap opera is about … .
a teenagers' lives b a mail carrier c a school in Sydney

4 There are … houses on Clifton Street.
a 15 b 20 c 100

5 There are … actors in the soap opera.
a 10 b 50 c 60

5 ☆☆☆ **Answer the questions.**

1 Which series do you like?

______

2 What are the most popular soap operas in your country?

______

GRAMMAR IN ACTION

Simple Present and Present Continuous

1 ☆ **Complete the chart with the time expressions in the box.**

~~always~~ at the moment every day
every week never right now
this afternoon today

Simple Present	Present Continuous
always	

2 ☆ **Complete the sentences with the simple present or present continuous form of the verbs in parentheses.**

1 She *'s waiting* (wait) for her favorite TV show to start.
2 Actors ______ (love) taking selfies with their fans.
3 It usually ______ (take) days to learn the words of a script.
4 We ______ (watch) the news together at the moment.
5 I ______ (not come) here very often.
6 They ______ (make) a new episode every week.

3 ☆☆ **Put the words in the correct order to make sentences.**

1 download / Internet / Do / always / from / you / the / movies / ?
Do you always download movies from the Internet?
2 drama / good / I'm / the / a / moment / TV / watching / at / .
______
3 outside / eat / sometimes / summer / We / lunch / our / the / in / .
______
4 talks / actors / to / sound engineer / the / The / never / .
______
5 you / listening / teacher / your / now / right / Are / to / ?
______
6 now / taking / Sydney / guided tour / a / My / is / sister / of / .
______

Adverbs of Manner

4 ☆☆ **Underline and correct one mistake in each sentence.**

1 My mother isn't a slowly driver. *slow*
2 Their little brothers are playing happyly.
______
3 Our parents teach us to say "thank you" nice.
______
4 Be carefully! That camera is very expensive!
______
5 You're doing your homework very good at the moment. ______
6 She's playing the guitar beautiful now.
______

5 ☆☆ **Choose the correct adjectives. Then complete the sentences with the adverb forms.**

1 My brother writes very *well* (good / bad). I enjoy reading his stories.
2 Leila speaks very ______ (loud / quiet). I can't hear what she's saying sometimes.
3 That movie starts ______ (slow / fast). The beginning is really boring.
4 Kitty is singing really ______ (loud / quiet). You can hear her in the street!
5 You work ______ (easy / hard). That's why you do well on your tests.
6 This book ends ______ (good / bad). I don't like the ending at all.

WRITING

A Description of a Celebrity

1 ☆ **Read the description. Why can you watch Mason Millerson videos with your parents?**

My Favorite Comedian

By Gabriel Costa

1 Mason Millerson is my favorite comedian. He's an Australian comedian, Internet personality, singer, writer, and actor. His comedy videos have over 2 billion views, and he has over 15 million subscribers.

2 In each video, Mason is really funny and very original. You can watch his videos on the Internet. On them, he just speaks to the camera in a very natural way, and you're laughing all the time. Sometimes I laugh so much that I cry! He talks about ordinary, everyday things, like eating dinner with family or waiting for a train, but he makes them special.

3 I really like Mason Millerson because he has a great imagination. His stories are funny, but they are never mean or offensive; so it's OK to watch Mason's videos with your parents. I think he's great!

2 ☆☆ **Read the description again and answer the questions.**

1 Where is Mason from? ______

2 How many people watch Mason's videos online regularly? ______

3 What sometimes happens when Gabriel watches Mason's videos? ______

3 ☆ **Match the start of each paragraph (a–c) with the topics (1–3).**

a In each video, Mason is … ☐

b I really like Mason Millerson because … ☐

c Mason Millerson is my favorite comedian. ☐

1 an introduction to the person and his videos

2 what the person's videos are usually about

3 why I like this person

4 ☆ **Complete the sentences from the description and match them with the rules (a–c).**

1 He's an Australian comedian, Internet personality, singer, writer, ______ actor. ☐

2 He talks about ordinary, everyday things … , ______ he makes them special. ☐

3 His stories are … never mean ______ offensive. ☐

a We use *but* to show different information.

b We use *or* when there is a choice of two or more things.

c We use *and* to add similar information.

PLAN

5 ☆☆ **Write a description of your favorite comedian or comedy actor. Take notes about these things.**

1 Who the person is: ______

What they do: ______

How many followers they have: ______

2 What they usually do in their videos or movies: ______

3 Why I like this person and their videos or movies: ______

WRITE

6 ☆☆☆ **Write your description. Remember to include three paragraphs using the information from Exercise 5, the correct present tenses, and adverbs, and *and*, *but*, and *or*.**

CHECK

7 **Do you …**

- use sentences with *and*, *but*, and *or*?
- give information about what the person usually does?
- explain why you like the person?

1 REVIEW

VOCABULARY

1 Match 1–8 with a–h.

1 I don't like cooking shows ☐
2 They're talking about the soccer match ☐
3 Disney is famous for ☐
4 Dad's watching a comedy, ☐
5 Ava's watching the documentary ☐
6 I love historical dramas about ☐
7 You can win a lot of money ☐
8 Do you usually watch the news ☐

a about animals in Africa.
b on some of these game shows.
c on TV or online?
d but he doesn't think it's funny.
e children's cartoons.
f on our favorite sports show.
g life in the 1500s.
h because I hate cooking.

2 Complete the sentences with the words in the box.

actor camera operator costume digital camera director lights makeup artist script set sound engineer

1 The ________ is filming the pandas up close and getting some great shots.
2 Carlos learns the words by reading his ________ many times.
3 Does a TV news anchor wear normal clothes or a ________?
4 The movie ________ tells everyone what to do and how to do it.
5 It can be very hot when you work under bright studio ________.
6 The ________ for my favorite series is a street in Mexico City.
7 A ________ changes people's appearances for movies.
8 The ________ knows when the actors are speaking very quietly.
9 The ________ who plays the son is only six years old.
10 I can make great home videos with my new ________.

GRAMMAR IN ACTION

3 Complete the conversation with the present continuous form of the verbs in parentheses.

PEDRO What [1] ________ (you / do)?
MARIA I [2] ________ (write) an email to my uncle. He [3] ________ (work) on a movie set at the moment.
PEDRO Wow! [4] ________ (he / film) any famous actors?
MARIA No, he isn't. He [5] ________ (travel) with the film crew and actors, and he [6] ________ (cook) their food. He's a chef.
PEDRO That's cool. So why [7] ________ (you / send) him an email?
MARIA I [8] ________ (hope) he can come to my birthday party and cook something good for me!

4 Complete the sentences with the simple present or present continuous form of the verbs in parentheses.

1 I __________ (write) to my friend in Los Angeles right now. I __________ (email) her every month.

2 We usually __________ (watch) the news on TV, but today we __________ (listen) to it in the car.

3 Henry __________ (save) money at the moment because he __________ (need) a new bike.

4 __________ you __________ (look) for my sister? She usually __________ (sit) over there.

5 Our mom __________ (not go) to work on Fridays, but she __________ (work) today.

6 My friends __________ (swim) at the beach today, but I'm not. I __________ (prefer) swimming pools.

7 __________ you __________ (wait) for Susie? She __________ usually __________ (not arrive) late.

8 I __________ (cook) pancakes for breakfast at the moment. I often __________ (make) them on the weekend.

5 Circle the correct options.

1 Please be *quiet / quietly*! Your baby sister is sleeping.

2 Sandra is a very *nice / nicely* girl, in my opinion.

3 The children are watching *Frozen 2* and eating ice cream *happy / happily*.

4 I always speak *loud / loudly*, but Grandpa still can't hear me.

5 When we work *quick / quickly*, we sometimes make mistakes.

6 He answered the questions *good / well* on the test.

7 Our music teacher plays the guitar *beautiful / beautifully*.

8 Catalina is wearing a very *pretty / prettily* costume in the show.

CUMULATIVE GRAMMAR

6 Complete the conversation with the missing words. Circle the correct options.

ANA Hi, Dan. 1 __________ your vacation?

DAN We 2 __________ a great time here. I 3 __________ with my friends and their family in their summer apartment.

ANA That's 4 __________. What do you think of it?

DAN It's 5 __________ and there's a pool.

ANA Lucky you! 6 __________ swimming every day?

DAN Well, my friends Tess and Rob 7 __________ every morning before breakfast.

ANA Great!

DAN Yeah, but actually I 8 __________ eating something first.

ANA Really?

DAN I'm always 9 __________ when I 10 __________ up!

ANA So when do you 11 __________ breakfast?

DAN Well, that's breakfast time for me – when I 12 __________ up.

	a	b	c
1	Enjoy you	Are you enjoying	You enjoy
2	have	has	're having
3	'm staying	stay	staying
4	nice	nicily	nicely
5	beautifully	beautiful	beautifuly
6	Are you go	Go you	Do you go
7	swims	are swiming	swim
8	prefer	'm preferring	'm prefer
9	hungrily	hungry	hungryly
10	'm waking	wakes	wake
11	usually eat	eat usually	usual eat
12	'm getting	gets	get

2 How was the past different?

VOCABULARY

The Weather

1 ☆ **Find 12 more weather words in the word snake.**

(snowy)foggycoldwindyhoticycloudyrainywarmsunnywetstormydry

2 ☆ **(Circle) the correct options.**

1 We have winter coats because it is a (cold) / *warm* day.
2 Be careful, don't run! It's *hot* / *icy* outside.
3 It's not much fun skiing when it's *rainy* / *snowy*.
4 The bus driver can't see the road. It's very *windy* / *foggy* today.
5 **A** Is it raining now? **B** No, but it's *wet* / *cloudy*.
6 Trees sometimes fall down in very *windy* / *warm* weather.

3 ☆☆ **Complete the sentences with the words in the box. Then match them with photos a–f.**

foggy	snowy	~~stormy~~	sunny	wet	windy

a
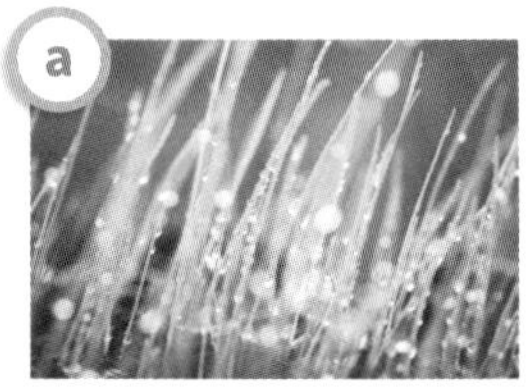
b

c

d

e

f

1 It's dangerous to go surfing in ___stormy___ weather. [f]
2 We can't have a picnic today. The grass is very ___________ because of the rain. [ ]
3 It's ___________, and they are lost because they can't see. [ ]
4 On a ___________ day, they wear their hats, gloves, and scarves. [ ]
5 This ___________ weather is perfect for sailing. [ ]
6 It's ___________, so don't forget your sunglasses! [ ]

4 ☆☆ **Complete the email with words from Exercise 1.**

TO: Jeremy
FROM: Calum

Dear Jeremy,

What's the weather like where you are? Here it's beautiful and ¹___sunny___, and I'm sitting under a tree with a sun hat and sunglasses on. There's no rain, so the fields are very ²___________. I like ³___________ weather – about 20 °C is fine, but 35 °C is very ⁴___________ and not great for me! We usually get a lot of ⁵___________ days in Oregon, so it's often very wet, but not this year. Actually, I can't wait for the winter, with some nice ⁶___________ weekends for skiing.

Talk to you soon,
Calum

5 ☆☆ **Write the noun forms of the adjectives.**

1 rainy ___rain___
2 cloudy ___________
3 icy ___________
4 sunny ___________
5 windy ___________
6 snowy ___________
7 foggy ___________
8 stormy ___________

Explore It!

Guess the correct answer.

The Sami people live in the far north of Norway, Sweden, Finland, and Russia. Language experts say that the Sami have at least *8* / *18* / *180* words for snow and ice.

Find another interesting fact about the Sami people. Write a question and send it to a classmate in an email, or ask them in the next class.

READING

Diary Extracts

1 ☆ **Read the text and diary extracts. What did Ollie and Jack find on their journey?**

____

Looking for Treasure

In 2010, an American man hid a big box full of treasure somewhere in the Rocky Mountains. His name is Forrest Fenn, and he was over 80 years old at the time. Fenn is an art expert, and he had a lot of old and very expensive objects. He filled his box with jewelry, diamonds, and gold, and then buried it in a secret place in the mountains. Why did he do that? He wanted to give families a reason to enjoy time in nature. In his opinion, children spend a lot of time on computers and need to do more outdoor activities. The result? Thousands of people are looking for Forrest Fenn's treasure. Below are diary extracts from two young treasure hunters.

Ollie's Diary: May 2, 2020

My friend Jack and I are on vacation in Yellowstone National Park, and we're looking for buried treasure with our parents. They planned this trip because they wanted us to enjoy hiking and camping in the spring. I just want to find the box! Forrest Fenn wrote a 24-line poem with clues about where to find it. He shared the poem on Instagram, so we know the box is somewhere in Wyoming or Colorado – two of the BIGGEST STATES in the U.S.A.!

Jack's Diary: May 11, 2020

Time to go home, but the roads are closed and there's deep snow everywhere. We're all staying in a hostel because it's not possible to camp out in this weather. It's very cold and there's no Wi-Fi here. And the worst thing is that we didn't find any treasure! I don't think this was a good idea after all!

2 ☆☆ **Read the text and diary extracts again and check the meaning of these words in a dictionary. Then complete the sentences.**

bury	clues	hides	~~jewelry~~	secret	treasure

1 That ___jewelry___ store sells beautiful earrings, necklaces, and bracelets.
2 That dog is making a hole in the ground to ________ the ball!
3 She usually ________ her diary under her bed.
4 Grandma keeps her diamond ring in a ________ place in her house.
5 They found a ship on the ocean floor with lots of ________ in it.
6 I always read the ________ carefully when I'm doing a crossword.

3 ☆☆ **Read the text again. Are the sentences *T* (true) or *F* (false)?**

1 Forrest Fenn hid expensive jewelry and gold in a box. ___T___
2 He hid the box because he doesn't want people to find it. ____
3 The boys' parents didn't go with them. ____
4 Fenn's clues are on the Internet. ____
5 The boys can't get home because of the weather. ____
6 Jack enjoyed hunting for treasure. ____

4 ☆☆☆ **Answer the questions with your own ideas.**

1 What outdoor activities do you do?

____

2 Do you like the idea of this treasure hunt? Why / Why not?

____

GRAMMAR IN ACTION

Simple Past

1 ☆ **Complete the sentences with the simple past form of the verbs in parentheses.**

1 The boys *hiked* (hike) for nine days.
2 They ________ (take) Fenn's clues with them.
3 They ________ (enjoy) listening to the poem about the buried treasure.
4 The adults and children ________ (read) the clues carefully.
5 Some people ________ (write) diaries about their journey.
6 Actually, the diary extracts ________ (be) very interesting.

2 ☆☆ **Complete the questions with the words in the box. Then match the questions with the answers from Exercise 1.**

did (x2) enjoy hike were write

a What *did* the adults and children read carefully? [4]
b How long did the boys ________ for? [ ]
c ________ the diary extracts boring? [ ]
d What did they ________ listening to? [ ]
e What ________ they take with them? [ ]
f What did some people ________? [ ]

3 ☆☆ **Write questions and short answers in the simple past.**

1 you / have a good vacation, Tina? (✓)
Did you have a good vacation, Tina? *Yes, I did.*
2 you / swim in the ocean? (✗)
________ ________
3 you all / go in the pool? (✓)
________ ________
4 your friends / like the food? (✓)
________ ________
5 Tomas / take lots of photos? (✓)
________ ________
6 Susie / want to come home? (✗)
________ ________

4 ☆☆ **<u>Underline</u> and correct one mistake in each sentence.**

1 Henry <u>seed</u> photos of the pioneers yesterday.
saw
2 We didn't enjoyed the bus trip. ________
3 Did you found a good tour guide last week?
____
4 I did went out in the stormy weather. ________
5 They stoped for food and drink. ________
6 Did she be late for class yesterday? ________

5 ☆☆ **Complete the conversation with the correct simple past form of the verbs in the box.**

become decide not have return
ride ~~see~~ stay take care of travel write

IVAN [1] *Did* you *see* the TV documentary about Dervla Murphy last night?

DARIA No, I didn't. Who is she?

IVAN An amazing traveler and travel writer. In 1963, she [2] ________ to cycle from her hometown in Ireland all the way to India. And in those days, people [3] ________ the kinds of bikes we have now!

DARIA [4] ________ she ________ her bike all the way to India?

IVAN Yes, she did, and she [5] ________ there for a year. She [6] ________ Tibetan refugee children there, and when she [7] ________ home, she [8] ________ her first book. She quickly [9] ________ a famous travel writer – there are more than 20 books by her. Dervla [10] ________ all over the world when she was younger, but she still can't drive a car!

VOCABULARY AND LISTENING Useful Objects

1 ☆ **Put the letters in the correct order to make words for useful objects.**

1 rrroim mirror
2 mpla ____
3 lktebna ____
4 onops ____
5 infek ____
6 wploli ____
7 wblo ____
8 krof ____
9 bcmo ____
10 letpa ____
11 ssssocir ____
12 upc ____
13 bhiraushr ____
14 htbtuhosor ____

2 ☆☆ **Match the photos with six words from Exercise 1.**

a
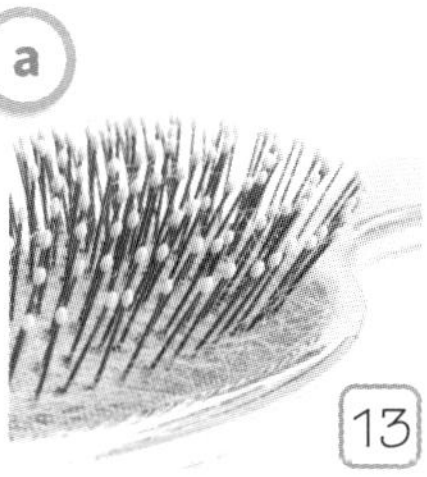
13

b
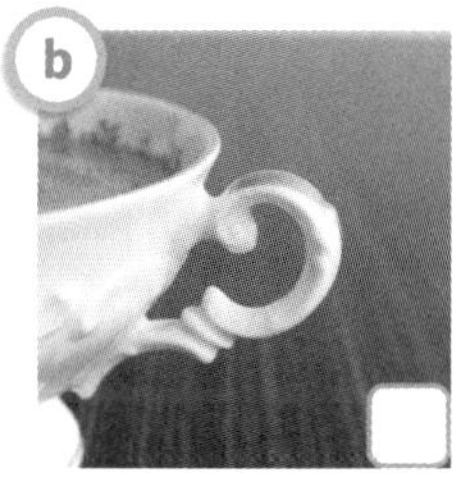

c
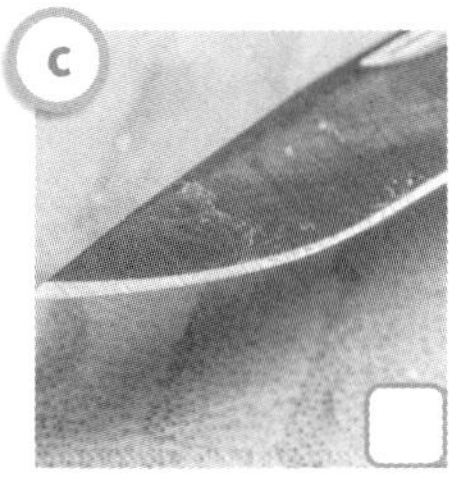

d
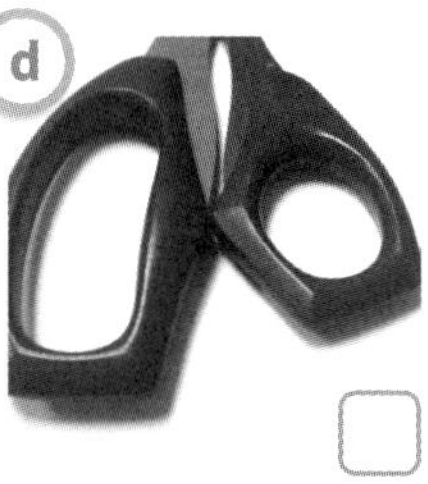

e
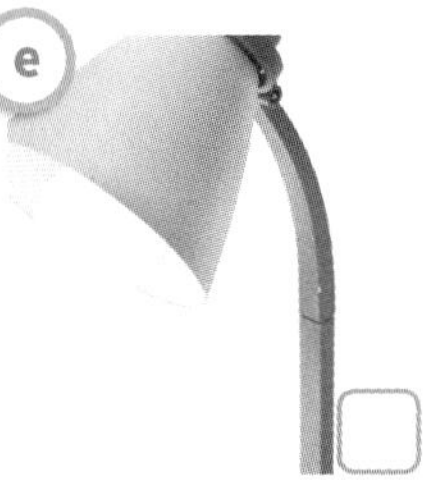

f
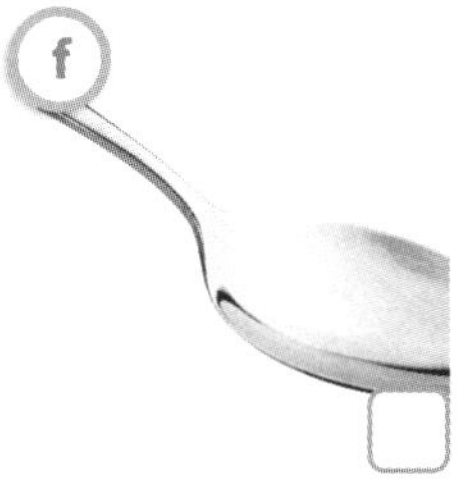

3 ☆ **Where do you usually find the objects from Exercise 1? Some words can go in more than one category.**

Kitchen	Bathroom	Bedroom
knife		

A Radio Show

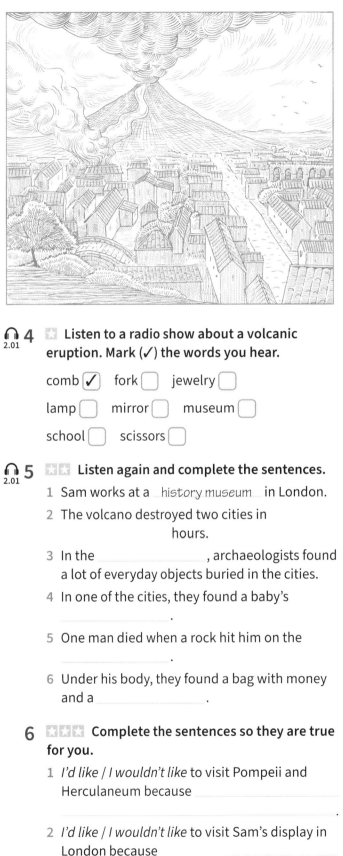

2.01 **4** ☆ **Listen to a radio show about a volcanic eruption. Mark (✓) the words you hear.**

comb ✓ fork ☐ jewelry ☐
lamp ☐ mirror ☐ museum ☐
school ☐ scissors ☐

2.01 **5** ☆☆ **Listen again and complete the sentences.**

1 Sam works at a history museum in London.
2 The volcano destroyed two cities in ____ hours.
3 In the ____, archaeologists found a lot of everyday objects buried in the cities.
4 In one of the cities, they found a baby's ____.
5 One man died when a rock hit him on the ____.
6 Under his body, they found a bag with money and a ____.

6 ☆☆☆ **Complete the sentences so they are true for you.**

1 *I'd like / I wouldn't like* to visit Pompeii and Herculaneum because ____.
2 *I'd like / I wouldn't like* to visit Sam's display in London because ____.

GRAMMAR IN ACTION

There Was/Were

1 Circle the correct options.

1 *There was* / *There were* a team of archaeologists in Naples.

2 *There was* / *There were* some kitchen furniture in the exhibition.

3 *Was there* / *Were there* any travelers in the storm?

4 *There wasn't* / *There weren't* any information about the objects.

5 *Was there* / *Were there* a school in Herculaneum?

6 *There was* / *There were* some old books in the box.

7 *There wasn't* / *There weren't* any clothes in the ruins.

2 Put the words in the correct order to make sentences.

1 wasn't / rain / month / There / any / last / .

There wasn't any rain last month.

2 display / any / There / the / weren't / interesting / in / things / .

______

3 people / exhibition / there / the / at / many / Were / ?

______

4 old / baby / with / an / woman / There / a / was / .

______

5 there / box / Was / any / the / jewelry / in / ?

______

6 Naples / hundreds / were / in / tourists / There / of / .

______

3 Match 1–6 with a–f.

1 There were some [e] — a interesting display of jewelry.

2 Was there a [ ] — b information about Herculaneum?

3 There weren't any [ ] — c useful objects in the kitchen?

4 There was an [ ] — d women on the team.

5 Was there any [ ] — e Roman bowls in the museum.

6 Were there any [ ] — f mirror in the woman's bag?

4 Complete the email with *some*, *any*, *a*, or *an*.

TO: Lily

FROM: Tom

Hi, Lily!

How are you? Just a quick email to tell you about our trip to Brazil! Yesterday, there was [1] a big storm, so we had a day of culture. We walked around the city, and there was [2] ______ fascinating museum called the Museum of Tomorrow, so we decided to go in. It's [3] ______ science museum in Rio, but [4] ______ architect from Spain designed it. There were [5] ______ amazing exhibitions about our planet, and there was [6] ______ very interesting information about it, too. There weren't [7] ______ postcards in the museum gift shop, but there was [8] ______ interesting little book, so I bought you that! Hope you like it!

Talk to you soon,
Tom

5 Look at the two museum displays and complete the texts with *there was(n't)/were(n't)*, *a*, *an*, *some*, or *any*.

Home | News | **Blog** | Lifestyle

[1] There was an interesting display with objects from a Roman kitchen at our local museum. [2] ______ some wooden bowls and [3] ______ knives and forks, but there weren't [4] ______ spoons. There was [5] ______ metal water bottle. There was also [6] ______ very old bread – over a thousand years old, in fact. Yummy!

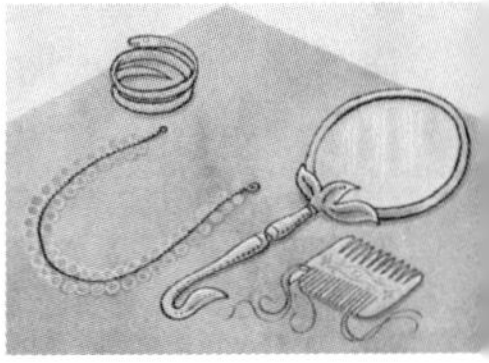

My favorite display had beautiful objects from a woman's bedroom. There was [7] ______ old mirror and [8] ______ gold jewelry. She was probably [9] ______ important person. [10] ______ a beautiful necklace and a bracelet, too, but [11] ______ any earrings. And there was a comb with [12] ______ human hair in it!

WRITING

A Fictional Account of a Journey

1 ☆ **Read the account and circle the best title.**

a Swedish Family Lost in Edale

b Help for Teenage Hikers in Sweden

c Safe Return of Lost Hikers

● ● ●

Three Swedish teenagers decided to do a famous long-distance hike from England to Scotland. [1] They set off on October 22, 2018, from Edale, a small village in northern England.

The walk is 412 km long, and Lucas, Sven, and Lilly wanted to complete it in three weeks. They wore big boots and carried heavy bags with their camping equipment. [2] ________ it was warm and sunny, but after two days, everything changed. [3] ________ cold and rainy. The hikers' boots got wet, and their bags got heavier.

The three friends didn't stop, but [4] ________ with the weather. On day four, it became foggy. The path was difficult to see and they got lost. Then Sven fell and broke his leg. There was no one to help them and no cell phone signal.

[5] ________ on October 27, a mountain rescue team found the friends, and they arrived home safely the next day. Now they are planning to do the hike again in the spring.

2 ☆☆ **Complete the account with the words and phrases in the box.**

At first, Finally, The weather was there were a lot of problems ~~They set off on~~

3 ☆ **Circle the correct options.**

1 The teenagers wanted to hike from *Scotland to England* / *England to Scotland*.

2 They hoped to do the hike in three *weeks* / *days*.

3 The weather was *good* / *bad* on the first two days.

4 *Lucas* / *Sven* had an accident.

4 ☆ **Match 1–6 with a–f.**

1 October 22, 2018 [b]

2 412 km [ ]

3 after two days [ ]

4 the three friends [ ]

5 October 28, 2018 [ ]

6 in the spring [ ]

a the day they arrived home

b the day they set off

c Lucas, Sven, and Lilly

d the length of the trip

e when the friends plan to start again

f the weather changed

PLAN

5 ☆☆ **Write a fictional account of a journey. Make notes for each paragraph.**

1 Who made the journey: ________

When and where it started: ________

Where they planned to go: ________

2 The first part of the journey: ________

The weather: ________

3 How the journey continued: ________

Any problems: ________

4 The end of the journey: ________

WRITE

6 ☆☆☆ **Write your fictional account. Remember to include the simple past, *there was/were*, and phrases from the *Useful Language* box (see Student's Book, p29).**

CHECK

7 **Do you …**

- use the simple past to talk about the past?
- put the events in the correct order?
- explain what the journey was like?

2 REVIEW

VOCABULARY

1 Complete the sentences with weather words. Use the first letter to help you.

1 When it's f________, it's difficult to see where you're going.
2 It's going to be r________, so don't forget your umbrella.
3 She wore a hoodie, a scarf, and gloves because it was very c________.
4 Don't run outside. It's i________ and you can easily fall.
5 The weather was nice and w________. We could swim every day.
6 A branch of the old tree broke on a very s________ night.
7 It's still c________, but it isn't raining anymore.
8 They could eat in the backyard because the weather was d________.
9 The sun was really h________, so Sally went inside.
10 I love winter evenings when it's s________ outside.
11 On one horrible w________ and w________ night, the rain blew into our tent.
12 Take your sunglasses because it's very s________ today.

2 Match the descriptions with the words in the box.

blanket bowl comb cup fork hairbrush lamp mirror pillow plate scissors spoon toothbrush

1 You can use these to cut hair or paper. ________
2 This helps you to see when it's dark. ________
3 Two objects you use for your hair. ________ ________
4 You need this to clean your teeth. ________
5 Two useful objects you use to put food in your mouth. ________ ________
6 You use this at night to keep warm. ________
7 You put soup in a ________ and a sandwich on a ________.
8 You put your tea or coffee in this. ________
9 Your head is on this when you're sleeping in bed. ________
10 You look into this when you're combing your hair. ________

GRAMMAR IN ACTION

3 Choose the correct verbs. Then write the simple past form of the verb.

Vasco da Gama, a Portuguese sailor and explorer, [1](work / arrive) ________ on the king's ships from 1492. In July 1497, he [2](leave / set) ________ off on a journey to India. He [3](want / become) ________ to find a route to the Far East. He [4](take / travel) ________ a total of 38,600 km. The journey [5](be / go) ________ dangerous, and the weather [6](like / be) ________ often stormy. Da Gama [7](take / carry) ________ 170 men with him, but only 54 [8](arrive / stay) ________ home safely in 1499.

4 Complete the sentences with the correct form of *there was/were* and *a*, *an*, *some*, or *any*.

1 ______ mirrors in the bathroom. (–)
2 ______ information about Egyptian mummies?
3 ______ interesting books in the museum gift shop. (+)
4 ______ article about dinosaurs in the newspaper. (+)
5 ______ good exhibitions in Berlin?
6 ______ clear answer to my question. (–)
7 ______ bowls in the kitchen. (–)
8 ______ visitors from Portugal in our school. (+)

CUMULATIVE GRAMMAR

5 Complete the conversation with the missing words. Circle the correct options.

SARA Hi, Katie. What [1] ______ at the moment?
KATIE I'm working really [2] ______! I need some ideas for my history project.
SARA [3] ______ the documentary about English kings and queens last Saturday?
KATIE No, I [4] ______ camping last weekend, so I missed it.
SARA That's a shame. It was very [5] ______.
KATIE [6] ______ information about the clothes they wore in the past?
SARA Yes, and [7] ______ interesting facts about jewelry. I [8] ______ about how they made gold and silver artifacts for my history project.
KATIE I know! I can write about everyday objects in the 16th century.
SARA [9] ______ exhibition in the city library last month called "At Home in the Past."
KATIE Really?
SARA And [10] ______ presentation by a famous history professor.
KATIE Oh, wow. I [11] ______ that, too. I really am a terrible student!
SARA Don't worry. I [12] ______ to that presentation, so I can help you.
KATIE Really? You're a great friend. Thanks, Sara!

1 a do you b did you do c are you doing
2 a hardly b hard c harder
3 a Saw you b Did you saw c Did you see
4 a went b go c didn't go
5 a well b good c better
6 a Was there any b Were there any c Was there an
7 a was there some b weren't there any c there were some
8 a write b 'm writting c 'm writing
9 a There's an b There was an c There was a
10 a there was a b was there a c there was an
11 a was missing b misses c missed
12 a go b went c going

3 What do stories teach us?

VOCABULARY
Adjectives of Feeling

1 ☆ **Read the clues and complete the puzzle. Then complete sentence 11 with your own idea.**

1 I feel … when I have nobody to talk to.
2 When you have nothing to do, you get … .
3 I don't like big spiders, and I feel … when I see one.
4 Before an important test or exam, you can feel … .
5 My parents sometimes get … when I arrive home late.
6 Do your teachers get … when you don't listen to them?
7 I was … to see my friend because she arrived a day early!
8 They were very … when they heard your sad news.
9 Young children get … about their birthdays.
10 You look … . Why don't you go to bed?
11 I feel embarrassed when ______________________
______________________.

2 ☆ **Circle the correct options.**

1 Leave the light on when you feel *afraid* / *angry* of the dark.
2 Was your brother *excited* / *angry* when you took his tablet?
3 Call a friend when you feel *tired* / *lonely* and want some company.
4 I'm never *excited* / *bored*; there's always something to do.
5 Julio was *embarrassed* / *lonely* because he didn't remember my name.

3 ☆☆ **Complete the email with the words in the box.**

excited nervous ~~surprised~~ tired upset

TO: Diana FROM: Kylie

Dear Diana,

Hi! How are you? I was [1] *surprised* when you weren't in class today. Are you [2] ______________ about the exam tomorrow? I can't study anymore tonight. I'm very [3] ______________ – I need to go to bed. My parents get [4] ______________ when I work late – they think I need more sleep! Don't worry about tomorrow. Just remember our camping trip when the exams are over – I'm [5] ______________ about that!

See you, Kylie

4 ☆☆☆ **Complete the sentences so they are true for you. Write them in your notebook.**

I feel nervous when … . I don't get upset when … .
I sometimes feel lonely when … .

Explore It!

Guess the correct answer.

If you have hippophilia, you love *hippos* / *spiders* / *horses* and they make you feel good.

Find another interesting thing that makes people feel good. Write a question and send it to a classmate in an email, or ask them in the next class.

READING

A Folk Tale

1 ☆ **Read the folk tale and match the names (1–3) with the people (a–c).**

1 Manata ☐ a the young man
2 Matakauri ☐ b the terrible giant
3 Matau ☐ c the beautiful girl

The Story of Lake Wakatipu

The Māori people of New Zealand have different stories about their country and how it began. One popular Māori story is about Lake Wakatipu. This lake is in the shape of the letter *S*, and there are high mountains all around it.

The story is about the beautiful daughter of a Māori chief. Her name was Manata, and she loved a young man named Matakauri. They wanted to get married, but Manata's father said no because Matakauri was not important. One day, a terrible giant named Matau came down from the mountains and took Manata. Her father was very upset and worried. "The man who rescues Manata can ask her to marry him," he said. Many men were afraid of the giant because he was very strong and dangerous. But Matakauri's love for Manata was strong, too, so he rescued her and she became his wife.

However, Matakauri was unhappy because the giant was still alive. One winter day, he went back to the giant's home. Matau was sleeping on a bed of dry leaves when Matakauri started a fire under him. Soon Matau's body was burning, although his heart was still beating. The giant's dead body made a big hole in the ground, in the shape of the letter *S*. The snow on the mountains melted because of the fire and ran into the hole. This created Lake Wakatipu.

Today, people still tell this story. The water in the lake goes up and down, and people say it is the beating heart of the dead giant!

2 ☆☆ **Read the folk tale again and check the meaning of the words in the box in a dictionary. Then complete the sentences.**

beat	~~burn~~	chief
giant	melts	rescue

1 Cook the vegetables on low heat. Don't *burn* them!
2 The ________ was the most important person in the village.
3 Ice cream ________ in the hot sun.
4 Heroes ________ people from dangerous situations.
5 Does your heart ________ faster when you're excited or nervous?
6 The ________ in the folk tale was ten meters tall!

3 ☆☆ **Are the sentences *T* (true) or *F* (false)?**

1 Manata's father wasn't an important person. *F*
2 Matakauri was a chief. ____
3 Matakauri and Manata got married after the giant died. ____
4 Matau died in the water when the snow melted. ____
5 Matau's body made a big hole that looked like a letter. ____
6 People tell the story to explain why the water in Lake Wakatipu moves. ____

4 ☆☆☆ **Choose from the options and complete the sentences in your notebook so they are true for you.**

1 I *think* / *don't think* Matakauri was an important person because ... .
2 I *like* / *don't like* the ending of this story because ... .
3 I *believe* / *don't believe* folk tales are just for young children because ... .

GRAMMAR IN ACTION

Past Continuous: Affirmative and Negative

1 Complete the sentences with the past continuous form of the verbs in parentheses.

1 I *was working* (work) all afternoon yesterday.
2 Yolanda ______ (make) sandwiches for our picnic.
3 My brother ______ (not sleep) in front of the TV.
4 We ______ (sit) in the car.
5 Clara ______ (look) for her phone.
6 They ______ (not shop) at the supermarket.

2 Look at the photos and correct the sentences. Use the past continuous.

1 
2 
3 
4 

1 She was playing soccer.
She wasn't playing soccer. She was playing tennis.
2 They were texting.
______
______
3 He was sleeping.
______
______
4 We were sitting on the bus.
______
______

3 Complete the email with the past continuous form of the verbs in the box.

feel	~~have~~	jump	listen	not dance	play	sleep

Dear Irina,

Happy New Year! I hope you [1] *were having* fun at midnight last night. I was at a party, and a DJ [2] ______ my favorite songs. I [3] ______ to the music, but I [4] ______ – I [5] ______ really tired. ☹ My friends [6] ______ up and down on the dance floor all night, though! What about you? Don't tell me that you [7] ______ ! ☺

Write back soon!

Jessie

4 Look at the picture and complete the story with appropriate verbs in the past continuous. There may be more than one possibility.

I had an interesting dream last night. I [1] *was sitting* outside. It was winter. Everything was white because it [2] ______, and I was very cold because I [3] ______ winter clothes. A big brown bear [4] ______ in front of me on two legs. It was very tall! It looked angry and dangerous. I don't know why, but I [5] ______ afraid at all. I [6] ______ nicely to the bear in a very friendly voice, but the bear [7] ______ to me! Then suddenly the bear [8] ______ a guitar and singing! In the end, I started to get angry with the bear. Then I woke up!

VOCABULARY AND LISTENING

Prepositions of Movement

1 ☆ **Complete the prepositions with the missing vowels.**

1 und*e*r
2 __p
3 __cr__ss
4 p__st
5 __ __t __f
6 thr__ __gh
7 __nt__
8 b__tw__ __n
9 d__wn
10 __l__ng
11 __v__r
12 __ff

2 ☆☆ **Complete the sentences with the prepositions in the box.**

~~along~~ into off over through under

1 I was walking *along* the river yesterday afternoon.
2 They were having a picnic ________ the trees.
3 Our dog was running after a cat, but it jumped ________ a wall.
4 When she lost her keys, she climbed into her house ________ the open window.
5 We can get ________ the bus here and walk to my house.
6 Mom walked ________ the store and asked the assistant for help.

3 ☆☆ **Look at the photos and complete the sentences with prepositions from Exercise 1.**

1 He was running *down* the stairs.
2 Shelia was getting ________ the taxi.
3 The sisters were walking ________ their parents.
4 Jodie was going ________ the table.
5 Dominic was jumping ________ the water.
6 Dan was walking ________ the street.

A Radio Phone-in

4 ☆ **Look at the picture. What do you think the story is about? Predict the words you might hear.**

____

3.01 **5** ☆ **Listen to Bruno's story. Do you hear any of your words from Exercise 4?**

3.01 **6** ☆☆ **Listen again and (circle) the correct answers.**

1 The radio show is about … things that happen to people.
  a dangerous (b) funny c embarrassing
2 When Bruno got off the bus, a man was running … .
  a across the street b into a bank c out of a bank
3 The man had a … .
  a knife in a bag b knife c bag
4 The alarm bells were ringing … .
  a in the bus b inside the bank c outside the bank
5 The people at the bus stop were … .
  a helping the man
  b not doing anything
  c helping the police officer
6 The police officer caught the man because … stopped him.
  a a woman b Bruno c some dogs

7 ☆☆☆ **Answer the questions.**

1 How do you think the people at the bus stop felt?

____

2 Did they do the right thing? Why / Why not?

____

GRAMMAR IN ACTION

Past Continuous: Questions

1 ☆ **Put the words in the correct order to make past continuous questions.**

1 you / watching / night / Were / last / news / the / ?
Were you watching the news last night?

2 the / long / a / wearing / woman / coat / Was / ?

3 down / Were / street / your / skating / friends / the / ?

4 through / people / many / park / were / How / the / walking / ?

5 into / Where / children / river / were / the / the / jumping / ?

6 off / bus / the / passengers / were / Why / the / getting / ?

2 ☆☆ **Write past continuous questions and short answers about the story from Exercise 5 on page 27.**

1 A the man / wear / a hoodie / ?
Was the man wearing a hoodie?
B *No, he wasn't.*

2 A he / carry / a black bag / ?
B

3 A alarm bells / ring / in the bank / ?
B

4 A the police officer / ride / a motorcycle / ?
B

5 A the people / help / the police officer / ?
B

6 A the dogs / run after / the man / ?
B

Simple Past and Past Continuous

3 ☆☆ **Circle the correct options.**

1 Our neighbor *fell* / *was falling* while he *walked* / *was walking* into the town.

2 While she *looked* / *was looking* for her bag, she *found* / *was finding* an old photo.

3 William *didn't hear* / *wasn't hearing* the man when he *stood* / *was standing* behind him.

4 We *cycled* / *were cycling* home when it *started* / *was starting* to rain.

5 She *had* / *was having* a problem when she *did* / *was doing* her homework.

6 *Did they sit* / *Were they sitting* on the bus when it *hit* / *was hitting* the car?

4 ☆☆ **Underline and correct one mistake in each sentence.**

1 Ann did her homework when her mother came into her room. *was doing*

2 My friend was looking at her phone when the teacher was seeing her.

3 While we were eating dinner, the cat was jumping onto the table and surprised us!

4 He was playing football when he was breaking his leg.

5 Weren't you answering the phone when it rang?

5 ☆☆ **Complete the text with the correct past continuous or simple past form of the verbs in the box.**

leave	not look	not see	play
stand	steal	take	~~wait~~	walk

Caught on Camera!

I [1] *was waiting* for a friend at the park. I [2] ________ under a small tree – that's why the girl [3] ________ me. She [4] ________ through the park quickly to where a man [5] ________ soccer with his son. The man's backpack was under a chair, and the girl [6] ________ it when he [7] ________ in her direction. While the girl [8] ________ the park, I [9] ________ a photo of her.

WRITING

A Story

1 ☆ **Look at the notes. What do you think Olive's story is about? Read the story and check your ideas.**

A Misunderstanding

By Olive Crooke

The other day, I was playing tennis with some friends after school, and I got home late in the afternoon. At first, I thought my parents were working, but then I noticed the car wasn't outside. There was no one in the house. Then I remembered they were all shopping.

I went to get a snack, and I saw a note on the fridge from my dad. It said, "We were waiting for you, but it got late. Your dinner's in the fridge. Back soon." I found a bowl of food and took it out. It didn't look very good, but I was hungry, so I started to eat it. Suddenly, I saw another note on the table from my mom. It said, "Please feed the cat – her food's in a bowl in the fridge." I was eating the cat's dinner!

I didn't feel well, so the next morning I didn't go to school. The next day, I told my my brothers what happened. They thought it was very funny, but I wasn't laughing!

2 ☆☆ **Read the story again. Are the sentences *T* (true) or *F* (false)?**

1 Olive's story happened yesterday. F
2 Her parents were at work. ____
3 Olive's parents expected her to arrive sooner. ____
4 She stayed at home the day after eating the cat food. ____
5 She thought it was a funny accident. ____

3 ☆☆ **Read the story again and put the events (a–g) in the correct order (1–7).**

a She didn't go to school the next day. ☐
b Olive was playing tennis. 1
c She found a note about her dinner. ☐
d She saw a note about the cat's dinner. ☐
e She found a bowl of food and started eating it. ☐
f She came home late and the house was empty. ☐
g She realized her mistake and felt sick. ☐

4 ☆☆ **Put the phrases in the order they appear in the story.**

a in the afternoon ☐
b The next day, ☐
c Suddenly, ☐
d At first, ☐
e the next morning ☐
f The other day, 1

PLAN

5 ☆☆ **Write a story. Think about a misunderstanding that happened to you, or invent one. Make notes about these things.**

1 What was happening before the main events started: ____

What happened first: ____

2 The main events of the story: ____

3 What happened in the end: ____

WRITE

6 ☆☆☆ **Write your story. Remember to include three paragraphs using the information from Exercise 5, the simple past and past continuous, and phrases from the *Useful Language* box (see Student's Book, p41).**

CHECK

7 **Do you …**

- have three paragraphs?
- explain the main events?
- explain what happened in the end?

3 REVIEW

VOCABULARY

1 Complete the sentences with adjectives of feeling. Use the first letter to help you.

1 I'm w__________ about my sister because she isn't feeling very happy.
2 He felt e__________ when he didn't understand the message.
3 Linda is busy all the time! She's never b__________.
4 Don't be n__________ about your exams. You'll be fine.
5 Are you a__________ of cows? They're big, and they can get angry!
6 We were s__________ when some old friends from Mexico suddenly came to our door!
7 Sara felt l__________ at first when she moved to a new town. She didn't have any friends there.
8 Do your parents get a__________ when you come home late?
9 Don't get so e__________! It's only a little birthday present!
10 They were all t__________ after running and doing exercise all day.
11 Don't be u__________ when you don't get 100% on a test. No one gets that!

2 Match 1–6 with a–f.

1 They ran quickly down ☐
2 She was sitting between ☐
3 When you walk past ☐
4 We jumped off the boat ☐
5 Tell the driver your address ☐
6 Look right, left, and then right again ☐

a when you get into the taxi.
b into the river.
c her two best friends.
d before you walk across the street.
e my house, you can always come in.
f the stairs and out into the street.

3 Look at the photos and circle the correct prepositions.

1

2

3

4

5

6

1 The boat went *across* / *under* the bridge.
2 Kim was running *down* / *across* the road.
3 He jumped *through* / *over* the wall.
4 The cat came *through* / *under* the kitchen window.
5 The movie star got *out of* / *off of* the car.
6 Lena climbed *over* / *up* a tree.

GRAMMAR IN ACTION

4 Complete the email with the past continuous form of the verbs in the box.

discuss	laugh	sing	talk	think

Dear Danny,

I'm sorry you were upset earlier today in music class. I'm embarrassed because when you were about to sing, Eva and I [1] __________ to each other pretty loudly. Then you [2] __________ really well and we [3] __________, but only because it was a funny song. Anyway, at a meeting yesterday, we [4] __________ our band. We decided we need a lead singer and, of course, the whole time we [5] __________ of you. Would you like to be our singer? Please say yes!

Emily

5 Write past continuous questions for the answers.

1 Why ______________________?
She was feeling nervous because she had an exam.

2 What ______________________?
They were talking about their new project.

3 Who ______________________?
He was visiting his grandparents.

4 Where ______________________?
I was camping in Costa Rica.

5 Why ______________________?
We were running because we were late.

6 How long ______________________?
She was waiting for more than an hour.

6 Complete the sentences with the simple past or past continuous form of the verbs in parentheses.

1 While we ____________ (wait) for our friends, we ____________ (start) to make tea.

2 He ____________ (hear) an announcement while he ____________ (sit) on the train.

3 Someone ____________ (call) you while you ____________ (take) a shower.

4 When their parents ____________ (return), a band ____________ (play) in their garage.

5 When the movie ____________ (end), everyone in the theater ____________ (cry).

6 While I ____________ (look) for my shoes, I ____________ (find) an old sandwich under my bed.

CUMULATIVE GRAMMAR

7 Complete the conversation with the missing words. Circle the correct options.

JAKE Hi, Bella! Are you OK? When I [1] ________ you yesterday, you looked really upset.

BELLA There were [2] ________ problems at home.

JAKE That's too [3] ________. What happened? Did you have a lot of homework?

BELLA No, I [4] ________. But I was angry with my little brother.

JAKE Really? What [5] ________?

BELLA Oh, he [6] ________ awful noisy video games all evening.

JAKE My sister [7] ________ playing those, too. What was the problem?

BELLA Well, he was making a terrible noise while I [8] ________ my favorite show.

JAKE Come on, Bella. Sometimes it can be difficult to play video games [9] ________.

BELLA I never [10] ________ video games!

JAKE OK, so what [11] ________ in the end?

BELLA Well, in the end, I [12] ________ Billy's game and hid it in a very secret place … in the kitchen.

JAKE You're kidding!

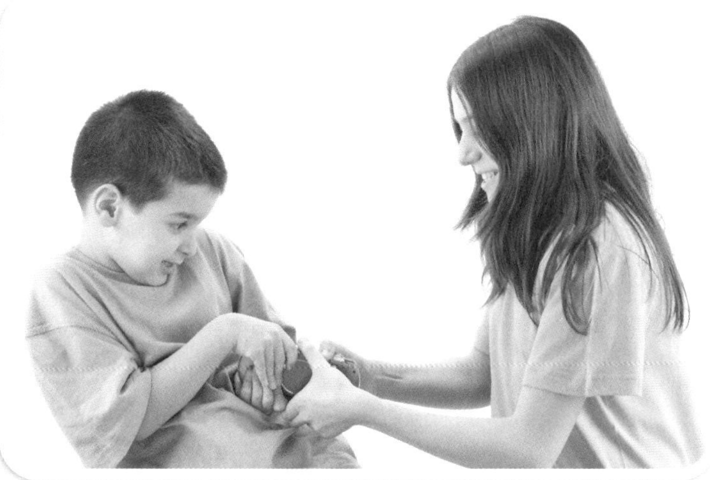

1	a seeing	b was seeing	c saw
2	a any	b some	c a
3	a bad	b well	c badly
4	a did	b do	c didn't
5	a did he do	b did he	c he did
6	a plays	b playing	c was playing
7	a loves	b is loving	c doesn't love
8	a watch	b was watching	c watched
9	a quietly	b quieter	c quiet
10	a am playing	b to play	c play
11	a happened	b was happening	c happens
12	a was taking	b take	c took

4 What do you value most?

VOCABULARY
Money Verbs

1 ☆ **Put the letters in the correct order to make money verbs.**

1 s o t c _cost_
2 n e h g c a ______
3 r n a e ______
4 r o o r w b ______
5 e p n d s ______
6 l e s l ______
7 y a p ______
8 d l n e ______
9 v a e s ______
10 e o w ______

2 ☆ **Circle the correct options.**

1 *Save* / *Spend* your money for something you really want.
2 Please can you *borrow* / *lend* me $5?
3 How much did that phone *sell* / *cost* you?
4 Harry *earns* / *spends* $2.50 when he washes his mom's car.
5 I don't like *changing* / *owing* my friends money.
6 She *sold* / *bought* her old bike to a friend from school.

3 ☆ **Complete the sentences with the words in the box.**

change	cost	~~earn~~	pay	sell	spend

1 You _earn_ money for work you do.
2 How much did those cool sneakers ______?
3 Can we ______ for our food with dollars on the plane?
4 Supermarkets ______ many different things to their customers.
5 Where can I ______ my Brazilian *reais* into dollars?
6 Don't ______ all your birthday money on video games and candy!

4 ☆☆ **Complete the text messages with money verbs from Exercise 1.**

I can't [1] _pay_ for my phone this month. Can I [2] ______ $10 from you, please?

But you [3] ______ me $5 from last month! ☹ I can't [4] ______ you any more. Sorry.

What can I do? It's impossible to [5] ______ money – I never have any left at the end of the week.

You can [6] ______ me your skateboard for $15. 😉

My skateboard [7] ______ $50 when I bought it!

Oh, well. Sorry, I can't help you then.

5 ☆☆ **Complete the definitions with the correct form of the similar words in each pair.**

1 You _lend_ some money to a friend. Your friend ______ money from you. (borrow / lend)
2 A sales assistant ______ something to you. You ______ something from a sales assistant. (buy / sell)
3 People ______ money for things they need later. They ______ money in a store or online. (save / spend)
4 You ______ money when you work. You ______ money in a competition or a lottery. (earn / win)

Explore It!

True or false?

In the U.S.A., they print more *Monopoly* money than real dollars every year.

Find another interesting fact about bills or coins. Write a question and send it to a classmate in an email, or ask them in the next class.

READING

A Newspaper Article

1 ☆ **Read the article. Which opinion in the last paragraph do you agree with?** ______

Goodbye to Weekend Jobs?

Fifty years ago, it was very common for a North American teenager to work part-time. These days, the number of teens with a weekend job is falling.

The most common jobs in the U.S.A. for young people are working in stores and restaurants. In the past, teens could easily get these jobs.

One reason for the fall in part-time teenage workers is that, in the past, they could have a part-time job and do their schoolwork. Now, success on exams is the most important thing, and there's more pressure to do well in school.

"Working part-time and doing well in school isn't easy," says 15-year-old sales assistant Cheryl Bates. "You need to organize your time and maybe do

some of your homework at lunchtime. It's harder than you think, but when I earn my own money, I feel more independent because I don't need to ask my parents to buy me things."

Fourteen-year-old server Martin Cox adds, "Having a job is the best way to learn the skills you need for the future. I was the quietest boy in my class, and I couldn't talk to people very well. Now, because I talk to customers at work, I'm much better in social situations."

So, can part-time work help to prepare young people for adult life, or does it put extra pressure on teens with already busy lives? What do you think?

2 ☆☆ **Read the article again and check the meaning of the words in the box in a dictionary. Then complete the sentences.**

common	employer	~~independent~~	part-time	pressure

1 Maisie is a very *independent* girl. She never needs much help.

2 Is there a lot of ______ to do well on all your exams at your school?

3 Fruit picking is usually a ______ job in the summer months. It's a very ______ job in a lot of countries.

4 Mrs. Preston is a good ______. All her teenage workers really like her.

3 ☆☆ **Read the article again. Are the sentences *T* (true) or *F* (false)?**

1 In the U.S.A., there weren't many young part-time workers in the past. *F*

2 Many teenagers work in restaurants. ______

3 There was more pressure to do well in school in the past. ______

4 Cheryl thinks earning her own money is easy. ______

5 For Martin, talking to people isn't a problem now. ______

4 ☆☆☆ **Answer the questions with your own ideas.**

1 Is part-time work for teenagers common in your country? Why / Why not?

______

2 How do you get the money to buy the things you want?

______

GRAMMAR IN ACTION

Could

1 ☆ **Match 1–6 with a–f.**

1 I had no money, e
2 Sara couldn't lend me $10 ☐
3 All the lights in the store went out, ☐
4 Mozart could play and write music ☐
5 My dad could run marathons ☐
6 The bank was closed, ☐

a because she didn't have any money.
b so they couldn't change their money.
c from the age of four.
d and we couldn't see anything.
e so I couldn't buy anything.
f when he was younger.

2 ☆☆ **Write sentences that are true for you when you were six. Use the pictures.**

1 When I was six, I couldn't ride a bike.
2 ______
3 ______
4 ______
5 ______
6 ______

Comparative and Superlative Adjectives

3 ☆ **Circle the correct options.**

1 The movie was *more exciting* / *the most exciting* than the book.
2 Samir was *happier* / *the happiest* in his old job than he is now.
3 Money isn't *more important* / *the most important* thing in life.
4 It was *more difficult* / *the most difficult* decision for him to make.
5 Today's class was *shorter* / *the shortest* than yesterday's.
6 The sales assistants were *more helpful* / *the most helpful* than they usually are.

4 ☆☆ **Put the words in the correct order to make sentences.**

1 yesterday / than / was / It's / today / it / hotter / .
It's hotter today than it was yesterday.
2 mine / phone / than / your / Was / expensive / more / ?
______
3 worse / What's / than / your / losing / wallet / ?
______
4 quietest / town / Monday / the / is / in / day / .
______
5 are / cheapest / store / the / jeans / These / in / the / .
______
6 best / life / Yesterday / of / the / my / day / was / .
______

5 ☆☆ **Complete the text with the comparative or superlative form of the adjectives in the box.**

exciting	expensive	~~famous~~	old	rich	successful

I got some money for my birthday, so I bought a ticket to a City game. Everyone knows City: they're [1] the most famous soccer team in the world. I think they're [2] ______ than the other clubs in the UK because my great-grandfather was a City fan when he was a kid, and that was a long time ago! And they have a lot of money, so they're definitely [3] ______. They play fast and score lots of goals, so they're [4] ______ to watch than other teams. I also think they are [5] ______ team because they win most of their games. The only bad thing is that I can't go to every game because the tickets are probably [6] ______ tickets in the world.

VOCABULARY AND LISTENING

Caring Jobs

1 ☆ **Complete the crossword. Use the clues.**

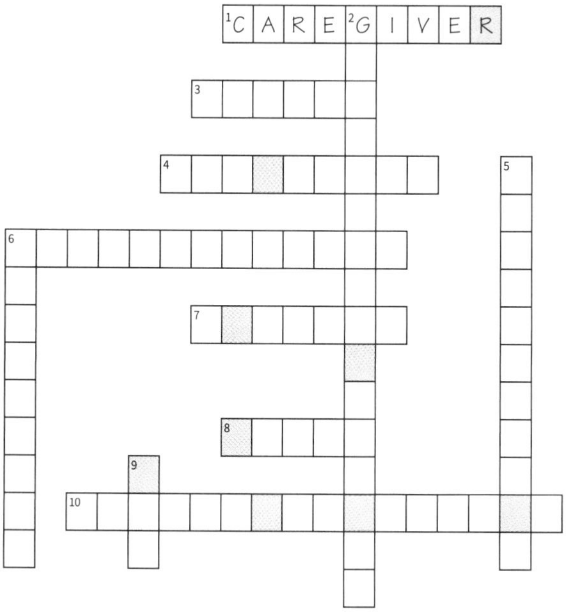

Across

1 A … helps old or sick people in their homes.

3 A … gives advice to people about the law.

4 A … takes care of swimmers.

6 A … helps to protect people from crime.

7 A … does operations in hospitals.

8 A … cares for sick people in hospitals.

10 A … teaches very young children.

Down

2 A … takes away the things we don't want.

5 A … rescues people from dangerous situations.

6 A … gives medical help to people before they get to a hospital.

9 A … is a doctor for animals.

Put the gray letters in the correct order to complete this clue: A ____________ works for no money.

2 ☆ **Circle the correct answers.**

1 The *lifeguard* / *firefighter* told us not to swim there.

2 When our dog was sick, we took it to the *vet* / *lawyer*.

3 The *paramedic* / *police officer* stopped the motorcycle because it was going very fast.

4 The *firefighter* / *garbage collector* climbed into the burning house through a window.

5 My neighbor is a *preschool teacher* / *caregiver* in nursing home.

Monologues

4.01 **3** ☆ **Listen to three people talking about their jobs. Which place connects all three speakers?** ____________

4.01 **4** ☆☆ **Listen again and circle the correct answers.**

1 Speaker 1 …
   a never has time for her family.
   b spent a long time studying.
   c doesn't spend much time working.

2 Speaker 1 …
   a receives help from her team.
   b prefers working alone.
   c thinks the nurses need to work harder.

3 Speaker 2 …
   a thinks his job is more important than a doctor's job.
   b didn't want to be a nurse when he was younger.
   c is doing the work he always wanted to do.

4 Speaker 2 thinks …
   a some nurses are leaving because the job doesn't pay well.
   b it's sad that nurses want more money.
   c nurses need more responsibilities.

5 Speaker 3 does her job …
   a on the weekend.
   b in the morning.
   c three days a week.

5 ☆☆☆ **Answer the questions in your notebook.**

1 Which job is the most tiring? Why?

2 Which job is the most important? Why?

GRAMMAR IN ACTION

Too, Too Much, Too Many

1 ☆ **Complete the sentences with *too* and the words in the box.**

busy	expensive	hard	hot	~~tired~~	young

1 The nurses were *too tired* to go out after work.
2 The hospital parking lot costs $10. That's ______________ .
3 Is John ______________ to stop working as a firefighter? He's 45.
4 It was ______________ in the sun, so I went inside.
5 Can you help me this morning, or are you ______________ ?
6 They couldn't answer the question because it was ______________ .

2 ☆ **Circle the correct options.**

1 The doctor gave us too (*much*) / *many* information when she called.
2 Were there too *much* / *many* people in the waiting room?
3 Most caregivers say they have too *much* / *many* work.
4 Don't put too *much* / *many* milk in my coffee, please.
5 Is it possible to have too *much* / *many* good ideas?
6 Do you think surgeons earn too *much* / *many* money?

3 ☆☆ **Complete the conversation with *too*, *too much*, or *too many*.**

CHRIS What a day! I have [1] *too many* children in my class.
LILY Me, too. Over 30 in my group and they all have [2] ______________ energy. It gets [3] ______________ noisy sometimes!
CHRIS True! And they say we give them [4] ______________ homework, and that it's [5] ______________ difficult.
LILY I know, but it's difficult for us, too – there are always [6] ______________ notebooks for us to look at!

(Not) Enough + Noun

4 ☆☆ **Put the words in the correct order to make sentences.**

1 enough / don't / Doctors / money / nurses / and / earn / .
Doctors and nurses don't earn enough money.
2 food / everyone / the / There / for / enough / is / in / world / .
____
3 volunteers / Are / organization / enough / your / in / there / ?
____
4 moment / enough / We / at / information / don't / have / the / .
____
5 in / Is / enough / classroom / space / this / there / ?
____

5 ☆☆ **Underline and correct one mistake in each sentence.**

1 Soccer players earn too <u>many</u> money, in my opinion. *much*
2 It's too noise in here for me; please be quiet.
____
3 The teacher gave us too much options to think about. ______________
4 There wasn't information enough on the poster.
____
5 She was much young to be a caregiver.
____

6 ☆☆ **Complete the text about a dream job with *too*, *too much*, *too many*, or (*not*) *enough*.**

My dream job is to be a paramedic. Everyone knows that there are [1] *n't enough* doctors, but [2] ______________ people forget about the paramedics. I don't want to spend [3] ______________ time studying when I finish school, and you don't need to take [4] ______________ exams in emergency medicine to do it. But of course, you need to take some exams, and you need to be a good driver. When the roads are [5] ______________ full of cars, you need [6] ______________ driving skills to get to the hospital safely and quickly!

WRITING

An Opinion Essay

1 ☆ **Read David's essay. Does he agree with the statement?**

____

It's good to have a weekend job while you're still in school. Do you agree?
By David Rodríguez

1 Nowadays, things cost a lot, and you need enough money to buy them. With a weekend job, you can earn your own money, but [1] ___in my opinion___, it's not a good idea.

2 [2] ______________, working in a supermarket or café can sometimes be boring. Also, a student often gets lower pay than an adult for the same type of job. Perhaps because of this, more students get these jobs, and there isn't enough work for older people with families who need money more than you.

3 Also, teenagers usually sleep longer and get up later on weekends. [3] ______________ that when you study hard at school all week, you need to relax on the weekend. I also think that enjoying free-time activities is more important than earning money.

4 [4] ______________, students need enough time for schoolwork, relaxing, and doing free-time activities. [5] ______________ it's better to rest on the weekend and spend more time doing your favorite things. We'll have enough time for work when we're older!

2 ☆ **Complete the essay with the phrases in the box.**

First of all	I believe that	In conclusion
~~in my opinion~~	Personally, I think	

3 ☆☆ **Read the essay again and answer the questions.**

1 What examples of part-time jobs does David give?
____

2 In David's opinion, why can part-time jobs for teens be a problem for adults?
____

3 According to David, what do teenagers typically do on weekends?
____

4 What does David say is more important than money?
____

4 ☆ **Match the paragraphs (1–4) with the summaries (a–d).**

a a first reason for your opinion ☐
b a summary of your opinion ☐
c an introduction to the topic and your opinion ☐
d a second reason for your opinion ☐

PLAN

5 ☆☆ **Write an opinion essay. Choose one of the following topics or use David's topic. Take notes for each paragraph.**

Weekend jobs teach you the skills you need for the future.
Hard-working teachers don't earn enough money.

1 Introduce the topic and give your opinion:
____

2 Give a reason for your opinion:
____

3 Give a second reason:
____

4 Summarize your opinion:
____

WRITE

6 ☆☆☆ **Write your opinion essay. Remember to include (*not*) *enough* and *too*, *too much*, *too many*, and the phrases from the *Useful Language* box (see Student's Book, p53).**

CHECK

7 **Do you …**
- have four paragraphs?
- give reasons for your opinions?
- summarize your opinion at the end?

4 REVIEW

VOCABULARY

1 Match 1–8 with a–h.

1 Henry lent his sister ☐
2 How much did you ☐
3 I borrowed $5 more from Ben, ☐
4 You can earn more money ☐
5 Are you saving money ☐
6 Do they sell ☐
7 How much does it cost ☐
8 I spend a lot of money ☐

a for anything special?
b when you work more hours.
c on presents for my friends.
d to change money here?
e pay for those tickets?
f so now I owe him $10.
g jeans in this store?
h some money for her lunch.

2 Circle the correct options.

1 *preschool teacher / paramedic*

2 *caregiver / lifeguard*

3 *vet / lifeguard*

4 *garbage collector / surgeon*

5 *nurse / volunteer*

6 *lawyer / police officer*

GRAMMAR IN ACTION

3 Complete the sentences with *could* or *couldn't*.

1 In the 1970s, people ______ send texts.
2 Roads were safer 50 years ago, so my grandpa ______ walk to school.
3 He ______ cycle because he didn't have a bike.
4 My great-grandma ______ play soccer because it was only for boys in those days.
5 My mom ______ play lots of sports at school. She played tennis, basketball, and volleyball.
6 Teenagers in 1950 ______ watch streaming series because there weren't any.

4 Complete the conversation with the comparative or superlative form of the adjectives in parentheses.

PABLO Hey, Laura. What's up?
LAURA My exam scores were [1] ______ (bad) than last time.
PABLO Oh, no. And your parents were [2] ______ (angry) than usual, right?
LAURA Right. Dad was [3] ______ (worried) about them than Mom, but I think I was the [4] ______ (upset).
PABLO I can understand that. You're the [5] ______ (hard-working) student in the class.
LAURA Thanks, but I think you're a [6] ______ (hard) worker than me.
PABLO OK, we both work hard. But doing well on exams is [7] ______ (difficult) than parents think. It isn't the [8] ______ (easy) thing in the world!

5 **Complete the conversation with *too*, *too much*, *too many*, or (*not*) *enough*.**

PAT Can you come swimming today? It's not [1] __________ busy on Sunday mornings.
JAMES Sorry, I can't. I don't have [2] __________ time.
PAT Really? We don't have [3] __________ homework this weekend, only a little bit.
JAMES No, but I have [4] __________ jobs to do at home.
PAT Why do you need to do jobs?
JAMES I don't have [5] __________ money, so my parents pay me to help with the chores on Sundays.
PAT Well, I need more money, too, but I'm [6] __________ lazy to do any extra work!

CUMULATIVE GRAMMAR

6 **Complete the conversation with the missing words. Circle the correct options.**

FRAN Excuse me, I [1] ________ older people for my school magazine. Can you answer a few questions, please?
NIGEL Sure. I hope you don't have [2] ________ difficult questions for me.
FRAN No, don't worry! The first question is the [3] ________ – do you still work?
NIGEL Well, I [4] ________ as a firefighter for many years, but I'm retired now.
FRAN I see. So now what [5] ________ every day? Do you like reading or doing sudoku?
NIGEL Certainly not! I have [6] ________ energy to sit around all day.
FRAN You're [7] ________ my grandparents, then, because that's all they do!
NIGEL Of course I enjoy my free time, but I get [8] ________ bored when I do nothing.
FRAN So are there [9] ________ special things you do, now that you're not working?
NIGEL I'm a volunteer at [10] ________ outdoor activity center, where I give talks about being safe.
FRAN That's great! In my opinion, [11] ________ retired people share their skills.
NIGEL Very true. It's definitely the [12] ________ way to stay active and healthy! Next question?

1 a interviewed b 'm interviewing c I was interviewing
2 a too much b too many c enough
3 a most easy b easy c easiest
4 a was work b working c worked
5 a do you do b did you do c are you doing
6 a much b enough c too much
7 a fittest than b fitter than c fittest that
8 a too b too much c not enough
9 a much b an c any
10 a some b a c an
11 a not enough b much c not much
12 a good b better c best

5 What is your dream house?

VOCABULARY
Furniture

1 ☆ **Look at the photos and complete the furniture words.**

1 a r m c h a i r
2 c _____ o _
d _______
3 c _______
4 s _______
5 p _______
6 b _________
7 d ____
8 f _____
9 c _________
10 w _________
11 c ______
12 f ______
13 s ____

1

2

3

4

5

6

7

8

9

10
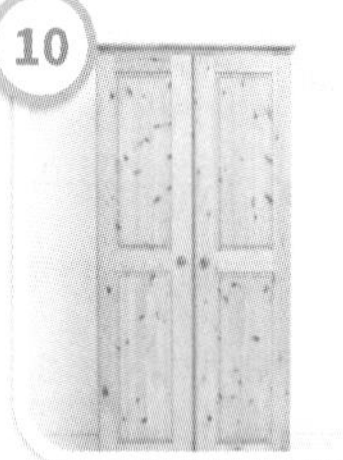
11

12
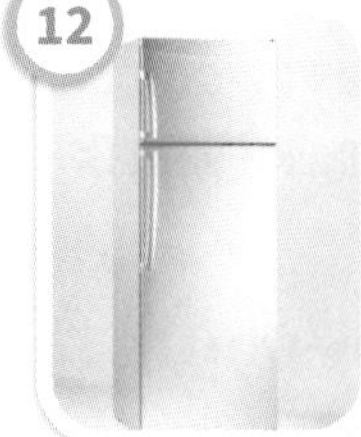
13

2 ☆ **Circle the correct options to complete the text.**

I love my bedroom and spend a lot of time in it. There's a nice warm [1] *cupboard* / (*carpet*) on the [2] *floor* / *ceiling*, and I have a comfortable old [3] *chest of drawers* / *armchair* by the window where I can sit and read. In the corner, there is a [4] *desk* / *sink* where I do my homework, and above it are some [5] *shelves* / *pictures* of my friends and family. I have a big [6] *fridge* / *wardrobe* for my clothes, but I sometimes leave them on my bed!

3 ☆☆ **Complete the sentences with words from Exercise 1.**

1 Sheila is very tall, so she can touch the *ceiling* in her bedroom.
2 Aunt Adie has an old _____________ of her grandparents on the wall.
3 He keeps his smaller clothes, like socks and T-shirts, in a _____________.
4 Don't come in with dirty shoes. I cleaned the kitchen _____________ this morning.
5 You can find tea and coffee in that _____________ next to the window.
6 We brush our teeth in the bathroom _____________.

Explore It!

Guess the correct answer.

The biggest hotel in Europe is the Izmailovo Hotel in Moscow. It has *3,500* / *7,500* / *9,500* beds.

Find another interesting fact about a hotel. Write a question and send it to a classmate in an email, or ask them in the next class.

READING

A Magazine Article

1 Read the article. In your opinion, which is the best place to live in? ________________

No Place Like Home

In this week's edition of *City Life*, we asked two 13-year-olds about living in London. What do they like about where they live? Is there anything they don't like?

"I live in an apartment building in Wembley, in the northwest of London. It has 21 floors! I live on the second to top floor. City life isn't as quiet as life in the country, but it's very quiet so high up, and the views are amazing. I can see Wembley soccer stadium from my bedroom window, and I can sometimes hear the crowd when they score a goal! We live near a canal, and I can cycle to school in five minutes along the canal path. It's great to live here. I only think my apartment isn't as good as a house when the elevator doesn't work!"

Kelly

"I live in a row of houses in a part of London called Camden. It takes me about ten minutes to walk to school from home. There's a famous market nearby called Camden Market. It's very popular with street musicians – and tourists, of course! The houses on my street are all painted different colors, but I don't like that very much. I think it's too colorful! My room is on the top floor of my house. The ceiling isn't as high as I'd like, but the room is big enough for just me. From my window, I can watch the boats and barges go by on the Regent's Canal at the end of our yard. I love living in my house."

Hasan

2 Read the article again and check the meaning of these words in a dictionary. Then complete the sentences.

barge canal crowd ~~floor~~ path row

1 We stayed on the top *floor* of an apartment building in New York.
2 We sat in the front ________ of chairs during the class presentations.
3 My Dutch friend lives in a houseboat on a ________.
4 A type of boat called a ________ transports things along rivers and canals.
5 To get to the village, follow this ________.
6 There was a big ________ of people outside of the concert.

3 Circle the correct answers.

1 *City Life* magazine asked Kelly and Hasan about … in London.
   a cycling
   b going to school
   (c) living
2 Kelly lives on the … floor.
   a 20th b 21st c 2nd
3 She likes … .
   a living high up
   b watching soccer
   c walking to school
4 Hasan's house is close to … .
   a a market
   b Wembley
   c the country
5 He doesn't like the … on his street.
   a tourists
   b musicians
   c colorful houses
6 From his bedroom, he can see … .
   a market stalls
   b boats and barges
   c colorful houses

4 Answer the questions with your own ideas.

1 How are the houses in the article similar to your house?
____
2 Name one good thing and one bad thing about living in a tall building.
____

GRAMMAR IN ACTION

(*Not*) *As* + Adjective + *As*

1 ☆ **Complete the sentences with the adjective in parentheses and (*not*) *as* … *as*. Then check your answers in the article on page 41.**

1 Hasan is *as happy as* (happy) Kelly with his home.

2 Kelly thinks country life is ________ (noisy) life in the city.

3 Kelly's trip to school is ________ (slow) Hasan's trip.

4 Hasan is ________ (old) Kelly.

5 The house is ________ (tall) the apartment building.

6 The apartment building is ________ (colorful) the houses in Camden.

2 ☆☆ **Look at the information and complete the sentences with *is* (*not*) *as* … *as* and an adjective from the box.**

big busy ~~expensive~~ fast good old

1 Tim's ticket = $10.00 / Liz's ticket = $12.00
Tim's ticket *isn't as expensive as* Liz's ticket.

2 house = 200 meters / apartment = 200 meters
The apartment ________ the house.

3 Juan's English exam = 8 out of 10 / Olivia's English exam = 8 out of 10
Olivia's exam score ________ Juan's exam score.

4 Saturday's market = 200 shoppers / Monday's market = 50 shoppers
The Monday market ________ the Saturday market.

5 a letter = two days / an email = two seconds
A letter ________ an email.

6 Luke = 15 years old / Nick = 15 years old
Luke ________ Nick.

(*Not*) + Adjective + *Enough*

3 ☆ **Complete the sentences with the adjectives in the box.**

~~fit~~ hot old safe well

1 I'd love to be *fit* enough to run a marathon, but I'm not.

2 See the red flag? The water here isn't ________ enough to swim in.

3 The soup isn't ________ enough. It needs five more minutes.

4 When are you ________ enough to drive a car in your country?

5 He was in the hospital, and he's still not ________ enough to go to school.

4 ☆ **Match 1–6 with a–f.**

1 You can take a shower [d]

2 This puzzle is too easy [ ]

3 Can I have some sugar, please? [ ]

4 We didn't understand because [ ]

5 He tried to park his car, [ ]

6 Her new coat is [ ]

a nice enough for the party.

b My coffee isn't sweet enough.

c the instructions weren't clear enough.

d when the water is warm enough.

e because the clues aren't hard enough.

f but the space wasn't wide enough.

5 ☆☆ **Complete the conversation with the phrases in the box.**

as comfortable as as expensive as as nice as as tall as ~~long enough~~ soft enough

SARA Here's a furniture store. Can we look for a new bed for me, Mom? My old bed isn't [1] *long enough* for me anymore.

MOM I know, you're nearly [2] ________ me now! OK, what about this bed?

SARA Mmm, it isn't [3] ________ for me – it's too hard. It isn't [4] ________ the one I have now!

MOM Look! This one isn't [5] ________ that one – it's a better price, and it's the right size.

SARA But it's not [6] ________ the first one. I'm not sure about the color. Oh, I can't decide, Mom!

VOCABULARY AND LISTENING

Household Chores

1 ☆ Circle the correct verbs to complete the household chores.

1 *mop* / *make* the floor
2 *make* / *do* the ironing
3 *do* / *make* the bed
4 *empty* / *dust* the furniture
5 *load* / *make* the dishwasher
6 *make* / *do* the dishes
7 *load* / *sweep* the floor
8 *empty* / *vacuum* the carpet
9 *do* / *make* the laundry

2 ☆ Match the photos with six of the phrases from Exercise 1.

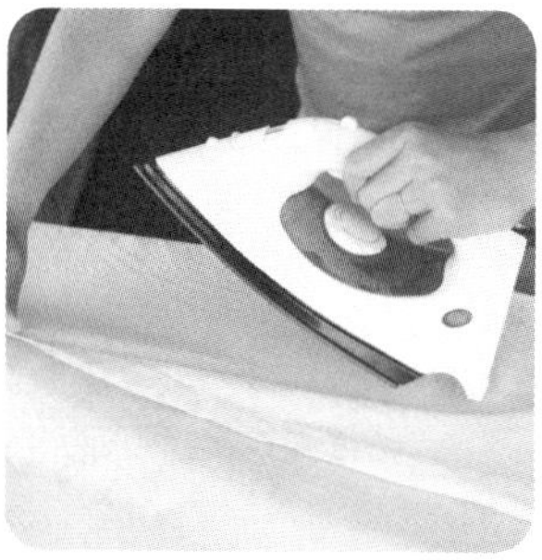
1 do the ironing

2 ______

3 ______

4 ______

5 ______

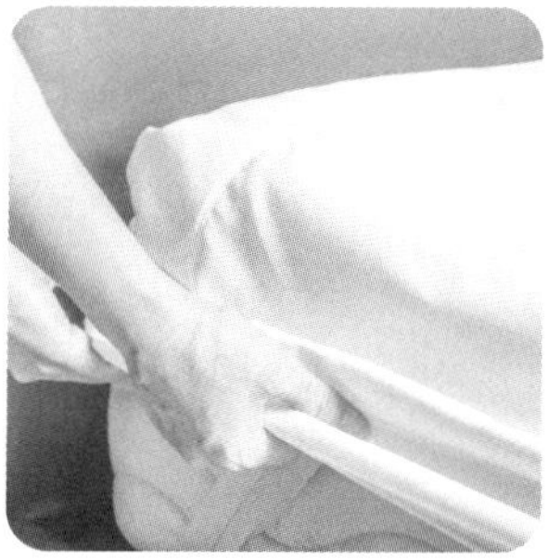
6 ______

Street Interviews

5.01 **3 ☆ Listen to an interview about how a family shares the chores at home. Who helps more: Daisy or Milo?**

______

5.01 **4 ☆☆ Listen again and circle the correct options.**

1 Daisy doesn't like *mopping the floor* / *dusting the furniture*.
2 Milo does the *laundry* / *dishes* on the weekend.
3 His parents *pay* / *thank* him for helping out with the chores.
4 The children's father does *all* / *some* of the cleaning.
5 Their mother *likes* / *doesn't like* cooking.
6 Milo and Daisy do *the dishes* / *their homework* after dinner.

5 ☆☆☆ Answer the questions.

1 What do you do to help out at home?

______

2 Who cooks in your family?

______

3 What chores do you like or hate doing? Why?

______

GRAMMAR IN ACTION

Have To

1 ☆ **Circle the correct options.**

1 I really (*have to*) / *don't have to* clean up my room because I can't find anything.

2 Pat *has to* / *doesn't have to* cycle to school because it's too far for her to walk there.

3 Most children *have to* / *don't have to* go to school on Sundays.

4 You *have to* / *don't have to* wash those jeans. They're clean.

5 There's no bread, so you *have to* / *don't have to* buy more.

2 ☆☆ **Complete the sentences with the correct form of *have to* and the verb in parentheses.**

1 Jake *has to run* (run) when he's late for school.

2 You ______ (make) your bed because I don't have time.

3 We ______ (shop) for food because Dad does that.

4 My three-year-old sister ______ (do) anything to help around the house. She's too young.

5 I ______ (wash) the car because we don't have one.

6 Bill ______ (help) his parents when they're too busy to do everything.

3 ☆☆ **Put the words in the correct order to make questions.**

1 shop / day / dad / Does / to / have / every / your / ?

Does your dad have to shop every day?

2 help / house / have / Do / around / you / to / the / ?

______

3 the / have / sleep / outside / Does / dog / to / ?

______

4 carpet / vacuum / have / Do / to / you / the / ?

______

5 children / bed / to / have / be / in / by / Do / nine / the / ?

______

6 Owen / Does / to / have / leave / breakfast / before / ?

______

4 ☆☆ **Look at the chart and complete the sentences with the correct form of *have to*.**

	 Tom	 Lisa	 Mike
Do the dishes	✗	✓	✗
Do the laundry	✗	✓	✗
Mop the kitchen floor	✗	✗	✗
Vacuum the carpet	✓	✗	✗
Make breakfast	✓	✗	✗
Make our beds	✓	✓	✓

1 Lisa *has to do* the dishes and the laundry.

2 Tom, Lisa, and Mike ______ the kitchen floor.

3 Mike's very little so he ______ much.

4 Mike only ______ his bed.

5 Tom ______ the carpet, but he ______ the dishes.

6 Tom ______ breakfast.

5 ☆☆☆ **Complete the text with the correct form of *have to* and the verbs in the box.**

carry	clean up	do
mop	put	take	~~work~~

My younger sister, Jenny, [1] *doesn't have to work* very hard at school because she's still little, but she and her classmates [2] ______ the classroom at the end of the day so it's clean. They [3] ______ their chairs on top of their desks, but they [4] ______ the floor, of course – the custodian [5] ______ that. Jenny has some heavy books, but she [6] ______ them home every day – she can keep them in the classroom. When there's homework, Jenny brings the book that she needs home, but she [7] ______ it back to school the next day. She's a very good student!

WRITING

A Description of a House

1 ☆ **Look at the photos and read the description. Which house does it describe: a or b?** ______

a

b

1 This vacation home is in a quiet place with great views, but it's [1]*also* / *too* close enough to a big town. You can drive to the stores, and there's a bus, [2]*as well as* / *too*.

2 The house is a long, modern building with four huge bedrooms upstairs. The living room has big windows, but the windows upstairs are big [3]*as well* / *as well as*. There's a beautiful tropical garden, and there are plants on the balcony, [4]*as well as* / *too*.

3 One very special thing about this house is the home movie theater. It's not as big as a real theater, but you don't have to leave the house! It's really cool because [5]*as well as* / *also* seats for ten people, there's a fridge and a cupboard for yummy snacks! It's the best vacation home in the world!

Daniel Bell (13), Los Angeles

2 ☆ **Circle the correct options (1–5) in the description.**

3 ☆☆ **Read the description again. Are the sentences *T* (true) or *F* (false)?**

1 The house is in the center of a big town. F

2 There's no public transportation near the house. ______

3 There are big windows upstairs. ______

4 The house is special because there's a movie theater in it. ______

4 ☆ **Match headings a–c with paragraphs 1–3.**

a What does the house have? ☐

b What is really special about the house? ☐

c Where is the house? ☐

PLAN

5 ☆☆ **Write a description of a vacation home. Find a photo of a vacation home online or in a magazine. Take notes about these things.**

1 Where the vacation home is: ______

Why you like it: ______

2 What rooms, furniture, and other things it has: ______

3 Why the vacation home is special: ______

WRITE

6 ☆☆☆ **Write your description. Remember to include adjectives with (*not*) *as … as*, *enough*, and *have to*/*don't have to*, and the phrases from the *Useful Language* box (see Student's Book p65).**

CHECK

7 **Do you …**

- have three paragraphs?
- describe what the vacation house has?
- explain why the vacation home is special?

5 REVIEW

VOCABULARY

1 Circle the correct options.

1 Ellie is sitting in a comfortable *carpet / armchair* and reading a graphic novel.

2 Take the cups out of the dishwasher and put them in the *cupboard / fridge*.

3 After he irons his shirts, Tom puts them carefully in his *desk / wardrobe*.

4 We need some more *shelves / carpets* above the sink in the bathroom.

5 Don't forget to clean the *floor / sink* after you brush your teeth.

6 There's milk all over the kitchen *ceiling / floor*. Did someone break a cup?

7 Mom has a special place in her *desk / chest of drawers* for scarves and gloves.

8 Berto was vacuuming the living room *shelves / carpet* when he found his lost key.

9 There's bread on the table and butter and cheese in the *fridge / sink*.

10 Ryan has a nice *desk / bookcase* in his room, but he never does his homework there.

2 Complete the household chores in the spidergram.

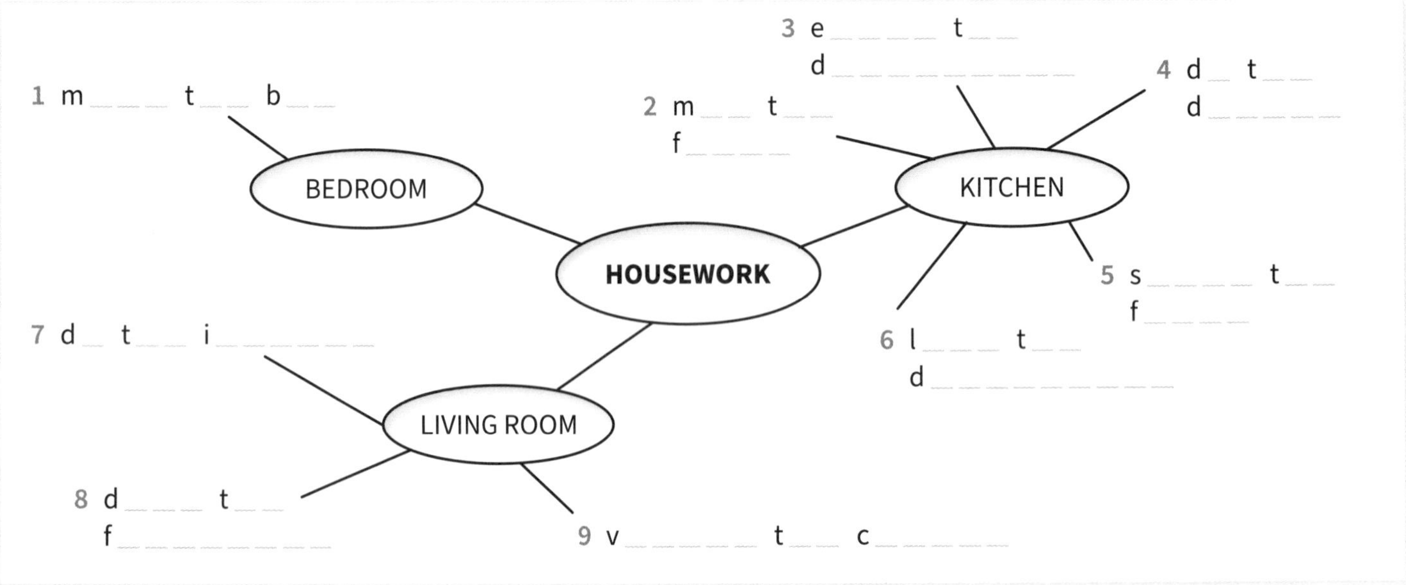

GRAMMAR IN ACTION

3 Rewrite the sentences with (*not*) *as … as* or (*not*) *enough* and the adjectives in parentheses.

1 Your house is the same size as my house. (big)
Your house ______________________.

2 The weather is warmer today. (cold)
The weather today ______________________.

3 Sam is more nervous than Jack. (relaxed)
Sam ______________________.

4 Nicky is too young to watch that movie. (old)
Nicky ______________________.

5 I don't need a bigger desk than this one. (big)
This desk ______________________.

6 Frank is stronger than his brother. (strong)
Frank's brother ______________________.

7 Is there enough sugar in your coffee? (sweet)
Is your coffee ______________________?

8 Sofia and her mother are 1.62 meters tall. (tall)
Sofia ______________________.

4 Complete the sentences with the correct form of *have to*.

1 We ______ do the dishes by hand. We have a dishwasher.

2 You ______ put the cups on the top shelf, not on the bottom.

3 Lisa ______ help in the yard. Her dad does that.

4 We ______ wash our clothes by hand. We use the washing machine.

5 You ______ give me a fork. I can use chopsticks.

6 Mr. Kelly ______ clean the school windows. That's his job.

7 You ______ help me, but thanks. I know what to do.

8 They ______ buy a new vacuum cleaner. Their old one broke.

CUMULATIVE GRAMMAR

5 Complete the conversation with the missing words. Circle the correct options.

DAD Hey, Kevin, come over here. I [1] ______ at some vacation websites.

KEVIN Oh, great. Can I take the tent you [2] ______ me for my birthday?

DAD Well, your mom [3] ______ camping.

KEVIN Oh, but Dad, tents are [4] ______ these days than they were in the past.

DAD Yes, but I [5] ______ about a vacation home, you know, with a pool.

KEVIN A vacation home isn't [6] ______ a campsite, Dad.

DAD [7] ______ where we stayed last summer?

KEVIN Yeah, it was nice, but it wasn't [8] ______ for me.

DAD A vacation home is definitely [9] ______.

KEVIN Yeah, but it's boring. There aren't [10] ______ other kids to hang out with.

DAD Well, I'm sorry your mother and I aren't [11] ______ for you, Kevin.

KEVIN No, Dad, I didn't mean that. But you [12] ______ agree: you're not as much fun as my friends!

1 a look b 'm looking c do look
2 a buy b buyed c bought
3 a not like b doesn't like c don't like
4 a better b good c best
5 a were thinking b was thinking c did thought
6 a as interesting as b more interesting as c interesting than
7 a Are you liking b Were you liking c Did you like
8 a enough exciting b very exciting enough c exciting enough
9 a most comfortable as b more comfortable c the more comfortable
10 a some b one c any
11 a cooler enough b enough cool c cool enough
12 a has to b don't have to c have to

6 How can I stay safe?

VOCABULARY

Accidents and Injuries

1 ☆ **Put the letters in the correct order to make words and phrases about accidents and injuries.**

1 tge ttneib *get bitten*
2 tih ______
3 usbrie ______
4 npsira ______
5 uct ______
6 tge gutsn ______
7 runb ______
8 lafl fof ______
9 psil ______
10 tarccsh ______
11 kebra ______
12 ptir vroe ______

2 ☆ **Circle the odd one out.**

1 break / bruise / (slip) **your arm**
2 fall off / sprain / trip over **a bike**
3 get cut / get stung / get bitten **by an insect**
4 hit / break / bruise **your head on the door**

3 ☆ **Match 1–6 with a–f.**

1 Jeremy got stung [*e*]
2 The bruise on my arm [ ]
3 You can't play soccer [ ]
4 I didn't see my bag, [ ]
5 They were running around the pool [ ]
6 He fell off his surfboard [ ]

a and I tripped over it.
b if you break your leg.
c when they slipped on the wet floor.
d and into the ocean.
e on his leg by a bee.
f is now black and blue.

4 ☆☆ **Complete the sentences with the correct form of the words and phrases from Exercise 1.**

1 Henry *sprained* his ankle running for the bus.
2 The cat ______ my arm when I picked it up.
3 You can easily ______ your hand while cooking.
4 You can ______ by mosquitoes when you camp near water.
5 My grandma ______ her finger on a sharp knife.
6 He ______ his head as he was getting out of the car.

5 ☆☆ **Complete the chat with the correct form of the words and phrases in the box.**

bruise	~~fall off~~	hit	not break
sprain	trip over		

< Back

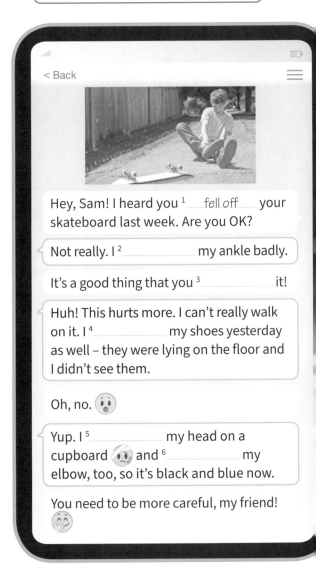

Hey, Sam! I heard you [1] *fell off* your skateboard last week. Are you OK?

Not really. I [2] ______ my ankle badly.

It's a good thing that you [3] ______ it!

Huh! This hurts more. I can't really walk on it. I [4] ______ my shoes yesterday as well – they were lying on the floor and I didn't see them.

Oh, no.

Yup. I [5] ______ my head on a cupboard and [6] ______ my elbow, too, so it's black and blue now.

You need to be more careful, my friend!

Explore It!

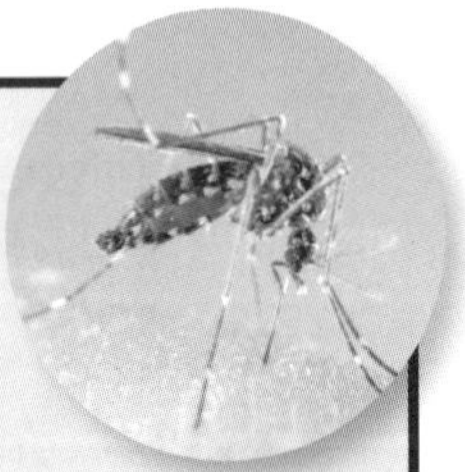

Guess the correct answer.

Both male and female / Only male / Only female mosquitoes bite humans.

Find another interesting fact about mosquitoes. Write a question and send it to a classmate in an email, or ask them in the next class.

READING

An Online Article

1 Read the article and write the headings in the correct places (1–4).

Burns | Do Not Eat or Drink! | Falls | Things Up Noses

DANGER AT HOME!

HOME | **STORIES** | PHOTOS

1 ______

You probably think that the most dangerous room in the house is the kitchen, but in fact, most accidents happen in the living room! Small children can get serious burns from hot drinks or open fires. Candles are also the cause of many accidents in the living room – a candle near a curtain can start a horrible house fire!

2 ______

Many people go to the hospital after getting poisoned, especially young children. Do you sometimes paint your bedroom? When you finish painting a wall, put the paints in a safe place so that young children don't try to drink them. Medicines, too, should be in a top bathroom cupboard – they shouldn't be easy for kids to get.

3 ______

This is a surprising accident but also a common one. Young children often put the strangest things up their noses: frozen peas, crayons, fries … . They think it's funny, but it can be serious. These objects get stuck, and it sometimes requires a hospital visit to get them out.

4 ______

Falling is the most common accident in the home. Be careful: climbing up a ladder to get something down from a high shelf can be very risky. This happens most often to people over 65 and kids under 15. And remember: young children must not play near open windows – thousands of children fall out of them every year, so watch out.

2 **Read the article again and check the meaning of these words in a dictionary. Then complete the sentences.**

candles | ladder | ~~medicine~~ | poison | risky | stuck

1 Judy was sick last year, and she's still taking a lot of *medicine* .
2 My little brother had seven ______ on his birthday cake.
3 Drinking dirty or polluted water can ______ you.
4 It's very ______ to light a candle and leave it near a young child.
5 We needed a ______ to get the boxes down from the top shelf.
6 My hand got ______ under the sofa, and I couldn't get it out.

3 **Read the article again. Answer the questions.**

1 Which room is the most dangerous, according to the article?
the living room
2 How can house fires start in the living room?
______
3 What's the best place to keep medicines?
______
4 Why do young children put things up their noses?
______
5 Which age groups have the most accidents with falls?
______
6 How can an open window be dangerous?
______

4 **Answer the questions with your own ideas.**

1 Which fact in the article surprised you the most? Why?
______
2 Do you light candles at home? When?
______

GRAMMAR IN ACTION

Should/Shouldn't and *Must/Must Not*

1 ☆ **Complete the sentences with *should* or *shouldn't*.**

1 You should always be careful with candles.
2 You ________ leave a lighted candle in an empty room.
3 Dad says that we ________ clean our shoes.
4 Maybe we ________ have a smoke alarm in the classroom.
5 You ________ take other people's medicine.
6 We ________ prevent as many accidents as we can.

2 ☆ **Complete the sentences with the words in the box.**

should be	should do	should send	shouldn't drink	shouldn't laugh	~~shouldn't swim~~

1 There's a red flag on the beach, so you shouldn't swim here.
2 My uncle had an accident at work. I ________ him a card.
3 It's very icy today, so you ________ careful that you don't slip.
4 Oliver got stung by a bee. You ________ at him – it's not funny!
5 My brother has a broken arm, so I ________ the dishes.
6 Hey, you ________ that! It's medicine, not fruit juice!

3 ☆☆ **Complete the poster with *should* or *shouldn't* and an appropriate verb.**

Can't sleep at bedtime?
Can't get up in the morning?

Here's some advice from SLEEP NURSE!

You [1] should do exercise in the fresh air every day.
You [2] ________ tea or coffee in the evening.
You [3] ________ to quiet relaxing music.
You [4] ________ scary movies in bed.
You [5] ________ your phone in a different room.
You [6] ________ off your light before you go to sleep.

4 ☆☆ **Complete the sentences about the signs using *must* or *must not*. Sometimes there is more than one possible answer.**

1 You must not park here.
2 You ________.
3 You ________.
4 You ________.
5 You ________.
6 You ________.

5 ☆☆ **(Circle) the best options to complete the conversation.**

PAULA I think you [1](should) / shouldn't / must come to judo class, Lola. It's really fun!

LOLA Do you really think I [2]*should / must / must not*? I'm not very athletic.

PAULA I know, but Mom says we [3]*should / shouldn't / must* do at least one after-school activity, so you have to choose one.

LOLA OK, what are the rules? What do I need to know?

PAULA First, you [4]*shouldn't / must / must not* be late because you can't come in once the class starts. Second, you [5]*should / must / must not* bring judo clothes – you can't wear normal clothes. And the most important thing: you [6]*should / must / must not* listen to everything the instructor says. Judo can be dangerous.

LOLA Mmm, it sounds kind of scary!

VOCABULARY AND LISTENING

Parts of the Body

1 ☆ **Find 11 more words for parts of the body in the word search. The words can be in any direction.**

A	K	E	E	H	C	C	L	V
R	(W)	D	O	C	H	I	N	N
F	(O)	R	E	H	E	A	D	M
Y	(B)	K	J	T	S	F	K	E
U	(L)	C	P	E	T	M	N	C
L	(E)	E	H	E	X	Z	E	I
A	C	N	S	T	T	O	E	A
W	R	I	S	T	V	N	W	N
R	E	D	L	U	O	H	S	R

2 ☆ **Circle the correct options.**

1 Marie's hair covered her (*forehead*) / *neck*, almost to her eyes.

2 The boys' *chins* / *cheeks* were red when they came in from the cold.

3 Joe walked on broken glass and cut his *wrist* / *heel*.

4 Our teacher wore a pretty, long scarf around her *neck* / *elbow*.

5 Olympic swimmers often have very wide *chests* / *elbows*.

6 The girl fell off her bike and bruised her *teeth* / *knee*.

7 Ballet dancers wear special shoes so they can dance on their *toes* / *elbows*.

8 She was wearing three gold bracelets around her *shoulder* / *wrist*.

A Radio Interview

3 6.01 ☆ **Look at the pictures about a story. What do you think happened? Listen and put the pictures in the correct order (1–6).**

a 

b 

c  1

d 

e 

f 

4 6.01 ☆☆ **Listen again. Are the sentences *T* (true) or *F* (false)?**

1 Toby was on the boat with a friend. F

2 Toby says dolphins can sometimes be dangerous. ____

3 The boys didn't know what the dolphins were doing. ____

4 The shark disappeared after about an hour. ____

5 One dolphin injured Toby's shoulder. ____

6 People can find more animal stories on the radio station's website. ____

5 ☆☆☆ **Answer the questions with your own ideas.**

1 Which other animals are especially smart?

____

2 Which other animals sometimes protect humans? How?

____

GRAMMAR IN ACTION

Zero Conditional and First Conditional

1 ☆ **Complete the zero conditional sentences with the correct form of the verbs in parentheses.**

1 People _don't swim_ (not swim) here when they _see_ (see) the red flag on the beach.
2 When sharks ________ (get) hungry, they ________ (be) a danger to swimmers.
3 Broken glass ________ (cut) your skin if you ________ (touch) it.
4 Swimmers ________ (get) very cold if they ________ (stay) in the ocean too long.
5 If the temperature ________ (fall) below 0 °C, water ________ (turn) into ice.
6 If a bee ________ (sting) you, it really ________ (hurt).

2 ☆☆ **Write zero conditional sentences.**

1 if / I / drink coffee at night / I / not sleep well / .
If I drink coffee at night, I don't sleep well.
2 if / we / study hard / we / do well on our tests / .
____
3 when / Helena / feel sick / she / not come to school / .
____
4 my little brother / fall down / if / he / run too fast / .
____
5 I / feel really bad / when / I / forget my friends' birthdays / .
____
6 if / you / call the doctor after nine / nobody / answer / .
____

3 ☆☆ **Complete the zero conditional sentences with the correct form of the verbs in the box.**

break	die	eat	fall	get	go	~~look~~	not rain	~~swim~~	walk

1 Ross always _swims_ in the river if it _looks_ safe.
2 Children ________ cavities in their teeth if they ________ too much sugar.
3 If it ________ all summer, enough plants and animals ________.
4 Older people ________ down easily when they ________ on ice.
5 You ________ to the hospital if you ________ your leg.

4 ☆☆ **Circle the correct options.**

1 I'll carry your bags if your shoulders *will hurt* / *hurt*.
2 If your cat scratches Laura, she *isn't* / *won't be* happy.
3 The roads will be dangerous if it *snows* / *will snow* tonight.
4 There will be an accident if they *aren't* / *won't be* more careful.
5 If she *will run* / *runs* too fast, her chest will start to hurt.

5 ☆☆ **Complete the first conditional sentences in the text with the correct form of the verbs in parentheses.**

Don't Get Lost!

If you [1] _walk_ (walk) a lot in the forest, it's possible that one day you [2] ________ (get) lost. If this happens, sit down and eat and drink something. If you [3] ________ (feel) calm, you [4] ________ (think) more clearly. Can you send a text or make a call? If you [5] ________ (make) contact with someone, [6] ________ you ________ (know) how to direct them to where you are? If you [7] ________ (look) around, you [8] ________ probably ________ (recognize) something. Remember to always take the correct equipment so you don't get lost in the first place. You [9] ________ (be) better prepared if you [10] ________ (pack) a map and a compass before you go!

WRITING

A Blog Post

1 ☆ **Read the blog post. Do you agree with the advice?** ______

The Climbers' Climbing Blog

Thanks for reading my blog! Here are a few of my readers' questions and my answers.

I always bruise my knees and elbows when I'm rock climbing. What should I do to avoid that? ***Spidergirl***

You should buy some knee and elbow pads. But [1] *make sure / that's why* that you climb in the correct way. You won't bruise anything if you're careful. [2] *If you ask me, / Make sure* you need some expert advice and maybe a lesson or two!

I'm 11, and I'd love to go climbing with my older brothers, but they say I'm too young. What's a good age to start climbing? ***Katya***

If you're tall and strong enough, you'll be able to climb now! [3] *That's why / I'd say* it's safe to start climbing at your age if you start with small climbs and you have good climbers with you. If you're careful, you'll be fine. Enjoy!

When's the safest time to go climbing? I only climb in the summer, but I want to do more. ***Barbara***

In the U.S.A., spring and summer are the best times. You'll slip and fall if you climb on wet rocks. [4] *Make sure / That's why* you shouldn't do it on rainy days. And of course, you must never climb in snowy or icy weather if you don't have special equipment.

That's all for now. Have fun, and happy climbing!

2 ☆ **Circle the correct options (1–4) in the blog post.**

3 ☆☆ **Read the blog post again. Write *S* (Spidergirl), *K* (Katya), or *B* (Barbara) for each sentence.**

1 She wants to know the best time for climbing. ______
2 The blogger thinks she should have classes. ______
3 The blogger says she should go with other climbers. ______

4 ☆☆ **Read the blog post again and circle the correct answers.**

1 Rock climbers should wear knee and elbow pads to avoid ... .
(a) bruises b falls c climbing incorrectly

2 Katya's brothers think she's not ... enough to start climbing.
a tall b old c strong

3 Katya should start with ... climbs.
a good b short c careful

4 Barbara doesn't climb on ... days.
a sunny b summer c winter

5 Climbers need special equipment in ... weather.
a summer b rainy c icy

PLAN

5 ☆☆ **Write a blog post to give safety advice. Choose an activity and think of three questions about doing it safely. Take notes for the answers in your notebook.**

1 ______
2 ______
3 ______

WRITE

6 ☆☆☆ **Write your blog post. Remember to include an introduction, three questions and answers, an ending, and phrases from the *Useful Language* box (see Student's Book, p77).**

CHECK

7 **Do you ...**

- answer each question?
- use *should/shouldn't* and *must/must not*?
- use vocabulary from this unit?

6 REVIEW

VOCABULARY

1 Complete the crossword. Use the clues.

Across

2 You … on icy roads.
7 A … around your eye is called a "black eye."
9 You … … objects on the floor if you don't see them.
10 Don't … your hand in the fire!
12 She … her head on the cupboard door.

Down

1 It hurts a lot when you … your ankle.
3 Don't stand on the wall or you'll … … !
4 Rugby players often … their noses.
5 You can … … by a bee if you make it angry.
6 You can … … by mosquitoes if you leave the window open.
8 Does your cat sometimes … you?
11 He … his foot on a sharp rock.

2 Complete the words for parts of the body with the missing vowels.

1 f _ r _ h _ _ d
2 h _ _ l
3 _ l b _ w
4 k n _ _
5 c h _ n
6 n _ c k
7 c h _ s t
8 s h _ _ l d _ r
9 c h _ _ k
10 t _ _ t h
11 w r _ s t
12 t _ _

GRAMMAR IN ACTION

3 Are the underlined words correct in the sentences? Correct the incorrect ones.

1 You must not drive on the right on U.S. roads. *must*
2 If she likes helping sick people, she should become a nurse. ______
3 You must not put metal in a microwave. ______
4 Cyclists must not stop when they see a stop sign. ______
5 Children should brush their teeth after eating candy. ______
6 You must not buy a ticket when you travel on public transportation. ______
7 You should go rock climbing in the rain. It's incredibly dangerous! ______

4 Put the words in the correct order to make conditional sentences. Add commas where necessary.

1 you get stung / it hurts / If / by a bee / .
______
2 warm clothes / we wear / We won't get cold / if / .
______
3 If / I won't / I see a red flag / go swimming / .
______
4 be happy / you wake him up / if / Nikita won't / .
______
5 When / soccer indoors / it rains / we usually play / .
______
6 you go cycling / to wear a helmet / when / It is safer / .
______

CUMULATIVE GRAMMAR

5 Complete the conversation with the missing words. Circle the correct options.

MARINA Do we [1] ________ go this way, Diego? Are you sure it's right?

DIEGO Yes, I'm sure. The map says if we [2] ________ the path, we get to the hostel.

MARINA Did you check the route before we [3] ________?

DIEGO Of course! But we [4] ________ hurry. It's getting dark. Come on!

MARINA If I try to run, I [5] ________ down. Ouch! Hey, Diego! Come back! Oh, no. My ankle!

DIEGO What's wrong? Why [6] ________ there?

MARINA I [7] ________ after you [8] ________ I fell and sprained my ankle. It hurts!

DIEGO Oh, no! You should be more careful! Does it feel better if you [9] ________ still? Or do you think you can walk on it?

MARINA Not sure. Is the hostel far from here?

DIEGO Well, I don't really know. Is your ankle still [10] ________ it was?

MARINA Yes, it is. We could call for help. Does the phone work up here?

DIEGO No, sorry. Listen, you stay here, and I'll go for help. I [11] ________ long if I run. But you [12] ________ move.

MARINA Don't worry, I can't! And please, hurry!

1	a must	b should	c have to
2	a follow	b will follow	c followed
3	a leave	b left	c were leaving
4	a must not	b shouldn't	c should
5	a won't fall	b 'll fall	c fell
6	a do you sit	b will you sit	c are you sitting
7	a ran	b was running	c 'm running
8	a when	b as	c while
9	a sat	b sit	c will sit
10	a as worse as	b worst	c as bad as
11	a won't be	b be	c 'm not
12	a must	b should	c must not

7 Are you connected?

VOCABULARY

Communication and Technology

1 ☆ **Find ten more communication and technology words and phrases in the word snake.**

(message)uploaddownloadappchipsocialmediadevicevideochatemojiscreensoftware

2 ☆ **(Circle) the correct options.**

1 I usually send my mother a *device* / (*message*) if I'm not home on time.

2 When his dad's working in the U.S.A., Thomas often does a *video chat* / *social media* with him.

3 You can listen to music on your tablet or any other mobile *emoji* / *device*.

4 Our IT teacher wrote some *chips* / *software* for checking homework.

5 Blogs and other types of *social media* / *video chat* are a lot of fun.

6 Iris dropped her phone and broke the *app* / *screen* on it.

3 ☆☆ **Match the definitions with words from Exercise 1.**

1 copy information to a computer system or to the Internet. *upload*

2 copy information onto a phone, tablet, laptop, etc. from the Internet or a computer. ______

3 the short word for an "application," for example, Spotify or Facebook. ______

4 a digital picture that shows a feeling or emotion. ______

5 a flat surface on a TV or computer where you can see words or pictures. ______

6 it's very small: the "brain" inside a computer or phone. ______

4 ☆ **Match the words to make different collocations. Sometimes there is more than one possible answer.**

computer, ~~download~~, social, electronic, send, upload

media, a message, devices, ~~software~~, screen, photos

download software, ______

______

______

5 ☆☆ **Complete the phone instructions with the correct form of words and phrases from Exercise 1.**

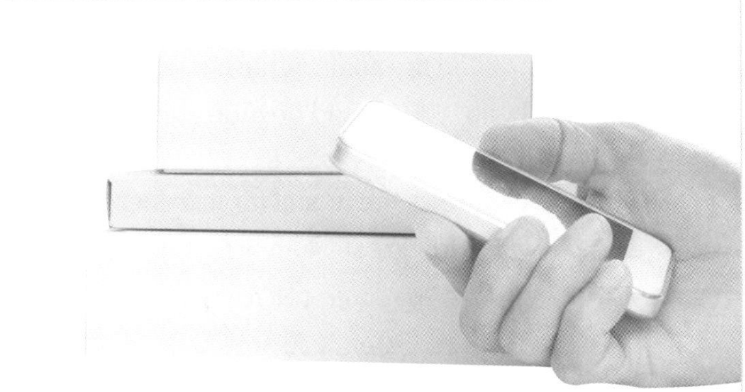

Thank you for buying a Techtime phone. When you turn on your new [1] *device* for the first time, you will see an icon for "Games Shop" at the bottom of the [2] ______. Here, you can [3] ______ all your favorite social media, music, and news [4] ______, like WhatsApp and Spotify. To write a [5] ______ using text or email, press one of your contacts on the contacts list. The Techtime 1000 also has an excellent camera, so [6] ______ with friends and family is easy!

Explore It!

True or false?

The average person checks their smartphone ten times a day.

Find another interesting fact about smartphones. Write a question and send it to a classmate in an email, or ask them in the next class.

READING

A Magazine Article

1 ☆ **Look at the photo and the title of the article. What do you think the article is about? Read the article and check your ideas.** ______

High-Tech or No-Tech?

Juan Carlos Garcia investigates how a school in California's Silicon Valley uses technology – or doesn't!

Silicon Valley in California has become the world center of technology, innovation, and social media. It's home to some of the world's biggest tech companies. So, with all this technology around, you probably think that all schools in Silicon Valley use lots of computers, laptops, and tablets in their classrooms, right? Wrong! In Masters Middle School, the school I visited, there isn't a tablet, screen, or smartphone anywhere. The classrooms have plants, traditional wooden desks, and even blackboards with colored chalks!

So why don't they use technology? The surprising thing is that the parents of these children – many of them technology experts at major tech companies – believe that bringing technology to class isn't a good idea! Many think that it doesn't help young people use their own minds. So, in this school, there are no electronic teaching devices in the classroom. Teachers here think that kids use their imaginations better without them!

This means that students don't use the Internet to study or upload apps to help them learn, and they use pens and paper to write, not tablets or laptops. They study their main subjects through artistic activities like music and painting. One student told me, "Our teachers believe that technology will only be helpful when we're older and we know how and when to use it properly."

So even the tech experts think that technology has its limits! High-tech or no-tech: which is the best? What do you think?

2 ☆☆ **Read the article again and check the meaning of these words in a dictionary. Then complete the sentences.**

expert	~~imagination~~	innovation
major	minds	properly

1 I'm not very good at writing stories because I have no imagination.
2 My aunt knows a lot about computers. She's a technology ______.
3 When you use this dictionary app ______, it's very easy to look up words.
4 This young company is famous for its ______ and new ideas.
5 My brother made a ______ decision to move to the U.S.A. to study.
6 People who develop software have creative ______.

3 ☆☆ **Read the article again. Are the sentences *T* (true) or *F* (false)?**

1 Juan Carlos visited the school to learn about new classroom technology. F
2 The school is home to technology and innovation. ______
3 Juan Carlos expected to find a lot of electronic teaching devices in the school. ______
4 Some parents think that classroom technology stops young people from thinking creatively. ______
5 Students learn through artistic subjects. ______
6 Teachers believe that technology will never help students learn. ______

4 ☆☆☆ **Answer the questions with your own ideas.**

1 How do some schools use technology in class?
______
2 What electronic devices do you use in class to help you learn?
______

GRAMMAR IN ACTION

Present Perfect: Affirmative and Negative

1 ☆ **Complete the chart with the correct past participles.**

be	was	1 *been*
change	changed	2 ______
choose	chose	3 ______
do	did	4 ______
hear	heard	5 ______
learn	learned	6 ______
design	designed	7 ______
see	saw	8 ______

2 ☆☆ **Complete the sentences with the present perfect form of the verbs from Exercise 1.**

1 Kim *has learned* to use her new phone.
2 Technology ______ the way we learn.
3 YouTube ______ a popular video app for many years.
4 I ______ the new *Mission Impossible* movie. Don't miss it, it's great.
5 The students ______ their subjects for next year.
6 We ______ our math and IT homework.
7 I ______ a website for our basketball team.
8 Paul ______ the news, so you don't have to tell him.

3 ☆ **Make the sentences negative.**

1 I've charged my phone.
I haven't charged my phone.
2 Sergey's forgotten his password.
______
3 Wanda's broken her watch.
______
4 We've bought a new computer.
______
5 They've turned on the TV.
______

4 ☆ **Write sentences with the present perfect.**

1 I / not finish / my homework for tomorrow
I haven't finished my homework for tomorrow.
2 Alex / not read / anything about Silicon Valley
______
3 we / look for / some better information
______
4 they / buy / a new computer online
______
5 he / use / the latest software
______
6 the boys / not call / their parents
______

5 ☆☆ **Choose the correct verbs in each pair. Then complete the email with the present perfect form of the verbs.**

Dear Jess,

Good news! I [1] *'ve thrown* (throw / push) away my old tablet! Mom and Dad [2] ______ (sell / buy) me a new laptop. I [3] ______ (upload / download) some great music software from the Internet, and I [4] ______ (decide / forget) to make a website for my band. I'm not sure if I told you, but I [5] ______ (stop / start) a band. Nick and I [6] ______ (write / listen) some music together. Nick [7] ______ (give / choose) the songs that we want to sing, but we still [8] ______ (not film / not record) anything.

More soon!

Theo

VOCABULARY AND LISTENING

Getting Around

1 ☆ **Complete the transportation phrases with the missing vowels.**

1 go on foot
2 g_t _n _ tr_ _n
3 g_t _ff _ b_s
4 g_t _ _t _f _ c_r
5 g_t _nt_ _ t_x_
6 g_ by tr_m
7 t_k_ _ pl_n_

2 ☆ **Match 1–6 with a–d.**

1 Our visitors got into [d]
2 We planned to catch [ ]
3 I usually go by [ ]
4 If you miss your bus, [ ]
5 Which tram stop should I [ ]
6 Is it better to cycle or go [ ]

a bike when it isn't raining.
b you can catch the next one.
c on foot?
d their car and drove away.
e a plane from JFK Airport.
f get off at?

3 ☆ **Circle the correct answers.**

1 I *get* / *go* by tram when I visit my friends in town.
2 Pete always goes to school *on* / *by* bike.
3 I get off the bus at this stop and go *by* / *on* foot from here.
4 My friend's *taken* / *gotten into* a plane to Peru.
5 Get *on* / *off* the train and find a seat by the window.
6 If you go *on* / *by* the subway, you get there quicker.
7 They can *catch* / *go by* a bus outside their house.
8 Marie got out *off* / *of* the car and hit her head on the door.

A Radio Interview

7.01 **4** ☆ **Listen to the interview. Do Ellie and Joe think space tourism is just science fiction?**

____

7.01 **5** ☆☆ **Listen again and circle the correct answers.**

1 The interview takes place … .
a in a radio studio
b at a school
c at a technology fair

2 Joe says he … to drive.
a loves
b hasn't learned
c doesn't need

3 Ellie likes the idea of … .
a driverless cars
b more bikes
c faster bikes

4 She's seen an exhibit about … in space.
a movies b astronauts c travel

5 Joe thinks rockets to space will be … today's jet planes.
a the same as b different from c similar to

6 In Ellie's opinion, tourist trips to Mars in the next 20 years are … .
a possible b impossible c a problem

6 ☆☆☆ **Answer the questions.**

1 In your opinion, is a vacation on Mars just science fiction? Why / Why not?

____

____

2 If it becomes possible to go to space on vacation, do you think you will go? Why / Why not?

____

____

GRAMMAR IN ACTION

Will/Won't, May, and *Might*

1 Complete the sentences with *will* or *won't*.

1 The photos you post online ___will___ stay there for a long time.
2 Workers worry that robots ________ replace them and take their jobs.
3 I ________ work in another country in the future – I hate traveling.
4 Cars ________ need drivers in the future because of new driverless technology.
5 I think cities ________ become more bike friendly in future years because of all the traffic.

2 Circle the correct options.

1 Maybe you should take a coat. It *will* / *(might)* be cold.
2 Smartphones will always be expensive. They *won't* / *might* get cheaper.
3 It's not certain, but we *will* / *may* go to school by helicopter in the future.
4 They *will* / *may* go by train, but they still haven't decided.
5 He *will* / *might* have his own bike one day – he's sure of that!

3 Circle the correct options below to complete the email.

TO: Josh | FROM: Lucy

Dear Josh,

I'm on a train with my mom and dad. They [1] ________ be away for the weekend, so I'm staying with my uncle Ted. It [2] ________ be much fun there – it never is, but I'm sure I [3] ________ chat with friends online. But then, who knows – there [4] ________ be Wi-Fi in his house – I haven't asked! I'm sure he [5] ________ have a TV, though – everyone has one! I [6] ________ talk to you online this afternoon, but I don't know yet. Uncle Ted wants to go birdwatching!

Lucy

1 (a) will	b won't	c might
2 a may not	b will	c won't
3 a may	b might	c will
4 a might not	b won't	c may
5 a won't	b will	c may
6 a may not	b will	c may

Infinitive of Purpose

4 Rewrite the sentences with the infinitive of purpose.

1 My sister and I went to New York. We wanted to visit the Transportation Museum.
My sister and I went to New York to visit the Transportation Museum.
2 First, my sister went online. She checked the train times.
____
3 We walked to the station. We bought the tickets there.
____
4 I left the house at 6 a.m. I wanted to catch the first train.
____
5 My sister wanted to stop at a store. She needed to buy some sandwiches.
____
6 We got on the train quickly. That's how we got the best seats.
____

5 Complete the text with the verbs and phrases in the box.

may buy	might fly	to drive	~~to get~~
to go	will travel		

I normally use public transportation [1] ___to get___ around. For example, [2] ________ to school, I get the bus, or I catch a tram. I [3] ________ a motorcycle when I'm old enough, or maybe a car. I really don't know how my children [4] ________ in the future. Maybe they will have amazing machines [5] ________ around in, or they [6] ________ through the air. Who knows?

WRITING

An Article

1 ☆ **Read the article. Then circle the correct answer below.**

Technology has changed the way we … our friends.

a make contact with
b take care of
c have fun with

STAYING IN TOUCH: THEN AND NOW

(1) The way we communicate with our friends has changed a lot. [1] For instance, when our grandparents were young, there were no cell phones, and what's [2] ________, some families didn't even have a telephone at home. To call a friend, people needed to use a public phone.

(2) In contrast, today there are lots of ways of contacting friends. For [3] ________, almost everyone can use a smartphone at any time and in any place. Posting status updates is easy with technology, such [4] ________ online chats and messaging apps. In [5] ________, we can send photos and videos to share special moments.

(3) Some people think that friends might never meet face-to-face in the future. However, I don't think that will happen. It may become easier to "see" each other without actually meeting up, but it will always be more fun to sit and chat together.

2 ☆☆ **Complete the article with the words in the box.**

addition	as	example	~~for~~	more

3 ☆ **Read the article again and match 1–5 with a–e.**

1 In the past, there were [d]
2 People needed to use a phone booth [ ]
3 Today we can use [ ]
4 It's easier now to share [ ]
5 It will always be more fun [ ]

a photos and videos with friends.
b smartphones to make calls at any time.
c to meet our friends face-to-face.
d no cell phones.
e to make contact with their friends.

4 ☆ **Read the article again and write the correct paragraph number (1–3).**

a Which paragraph is about what might happen in the future? ________
b Which paragraph mentions old technology? ________
c Which paragraph describes ways of communicating today? ________

PLAN

5 ☆☆ **Write an article about doing homework. Think about homework in the past, present, and future. Take notes for each paragraph.**

1 How people did homework in the past:
____
2 Technology for doing homework today:
____
3 Predictions for the future:
____

WRITE

6 ☆☆☆ **Write your article. Remember to include past and present tenses, predictions with *will/won't* and *may/might* (*not*), and phrases from the *Useful Language* box (see Student's Book, p89).**

CHECK

7 **Do you …**
- have three paragraphs?
- make certain and uncertain predictions for the future?

7 REVIEW

VOCABULARY

1 Put the letters in the correct order to make communication and technology words.

1 p a p ______
2 d v o i e t c a h ______
3 j i o m e ______
4 d o u l a p ______
5 l o i s c a d m i a e ______
6 w r o s t e f a ______
7 c r e n e s ______
8 p i h c ______
9 o w o d n l d a ______
10 v i e e d c ______
11 s g a e s e m ______

2 Look at the photos. What are the people doing? Complete the sentences with phrases for getting around.

GRAMMAR IN ACTION

3 Complete the conversation with the present perfect form of the verbs in parentheses.

DAD Jon, stop playing computer games now. It's time to eat.

JON I [1] ______ (not play) any games this evening, Dad! And I [2] ______ (finish) my homework.

DAD Oh, OK. Well, that's good. I [3] ______ (make) your favorite dinner.

JON Great, thanks. I [4] ______ (send) Mom a message, but she [5] ______ (not reply).

DAD Well, she [6] ______ (fly) to Lisbon, so there's a time difference. I [7] ______ (check) my emails, too, but I [8] ______ (not hear) from her either. I'm sure she'll call us later.

1 Anna is *going on foot*.

2 Charlie is ______.

3 Helga is ______.

4 Kazuyo and Haru are ______.

5 David is ______.

6 Maria is ______.

4 Complete the dialogues with the infinitive of purpose or *will/won't*, *may*, or *might* (*not*). Use the verbs in the boxes. Sometimes there is more than one possible answer.

buy not have print

A Can I use your printer [1] ____________ these photos, please?

B Not sure. I [2] ____________ any paper. If there isn't enough, I think Dad [3] ____________ some.

get not take

A What time do we have to leave [4] ____________ to the movie theater by six?

B There's no rush. We have time, and it [5] ____________ long to get there.

be able to play

A Do I need to download an app [6] ____________ this game?

B You [7] ____________ play it without one. Let's check!

be edit

A What software does Sam use [8] ____________ photos?

B I don't know, but he [9] ____________ here in a minute, so you can ask him. OK?

CUMULATIVE GRAMMAR

5 Complete the conversation with the missing words. Circle the correct options.

CLAIRE Friday, at last! I'm happy it's over. I [1] ________ a tiring week. OK, see you later!
MARIK Hey, where [2] ________? Aren't you walking home?
CLAIRE No, I have a new bike. Didn't I tell you?
MARIK No, you [3] ________. When did you get that?
CLAIRE Last Saturday. It's great! It's the [4] ________ way to get around!
MARIK You [5] ________ really get a helmet, Claire! If you [6] ________, you'll hurt yourself.
CLAIRE I [7] ________ fall off, don't worry. I [8] ________ a helmet, but I just forgot it today.
MARIK Which one is your bike, then?
CLAIRE That blue one. It [9] ________ pretty cheap because I [10] ________ afford to spend much.
MARIK It's nice. You know, I [11] ________ get a bike. Then we can cycle to school together.
CLAIRE Good idea! But you'll need to ride fast [12] ________ with me! See you later!

1 a 've had b was having c 's had
2 a are you going b do you go c have you gone
3 a did b not c didn't
4 a best b good c better
5 a shouldn't b may c should
6 a fell off b 'll fall off c fall off
7 a don't b won't c must not
8 a bought b 'm buying c was buying
9 a were b was being c was
10 a couldn't b can c couldn't to
11 a might b might not c won't
12 a cycling b to cycle c for cycle

8 What is success?

VOCABULARY

Exceptional Jobs and Qualities

1 ☆ **Complete the puzzle with words for jobs and qualities. Use the clues. What's the secret word in gray?**

1 He works for a company or organization, like a bank.
2 If you have this, you don't stop until you get what you want.
3 This person has ideas to make something completely new.
4 A runner, swimmer, high-jumper, etc.
5 This person designs and builds things.
6 This person writes music.
7 You need this to make something new and imaginative.
8 This person does experiments in a lab.
9 This person might produce books or songs.
10 With this, you can learn, understand, and form opinions.
11 You can do an activity or job well if you have this.
12 A natural ability to do something well.
13 You have this if you are strong, physically or mentally.

2 ☆☆ **Complete the sentences with words for qualities from Exercise 1.**

1 It takes a lot of ___skill___ to operate on a person's heart.
2 She won the prize for __________ for her original ideas. She has a great imagination.
3 Maya always shows great __________ and never stops trying to do her best.
4 The __________ of a chimpanzee is similar to a human's: chimpanzees are clever!
5 Hercules was famous for his __________. He could lift very heavy objects.

3 ☆☆ **Complete the sentences with words for jobs from Exercise 1 and the names in the box.**

Adele	~~Isaac Newton~~	Marie Curie
Suzanne Collins	Tim Berners-Lee	Usain Bolt

1 ___Isaac Newton___ was a ___mathematician___ at Cambridge University in the 1600s.
2 The __________ of the World Wide Web is named __________.
3 __________ is the __________ of the song "Hello" from 2015.
4 __________ was a __________ who won two Nobel Prizes for important work on radioactivity.
5 __________ is a Jamaican __________ who was an Olympic champion in three different Olympic Games.
6 *The Hunger Games* series of novels is by a __________ named __________.

Explore It!

Guess the correct answer.

Ashrita Furman has the world record for world records. He has over *100* / *200* / *300*.

Find another interesting fact about a world record. Write a question and send it to a classmate in an email, or ask them in the next class.

READING

Online Comments

1 ☆ **Read the online comments. Who has something in common with their hero?** ______

● ● ●

HOME	PROFILE	BLOG	PHOTOS

FROM EARLY CHALLENGES TO ADULT SUCCESS!

Many of you liked our article last week about young adults who faced difficult times when they were kids but never stopped trying. Comments have flown in from all over the world!

An astrophysicist when he was still a teenager, Jake Barnett has made the biggest impression on me. Doctors said he had autism when he was two and that he might never speak. But he did, and he has shown an amazing talent for math. As an adult, Jake has an incredible memory and remembers every math problem he has ever solved!

Hooper 30 minutes ago

His name is Aaron "Wheelz" Fotheringham, and he's an amazing athlete. Now an adult, he needed a wheelchair when he was eight. He wanted to do tricks like his friends on skateboards and BMXs, so he took skateboard and BMX tricks and invented his own wheelchair tricks. You need strength and determination to become an extreme athlete when you can't use your legs. I use a wheelchair, and Aaron's had a big effect on me.

cre8tiv 35 minutes ago

Bethany Hamilton was 13 and already a great surfer when a shark attacked her and bit off her left arm. Three weeks after the accident, she got back into the water and continued surfing with only one arm! She wrote a book at 14, and a movie, *Soul Surfer*, followed. Now, as an adult, Bethany works hard helping others to face their challenges.

daisymay 45 minutes ago

2 ☆☆ **Read the comments again and check the meaning of these words in a dictionary. Then complete the sentences.**

~~autism~~ extreme face tricks wheelchair

1 A child with __autism__ might not have good communication or social skills.
2 My brother used a ______ for a while after he broke both his legs.
3 We have to ______ our problems if we want to solve them.
4 Rock climbing is exciting and dangerous – it's one of the oldest ______ sports.
5 We've learned to do some great new ______ on our skateboards.

3 ☆☆ **Read the comments again. Are the sentences *T* (true), *F* (false), or *DS* (doesn't say)?**

1 Jake has an unusual talent for remembering numbers. __T__
2 He's doing research in astrophysics. ______
3 Aaron invented new skateboard and BMX tricks. ______
4 A lot of people watch Aaron's wheelchair tricks online. ______
5 Bethany got back into the water three weeks after the shark attack. ______
6 First there was a movie about her, and after that she wrote a book. ______

4 ☆☆☆ **Answer the questions with your own ideas.**

1 Which person in the comments has faced the biggest challenge? Why?

______

2 Have you faced a big challenge? What was it?

______

GRAMMAR IN ACTION

Present Perfect for Experience

1 ☆ **Complete the sentences with the present perfect form of the verb in parentheses.**

1 I *'ve* never *heard* (hear) of Alexander Rybak.
2 A girl in my class ______ (win) a talent show.
3 Jess ______ (not be) to Spain.
4 They ______ (not see) *The Avengers*.
5 We ______ (raise) a lot of money for charity.
6 Max ______ (cycle) from Los Angeles to San Diego.

2 ☆ **Match 1–6 with a–f.**

1 Have you ever drunk [d]
2 Which European cities [ ]
3 Our team has won [ ]
4 I've never read [ ]
5 Have you ever replied [ ]
6 We've seen their band, [ ]

a but only on YouTube.
b to an email in English?
c has she visited?
d carrot juice?
e the book he gave me.
f the championship three times.

3 ☆☆ **Write questions with the present perfect. Then look at the pictures to answer them.**

1 they / ever fly in a helicopter?
A *Have they ever flown in a helicopter?*
B *No, they haven't, but they've flown on a plane.*

2 Fiona / ever sing in a band?
A ______
B ______

3 they / ever swim in the ocean?
A ______
B ______

4 your dad / ever make a cake?
A ______
B ______

4 ☆☆ **Underline and correct the mistake in each sentence.**

1 Have you ever swim with dolphins? *swum*
2 They never have been to the U.S.A. ______
3 Never you have ridden a horse. ______
4 Have she ever broken her phone? ______
5 Stayed you ever in a five-star hotel? ______
6 I'm happy to say I have ever lost my house keys. ______

5 ☆☆ **Complete the email with the present perfect form of the verbs and phrases in the box.**

be	do	~~fly~~	never explore
never surf	ever try		

Mailboxes Inbox Sent New

Hi, Harry.
How are you? I'll be in Mexico in two weeks! I [1] *'ve flown* into Mexico City Airport before, but I [2] ______ the country. My parents [3] ______ on a lot of Mexican vacations, so they want to go to some new places. But they're also happy to revisit some of their favorite surfing beaches – they know I love the ocean! I [4] ______, and I really want to learn. It can be dangerous, but I think I'll be OK! And [5] ______ you ______ kite-surfing? My dad [6] ______ it lots of times. I'm looking forward to watching him!
Bye for now!
Ava

VOCABULARY AND LISTENING

Phrasal Verbs: Achievement

1 ☆ Match the phrasal verbs with the meanings.

1 work out [e]
2 look up to [ ]
3 give up [ ]
4 set up [ ]
5 come up with [ ]
6 take part in [ ]
7 show off [ ]
8 keep up with [ ]

a admire and respect someone
b act to attract attention, usually in a bad way
c start a new business
d join in an activity or event
e calculate something to get a result
f suggest or think of an idea or answer
g do what is necessary to stay equal or at the same level
h stop doing or having something

2 ☆☆ Complete the sentences with the correct form of phrasal verbs from Exercise 1. Then match them with photos (a–f).

1 Susie likes *working out* hard math problems. *e*
2 It was so difficult that Hector decided to ________ . ____
3 Benjie ________ his dad and wants to be like him. ____
4 Robin always ________ to the other band members. ____
5 My little brother is a fast runner – no one can ________ him. ____
6 Tanya really enjoyed ________ the race. ____

a

b
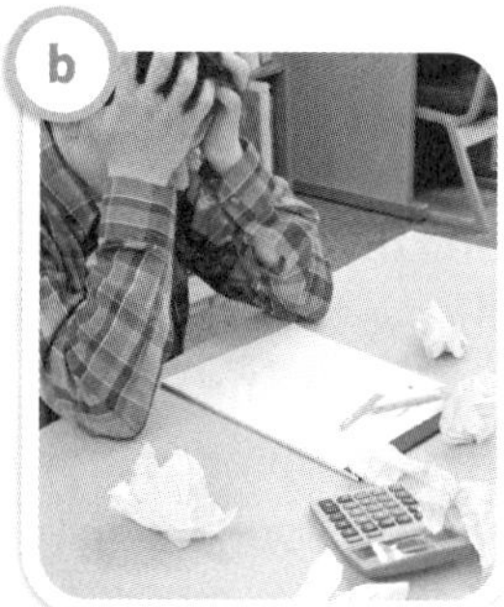

c

d

e

f

A Talk

3 ☆ Check the meaning of these words in a dictionary. Which words can you see in the photos?

antibiotic	bacteria	mold
Petri dish	reflect	shine

a

b

____

____

4 ☆ Listen to the talk. What do the two discoveries have in common? (8.01)

____

5 ☆☆ Listen again and circle the correct options. (8.01)

1 The speaker describes the inventions as happy *accidents* / *experiments*.
2 The "cat's eyes" help drivers to see *other drivers' lights* / *the middle of the road*.
3 The inventor saw his car lights reflecting in *a glass object* / *an animal 's eyes*.
4 Sir Alexander Fleming was studying *bacteria* / *mold* in a London hospital.
5 A person left the Petri dish open when Fleming was *in hospital* / *on vacation*.
6 Some mold was *growing* / *killing* the bacteria in the Petri dish.

6 ☆☆☆ Choose one of the discoveries, cat's eyes or penicillin, and take notes for each heading in your notebook.

- name and nationality of the inventor
- country and place of discovery
- how the inventor discovered it
- why the discovery is important

GRAMMAR IN ACTION

Reflexive Pronouns

1 ☆ **Circle the correct options.**

1 Peter is always looking at (*himself*) / *themselves* in the mirror!
2 You two should prepare *yourself* / *yourselves* for the test.
3 Have you ever taught *myself* / *yourself* a new skill?
4 The cat washes *yourself* / *itself* carefully every morning.
5 We embarrassed *ourselves* / *themselves* by showing off.
6 The girls entertained *themselves* / *herself* with video games.

2 ☆☆ **Complete the sentences with reflexive pronouns and the correct form of the verbs in the box.**

enter	imagine	make	~~switch off~~	take care of	teach

1 The computer screen switches itself off automatically.
2 Those kids are old enough to ______________ .
3 Lauren and I ______________ some new yoga exercises last week.
4 He ______________ for three races in our sports event: running, cycling, and swimming.
5 Monica ______________ a good lunch yesterday.
6 We often ______________ as famous inventors.

Indefinite Pronouns

3 ☆☆ **Put the words in the correct order to make sentences.**

1 anyone / Mars / think / has / don't / walked / I / on
I don't think anyone has walked on Mars.
2 phone / everywhere / her / She's / for / looked
____
3 will / tonight / Nobody / happen / what / knows
____
4 nowhere / on / to / bus / was / There / sit / the
____
5 new / broken / has / camera / Someone / my
____
6 do / help / Is / anything / I / there / can / to / ?
____

4 ☆ **Match 1–6 with a–f.**

1 Has anyone seen [b]
2 Mr. Kellogg invented [ ]
3 Everyone at the party [ ]
4 Olivia hasn't been [ ]
5 I get bored when [ ]
6 Everything was ready [ ]

a anywhere nice this summer.
b that documentary about inventors?
c I have nothing to do.
d when the first guests arrived.
e something by accident.
f had a great time.

5 ☆☆ **Complete the text with the words in the box.**

everyone	everywhere	himself
nobody	~~someone~~	something
somewhere	themselves	

Most of us admire [1] someone who faces challenges and achieves great things. That's why [2] ______________ I know looks up to the scientist Stephen Hawking. He lived [3] ______________ near London until he went to Oxford University. There, he quickly proved [4] ______________ to be a math genius. However, when he was only 21, doctors told him that he had [5] ______________ called motor neurone disease (MND). [6] ______________ usually lives long with MND, but Hawking didn't give up and, in fact, he lived another 55 years. When he couldn't walk, he used a wheelchair. Soon he lost his voice, so then he used a computerized voice to speak and write his books. He traveled [7] ______________, giving talks and showing the world what people can achieve when they believe in [8] ______________.

WRITING

A Competition Entry

1 ☆ **Read the advertisement. What do you have to do to enter the competition?**

____

YOUNG HEROES CLUB ANNUAL COMPETITION

Send us your entry! Describe how you have helped someone who has faced a challenge. Tell us:

- the greatest help you have given someone
- how you did it
- what advice you have for other young helpers

The best entry will receive a special award from a mystery celebrity!

2 ☆ **Read the competition entry. What has Gabriela's brother achieved?**

____

My name is Gabriela. My brother Jamie has learning difficulties, and he has faced many challenges.

One of Jamie's [1] ________________ is learning to make friends. He can't speak clearly, and because of this it's sometimes difficult for him to make new friends. At first, he was very shy, so I decided to help him. However, after [2] ________________, I've managed to bring a group of friends into Jamie's life.

How [3] ________________ it? First of all, I asked our parents to get Jamie a drum. He has always loved music, so he loved the drum! One day, I invited some musician friends to our house. They introduced themselves to Jamie and then just played some music. Soon Jamie started to play with them. Two of these friends have now formed a band, and Jamie is their drummer.

If you want to help someone make friends, my [4] ________________ is to find something they love doing and help them meet people with the same interest. And never give up!

3 ☆ **Complete the competition entry with the phrases in the box.**

a lot of effort	advice to you
did I do	greatest achievements

4 ☆☆ **Read the competition entry again and answer the questions.**

1 What challenge does Jamie face?

____

2 Why did his sister decide to help him?

____

3 What did Jamie's parents buy him?

____

4 How many people are in Jamie's band?

____

PLAN

5 ☆☆ **Write a competition entry. Take notes about how you helped a person for the competition in Exercise 1.**

1 Introduce yourself and the person you helped: ________________

2 Explain what you did: ________________

3 Explain how you did it: ________________

4 Give advice for other people: ________________

WRITE

6 ☆☆☆ **Write your competition entry. Remember to include the present perfect, reflexive pronouns, vocabulary from this unit, and phrases from the *Useful Language* box (see Student's Book, p101).**

CHECK

7 **Do you …**

- have four paragraphs?
- explain your achievement clearly?
- give useful advice?

8 REVIEW

VOCABULARY

1 Look at the pictures and circle the correct options.

1 *athlete / engineer*

2 *inventor / composer*

3 *engineer / writer*

4 *businesswoman / mathematician*

5 *athlete / scientist*

6 *composer / writer*

7 *mathematician / writer*

8 *businesswoman / athlete*

2 Put the letters in bold in the correct order to make words for qualities.

1 She admired the **vaiittcyre** of the architect who designed her new home. ________
2 Carlos Acosta showed great **letant** as a dancer from an early age. ________
3 Rock climbers need physical **gshtnert**. ________
4 Her **eignelelictn** was clear from the clever answers she gave. ________
5 His **ndoeittearnmi** to win made him practice for hours. ________

3 Circle the correct options.

1 My sister finishes her homework so fast. It's hard to *keep up / come up* with her.
2 We all *look up to / keep up with* our teachers and listen to their advice.
3 If you want to *show off / take part in* the competition, fill out this entry form.
4 Can you help me *give up / work out* this problem?
5 Let's *give up / set up* a volunteer organization to help our community.
6 If I don't *come up with / keep up with* a good idea soon, I'll *show off / give up*.

GRAMMAR IN ACTION

4 Complete the sentences with the present perfect form of the verbs in the box.

be	break	hear	read	see

1 ________ you ever ________ of a mathematician named Maryam Mirzakhani?
2 I ________ never ________ a book about astrophysics.
3 He ________ never ________ a world record, but I'm sure he will one day.
4 ________ Philip ever ________ a Studio Ghibli movie?
5 ________ we ________ here before? I don't remember it.

5 Correct the underlined reflexive and indefinite pronouns.

1 My cat has taught myself to open the fridge door. ______
2 Mrs. Howe is nobody who I've always looked up to. ______
3 Mary Ann saw themselves in a video clip on YouTube. ______
4 We've looked anywhere for our lost door keys. ______
5 You often talk to ourselves when you're alone. I've heard you! ______
6 I think there's anything wrong with my computer. ______
7 I've noticed that my brother looks at herself in the mirror a lot. ______
8 There was anybody in the house; it was empty. ______

CUMULATIVE GRAMMAR

6 Complete the conversation with the missing words. Circle the correct options.

JILL Oh, no. I [1] ______ to write a 500-word essay for Mr. Jenkins.
PETE Uh, and you've come to me [2] ______ some ideas, right?
JILL Yes, please! The title is "[3] ______ Creative Person I Know".
PETE Can't you think of [4] ______ ?
JILL Well, [5] ______ my aunt Louella?
PETE I think I saw her once when she [6] ______ with you.
JILL Maybe. She [7] ______ us very often, but it's possible.
PETE I'll probably remember her if you [8] ______ her.
JILL She's my mom's sister. She's [9] ______ tall as Mom, but she's slim and blond. Anyway, I look up to her because she's achieved a lot, and she hasn't had [10] ______ easy life.
PETE Really?
JILL Well, no. She was often sick as a teenager, and she didn't go to college, but she taught [11] ______ to paint. Now she has exhibitions [12] ______ .
PETE So, I think you have your topic, Jill, without any help from me!

1 a must	b have	c don't have
2 a getting	b and get	c to get
3 a The Most	b Most	c The More
4 a nobody	b anybody	c nothing
5 a have you met ever	b have you ever met	c did you ever met
6 a is staying	b stays	c was staying
7 a doesn't visit	b don't visit	c isn't visiting
8 a may describe	b describe	c will describe
9 a not as	b more	c not the
10 a some	b any	c an
11 a herself	b her	c himself
12 a nowhere	b everywhere	c somewhere

9 How do you express yourself?

VOCABULARY

Musical Instruments and Genres

1 ☆ **Put the letters in the correct order to make musical instruments and genres. Then complete the chart with the words.**

~~honroicpem~~ ~~garege~~ olivin ssab lkfo ssiclacal ugarit orkc phaxosone rumsd phi-oph rpumtet bekyarod azjz

Instruments	Genres
microphone	reggae

2 ☆☆ **Look at the band members (1–8) in the picture and complete the text with words from Exercise 1.**

HOME ABOUT ME ARCHIVE FOLLOW

There are eight of us in our band. Bruno plays the 1 drums. We have Janina on 2 __________, and her brother Stefan plays the 3 __________. Rob plays the 4 __________, and he's really good! Sally's just started to play the 5 __________, but we love her, and she's learning fast. Simon's a classical musician, but he plays an electric 6 __________ with us. He's really talented. Ramon plays the 7 __________, and that's Katie at the front. She's our singer, of course, and she doesn't really need that 8 __________ – she has a great voice!

3 ☆☆ **Match the photos with the musical genre words from Exercise 1.**

1 rock

2 __________

3 __________

4 __________

5 __________

6 __________

4 ☆☆ **Which word in each group does not follow the same stress pattern?**

1 (●) folk bass reggae drums
2 (● •) reggae guitar trumpet keyboard
3 (● • •) violin classical microphone saxophone

5 ☆☆☆ **Think of an example of a song or piece of music for each musical genre from Exercise 1. Use the Internet to help you if necessary.**

____
____
____
____

Explore It!

Guess the correct answer.

The world's longest officially released song is *The Rise and Fall of Bossanova*. It is about *3 / 13 / 23* hours long.

Find another interesting fact about a song. Write a question and send it to a classmate in an email, or ask them in the next class.

READING

An Events Guide

1 ☆ **Read the events guide. Do you think this is a good school party? Why / Why not?**

____

END-OF-YEAR PARTY

Friday, June 4, 7:00 p.m.–10:00 p.m.
Ticket price: $4 online, $5 at the door

It's been a long year, but it's finally the end! Join us at the school end-of-year party in the gym. We're going to have music, dancing, food, and a special guest!

7:00 p.m. Welcome! Feeling hungry? The school's Picnic Club will provide the evening's food: sandwiches, cookies, chips, and other yummy snacks will be available. And there will be a Super Fruit Juice Bar all evening for all you thirsty dancers!

7:30 p.m. DJ Quin is going to be with us with his unique mix of lights and sound. He'll be a star DJ one day, so don't miss this opportunity to dance as he plays the latest hits. He'll finish off his set with a "Happy Half-Hour" – when he'll play any song you want!

8:30 p.m. You won't believe it when you see our special guest. In his solo performance, he's going to tell us jokes and make us laugh (we hope!). But he isn't going to stop there: for one night only, he's also going to play the trumpet! Here's a clue: he's everyone's favorite geography teacher …

9:00 p.m. The evening's going to end with the band Born to Be Wild. This talented family of musicians will amaze you with the number of instruments they play: bass, saxophone, drums, violin …

So, don't miss the year's best party. See you on Friday!

2 ☆☆ **Read the events guide again and check the meaning of these words in a dictionary. Then complete the sentences.**

available	~~joke~~	latest	mix	provide	set

1 I never know if Juan's being serious or telling a *joke*.
2 The band began their ______ at eight and finished playing at nine.
3 We will ______ all the information you need for your trip.
4 Tickets for next week's concerts are now ______ online.
5 I think the ______ hit from Catfish is the best song they've ever written.
6 Tina's music is a ______ of hip-hop and reggae.

3 ☆☆ **Read the events guide again. Answer the questions.**

1 How much are tickets if you buy them before you go to the party?
____
2 Is the party indoors or outdoors?
____
3 What can the students drink?
____
4 What can the students do in the last 30 minutes of DJ Quin's set?
____
5 Why will people be surprised by the special guest?
____
6 What is special about the band Born to Be Wild?
____

4 ☆☆☆ **Answer the questions with your own ideas.**

1 In your opinion, which performer at the party will be the best?
____
2 Have you ever had an end-of-year party at school? What was it like?
____

GRAMMAR IN ACTION

Going To

1 ☆ **Write sentences with *going to*.**

1 I / take some photos

I'm going to take some photos.

2 She / watch TV

______

3 He / not answer the phone

______

4 Faye / play the piano

______

5 They / record a song

______

2 ☆☆ **Complete the sentences with *going to* and the verbs in the box.**

be	bring	not tell	~~organize~~	see

1 I *'m going to organize* a party for my best friend.
2 We ______ her anything about it.
3 Carmen ______ food and drinks to the party.
4 We ______ a folk-rock concert.
5 The party ______ in my garage.

3 ☆☆ **Write sentences about the people with *going to* and the phrases in the box.**

enter a talent competition	~~get a job as a DJ~~	get free concert tickets	run a marathon	study singing

1 Nasrin loves making playlists and discovering new music.

Nasrin's going to get a job as a DJ.

2 I've always wanted to go to music college.

______

3 Lily dreams of becoming a comedian.

______

4 Finn and Livvy run and train hard every day.

______

5 Max and I are lucky: we have a friend in the band.

______

Will and Going To

4 ☆ **Complete the sentences with *will* or *won't*.**

1 He's sure it *will* be a great event because the guide looked interesting.
2 I ______ pay $150 for a ticket – that's too much.
3 Your parents ______ get angry if your music is too loud, so turn it down.
4 ______ all three sisters sing in the same band?
5 It ______ be cold at the party, so you don't need a coat.

5 ☆☆ **Decide if the sentences are predictions or intentions. Then circle the best options to complete the conversations.**

1 **A** What *are you going to* (circled) / *will you* do this evening?
B *I'm going to* / *'ll* see a show at the City Hall.

2 **A** What *are you going to* / *will you* sing? Have you decided?
B No, but I promise you*'ll* / *'re going to* like it!

3 **A** *I'm going to* / *will* learn the saxophone.
B You*'ll* / *'re going to* be good at that. I just know it!

4 **A** The Headsets *aren't going to* / *won't* tour anymore.
B Oh, no. That *won't* / *isn't going to* be very popular with their fans.

6 ☆☆ **Complete the chat with the correct form of *will* or *going to* and the verbs in parentheses.**

[1] *Are* you *going to be* (be) at home later?

No, I [2] ______ (meet) my dad at the music store. I've decided: I [3] ______ (ask) him to buy me that guitar I saw in the window.

Really? You know you [4] ______ (get) a better price online.

Yeah, but I [5] ______ (try) it before we buy it – that's my plan anyway.

Well, OK, but do you play the guitar?

No, I don't, but I'm sure I [6] ______ (learn) fast! It can't be that difficult.

VOCABULARY AND LISTENING

Dance Styles

1 ☆ **Match five of the dance styles in the box with the shoes the dancers wear.**

~~ballet dancing~~ ballroom dancing breakdancing folk dance disco dancing modern dance salsa dancing swing tap dancing Zumba

1 ballet dancing

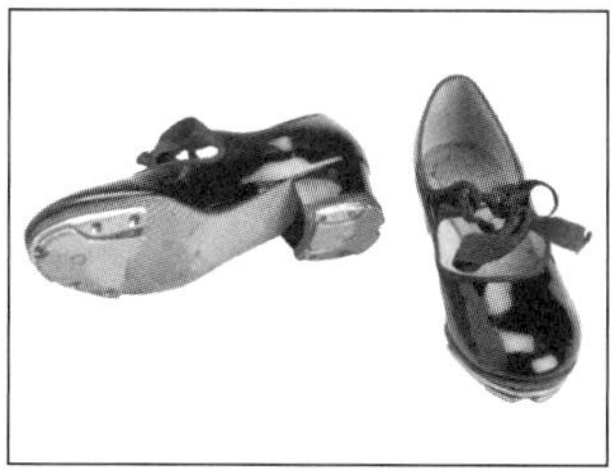

2 ______

3 ______

4 ______

5 ______

2 ☆ **Circle the correct options.**

1 In the 1970s, (*disco*) / *ballet* dancing was a popular dance in nightclubs.

2 *Salsa* / *Tap* dancing is a type of dance from Latin America.

3 *Breakdancing* / *Swing* is a strong, exciting style of jazz dancing with a partner.

4 My grandparents don't like *modern* / *folk* dance. They prefer more traditional performances.

5 *Swing* / *Zumba* is a type of exercise, often in a class, with dance movements.

A Discussion

9.01 **3** ☆☆ **Listen to the discussion and answer the questions.**

1 How many speakers do you hear? ______

2 How many are male and how many are female?

______

______

9.01 **4** ☆☆ **Listen again. Are the sentences *T* (true) or *F* (false)?**

1 The class is going to report back on their discussion next week. F

2 The after-school classes start next week. ______

3 One of the teachers is planning a school talent show. ______

4 Jessica wants to do modern dance. ______

5 Camila wants to do sports next semester. ______

6 Enzo wants to have a PE class after school. ______

5 ☆☆☆ **Answer the questions.**

1 What music or dance activities can you do at your school?

______

2 What other after-school activities or clubs does your school have?

______

GRAMMAR IN ACTION

Present Continuous for Future

1 ☆ **Complete the sentences with the present continuous form of the verbs in parentheses.**

1 Our school *'s performing* (perform) a musical next term.
2 Katie ______ (help) with the costumes after school.
3 Ms. Wilson ______ (teach) us the dance moves next week.
4 Who ______ (write) the programs for the new musical?
5 I ______ (not play) in the orchestra next time.
6 ______ you ______ (come) to watch the show tonight?

2 ☆ **Write sentences with the present continuous.**

1 the musicians / leave for New York tomorrow
The musicians are leaving for New York tomorrow.
2 they / perform three evening concerts in July
______
3 a journalist / interview the lead singer later
______
4 a TV camera operator / record tomorrow's show
______
5 the drummer / not play with the band tonight
______
6 he / fly to New York next week to study music there
______

3 ☆☆ **Complete the sentences with the present continuous form of the verbs in the box.**

arrive	cook	~~help~~	not come	not do	watch

1 Jonny *is helping* his sister with her homework later.
2 The boys ______ a movie after school.
3 I ______ pasta tonight. Who wants to come?
4 Helena's busy, so she ______ to the theater with us.
5 When ______ the stars of the show ______?
6 We ______ anything special tonight.

Simple Present for Future

4 ☆ **Complete the sentences with the simple present form of the verbs in parentheses.**

1 The next show *starts* (start) at eight.
2 The singers ______ (arrive) at five in the afternoon.
3 Our train ______ (leave) at six the next morning.
4 Tomorrow's rehearsal ______ (not end) until the evening.

5 ☆☆ **Write questions for the answers from Exercise 4.**

1 What time *does the next show start*?
2 When ______?
3 What time ______?
4 When ______?

6 ☆☆ **Circle the correct options.**

ADAM [1]*Are you doing* / *Do you do* anything this afternoon?
AVA Yes, my big brother and I [2]*meet* / *are meeting* our cousin Greg outside the club. He [3]*'s coming* / *comes* to stay with us after his performance.
ADAM Oh, yes – the rapper! [4]*Don't you watch* / *Aren't you watching* his show?
AVA I've seen it twice! We [5]*'re getting* / *get* something to eat on the way home.
ADAM What time [6]*is the show ending* / *does the show end*?
AVA It [7]*ends* / *'s ending* at 7:30, so we [8]*'re going* / *go* to that new Italian place. We [9]*buy* / *'re buying* pizza to take home for dinner!

WRITING

A Review

1 ☆ **Read the review. Where is the performance taking place?** ________________

Twelve – the Musical! ★★★★★

This year's 12th grade students have formed a unique song and dance group. Their show, called *Twelve – the Musical!*, tells the story of Kurt Goldberg, a theater director, and the dancers who want to perform in his show. The music is a mix of disco and swing. Some of 12th grade's best musicians also play their own songs.

It's a classic story of dancers who come to the city to become famous. I was <u>very impressed</u> by the beautiful costumes and creative makeup, and Chris Randall is superb as Kurt Goldberg. However, the <u>highlight</u> of the show was the singing. Chris has a powerful voice, and the dancers' songs were often funny. On the <u>downside</u>, the set was not very exciting.

Twelve – the Musical! is on again in the auditorium next Friday and Saturday. After graduating, Chris is leaving to study opera, and others in the group are continuing their theater studies at different colleges in the U.S.A. <u>All in all</u>, <u>if you love</u> music, this unique musical is <u>a must-see</u>.

2 ☆ **Complete the sentences with the <u>underlined</u> phrases in the review.**

1 I was *very impressed* by the funny script.
2 So, ________________ hip-hop, this show is for you.
3 The ________________ of the show was the superb tap dancing. I loved it!
4 For anyone who enjoys jazz, this show is ________________ .
5 On the ________________, the lead guitarist didn't play well.
6 ________________, it's a show you mustn't miss.

3 ☆☆ **Which things do these adjectives describe?**

1 unique *the song and dance group*
2 classic ________________
3 beautiful ________________
4 creative ________________
5 superb ________________
6 powerful ________________
7 funny ________________
8 not exciting ________________

PLAN

4 ☆☆ **Write a review of a school show that you have seen or been in. Take notes about these things.**

1 A general description of the show:
____
2 Details about the dancing, music, costumes, etc., and what you liked / didn't like:
____
3 A summary of your opinion:
____

WRITE

5 ☆☆☆ **Write your review. Remember to use adjectives, the simple present to describe the show, the simple past for your opinion, and phrases from the *Useful Language* box (see Student's Book, p113).**

CHECK

6 **Do you ...**

- use three paragraphs?
- say what you liked and didn't like?
- summarize your opinions at the end?

9 REVIEW

VOCABULARY

1 Look at the photos and complete the descriptions below with words for musical instruments and genres.

1

2

3

4

5

6

1 Katrina plays the ________________. She has studied ________________ music.

2 Bryony loves ________________ music and plays the ________________ in the park.

3 Marius is a great ________________ artist. All he needs is his ________________ to speak into.

4 Monica plays the ________________ in a reggae band, and Milton plays the ________________.

5 Ella plays the ________________, and Joe plays the ________________ in their band.

6 Our music teacher plays the ________________ at a ________________ club.

2 Find ten dance styles in the wordsnake.

discosalsatapballroombreakdancingZumbaswingfolkballetmodern

GRAMMAR IN ACTION

3 Complete the email with the correct form of *going to* or *will* and the verbs in the box.

be	bring	cost	finish	go
have	meet	not rain		

TO: Jed

FROM: Liam

Dear Jed,

Aidan and I 1 ________________ to a music festival on the weekend. Do you remember Jake and Ida? They 2 ________________ us there. I 3 ________________ all my homework first so I can really relax and enjoy myself! Aidan 4 ________________ sandwiches and hot drinks because we think the festival food 5 ________________ a lot – it's always expensive! I hope it 6 ________________ on Friday, but I bet it 7 ________________ cloudy all weekend. I'm not worried about that – I'm sure we 8 ________________ fun.

Hope your weekend's fun, too!

See you soon,
Liam

4 Circle the correct options.

1 *I'm not doing / don't do* anything special this afternoon.
2 The program says the music *starts / is starting* at 8:30 p.m.
3 People *are arriving / arrive* at seven tonight for the party.
4 *Are you using / Do you use* that microphone tonight?
5 Who*'s writing / writes* the songs for next year's show?
6 The ticket office *opens / is opening* tomorrow at 9 a.m.
7 A really exciting event *is happening / happens* at our school next week.
8 You'll have to run for the last bus because the show *isn't ending / doesn't end* until 10:30.

CUMULATIVE GRAMMAR

5 Complete the conversation with the missing words. Circle the correct options.

HARRY Have you [1] ________ of SoGood Sounds?
TINA If they [2] ________ a reggae band, I won't know them. I don't know as much about that kind of music [3] ________ you do.
HARRY No, no, there's an organization called SoGood Sounds. [4] ________ of them?
TINA No. What [5] ________?
HARRY They organize outdoor music festivals [6] ________ money for charities. They're all musicians, and they raise money for disabled people because some of them need assistance to take care of [7] ________.
TINA Oh, I see. Do you know [8] ________ more about the music they play?
HARRY Not really. I think that there [9] ________ be one of their concerts next weekend, but I'm not sure. I [10] ________ to look on the website tonight.
TINA OK, so when you get [11] ________ information, can you text me?
HARRY Of course. I'll do that if I [12] ________, no problem!

1	a heard ever	b ever heard	c ever hear
2	a are	b will be	c won't be
3	a like	b than	c as
4	a Did you hear	b Have you heard	c Were you hearing
5	a they do	b are they doing	c do they do
6	a to raise	b for raise	c for raising
7	a itself	b themselves	c theirselves
8	a anything	b anywhere	c anyone
9	a has to	b might	c might to
10	a will	b 'm going	c should
11	a an	b a	c some
12	a 'm remembering	b 'll remember	c remember

EXAM TIPS: Reading Skills

Reading: Multiple Choice

You will read a long text, which is often based on a newspaper or magazine article. This tests your understanding of the most important ideas and some details of the text. The title tells you what the topic is. There are multiple-choice questions. To answer the questions, you need to choose the correct answer, A, B, or C.

Example:

How does Estefania feel about the school exchange trip?

A She's excited to meet new people.

B She's worried about speaking a new language.

C She's nervous about being away from home for the first time.

Exam Guide: Multiple Choice

- Start by reading the title of the text so you know what the topic is.
- Read the whole text quickly first to find out more about the topic and to get a general understanding.
- Read the text again more carefully to get a better understanding. Use the context to work out the meaning of any new vocabulary, but don't spend too much time worrying about unfamiliar words at this point.
- Now read all the questions carefully and underline the important "key" words in the questions. This helps you when you look for the same information in the text.

  Example:

  How does Estefania feel about the school exchange trip?
- Read the first question again. Then look for the part of the text where you think you might find the answer. If you remember something from when you read through the text, go back to that part first to check. If not, read from the beginning until you find what you need.
- When you find the relevant part of the text, underline the words and write the number of the question next to the words you underlined. Then circle the option in the question, A, B, or C, that most closely matches the meaning in the text. Use the key words in the question to help you.

  Example:

  I'm really happy to go to Chicago to learn English and stay with an English-speaking family, and I don't mind being away from home, but I hope I won't forget the English I already know and I can understand everyone!
- Remember to check the other two options as well to decide why they aren't correct.
- Now read the other questions and repeat the process until you finish.

REMEMBER!

The text often mentions information from all three options in the question, but only one option is correct. Read the text carefully and match the meaning, not the words.

Reading Practice: Multiple Choice

> **Tip!**
> "Key" words carry the meaning in a sentence: they are usually nouns, adjectives, verbs, adverbs, and question words. Underlining these words in questions can help you to focus on the information you need to find in the text.

1 **Underline the key words in the questions.**

1 *What after-school activities does Lena like doing on Mondays?*
2 What day does Tom prefer playing tennis with his brother?
3 Why does Mason think art classes are difficult?
4 Who prefers studying alone to studying with other people?
5 How did Eva feel on the morning of her exam?
6 What, according to Josh, is the best thing about eating lunch at home?

2 **Underline the key words in questions 1–5. Then match 1–5 with A–E.**

1 What's Ben doing with his friends now? ☐
2 What did Ben do last weekend with his aunt? ☐
3 Where did Ben arrange to see his friend last week? ☐
4 What does Ben do Monday to Friday after school? ☐
5 Where does Ben go on Saturdays? ☐

A He met him in the park on Friday.
B He plays basketball during the week.
C Today, they're at the gym.
D He goes to computer club every weekend.
E On Saturday, he went to the movies with her.

3 **Choose the option, A, B, or C, which has the same meaning as each sentence (1–3). Then underline the words and phrases which helped you to match the sentences.**

> **Tip!**
> Look out for words or phrases which look different in the questions and text but have the same meaning; for example, synonyms, or antonyms with a negative verb.

1 *Lily hates going to her grandma's after school.*
(A) Lily really doesn't like going to her grandma's after school.
B Lily doesn't mind going to her grandma's after school.
C Lily likes going to her grandma's after school.

2 Harry was nervous about the exam scores.
A Harry wasn't worried about the exam scores.
B Harry felt worried about the exam scores.
C Harry was excited about the exam scores.

3 We were tired after the trip.
A We didn't have much energy after the trip.
B The trip was tiring, but we felt OK after it.
C We were full of energy after the trip.

4 My parents are upset with me.
A My parents aren't unhappy with me.
B My parents aren't angry with me.
C My parents aren't very happy with me.

4 **Read the text and match the words in bold with the synonyms 1–5.**

Last night our neighbors were on a game **show** on TV! Mr. and Mrs. Jackson seemed pretty **worried** at the beginning of the show because they were losing. Mr. Jackson looked **scared** and couldn't answer his questions very well, but Mrs. Jackson answered her questions **with no difficulty**. The final question was for the Jackson team, and they thought about it **with care** before answering. They got the answer **right** and won the game in the end, which was fantastic!

1 *nervous* *worried*
2 easily ________
3 carefully ________
4 program ________
5 correct ________
6 afraid ________

EXAM TIPS: Reading Skills

Reading: Open Cloze

You will fill in blanks in a short, simple text using one word only per blank. All words must be spelled correctly. This tests your knowledge of parts of speech such as verbs, determiners, prepositions, and pronouns. There is one example in the text, marked "0."

Example:

Have you (0) ______________ *the new* Fantastic Beasts *movie?*

Exam Guide: Open Cloze

- First, read the text quickly to find out the topic and understand the general meaning.
- Think about the possible words that might go in the blanks as you read through.
- Look carefully at the words before and after each blank, and read the whole sentence before deciding on an appropriate answer. Underline any important words.
- If you are not sure of an answer, move to the next item. You can do the ones you find easiest first and come back to the more difficult ones at the end.
- For difficult items, use the words before and after the blank to try to figure out the part of speech. For example, if the blank is preceded by a subject pronoun, the missing word is probably a verb. If it comes after a verb or a noun, it may be a preposition.
- If you think that more than one answer is possible, think very carefully about the sentence and the structure again. Read the sentence over in your head with both alternatives. Choose the word you feel fits best. Sometimes there is more than one possible answer, but remember you can write only ONE of these correct words in the blank.

  Example:

  Have you ***seen*** *the new* Fantastic Beasts *movie yet?*

  Have you ***watched*** *the new* Fantastic Beasts *movie yet?*
- When you have fill in all the blanks, read the whole text again carefully to check your answers and spelling.

REMEMBER!

The most common parts of speech are pronouns (e.g., *her*), determiners (e.g., *some*), conjunctions (e.g., *because*), time expressions (e.g., *since*), auxiliary verbs (e.g., *would*), and prepositions (e.g., *in*).

Reading Practice: Open Cloze

> **Tip!** Look at the words before and after the blank to decide what part of speech the missing word is.

1 What type of word is missing in each sentence? Choose the correct parts of speech.

1 *We saw ______ great movie last night.* — *(article) / verb*
2 Noel fell ______ his skateboard and hurt his knee. — *preposition / verb*
3 He bought ______ girlfriend a new pair of shoes. — *preposition / possessive adjective*
4 You don't ______ to come if you don't want to. — *verb / determiner*
5 She's put too ______ salt in the food. — *determiner / conjunction*
6 ______ does Lisa live? — *time expression / question word*
7 Let's buy Lucy a present ______ it's her birthday. — *conjunction / pronoun*

2 Complete the sentences in Exercise 1 with the correct missing words.

> **Tip!** Remember to read the whole text again when you finish. Check that you have used the correct verb forms, e.g., *She ~~have~~ **has** never been to Boston.*

3 Read the text and correct the words in bold.

[0]**Does** you know Corey's cousin, James? He's [1]**a** athlete! He [2]**win** two gold medals for [3]**her** school last year, and he wants to [4]**running** in the county championships next month. He exercises five times a week [5]**on** the gym, and he always tries to do [6]**best** each time. He's [7]**so** talented as the other athletes, and I believe he can win the championships [8]**on** the future.

1 Do 3 ______ 5 ______ 7 ______ 9 ______
2 ______ 4 ______ 6 ______ 8 ______

4 Choose the correct missing words to complete the sentences.

	a	b	c
1 *… it rain last night?*	*Has*	*(b) Did*	*Was*
2 I can't do this question. It's … hard!	too	enough	as
3 Kerry did very … on the exams.	good	bad	well
4 The alarm went off … our math class.	at	during	while
5 You … run in the school hallways.	don't	must	shouldn't
6 Were you … to call me just now?	trying	tried	try

5 Match one word from each box with each blank.

can ~~if~~ need on very what

could have off really ~~when~~ which

> **Tip!** Sometimes more than one word can be used to fill in a blank – though this isn't very common. When you think there is more than one possibility, write only one in the blank. Try to choose the option which you think is the most common.

1 *… you heat ice, it melts.* If When
2 I thought I did badly on the test, but I got a … good score! ______ ______
3 … country did you go to on vacation? ______ ______
4 We … to get to the station by ten o'clock to catch the train. ______ ______
5 … you open the window, please? ______ ______
6 Do you know how to turn … this computer? ______ ______

EXAM TIPS: Listening Skills

Listening: Matching

You will listen to a conversation between two people who know each other and match information in two lists of items. You will hear the conversation twice. This tests your understanding of detailed information. Before you listen to the conversation, you will hear instructions explaining who is speaking and what they are talking about.

Example:

*You will hear **Josh and Stella** talking about **the band for a new school musical**.*

You need to match the items in the first list with the correct items in the second list. There are five items in the first list and eight in the second: there are three extra items you don't need.

Example:

You will hear Josh and Stella talking about the band for a new school musical. Which musical instrument is each person going to play?

1	*Josh*	*A*	*keyboard*
2	*Stella*	*B*	*drums*
3	*Kristie*	*C*	*guitar*
4	*Ella*	*D*	*piano*
5	*Adam*	*E*	*trumpet*
		F	*violin*
		G	*bass guitar*
		H	*saxophone*

Exam Guide: Matching

- You will have time before you listen to read the question and look at the lists. Read them carefully and think about the context so you know what you can expect to hear.
- You will see that all the words in each list belong to the same vocabulary group. The first list is usually people and the second list is a group of nouns such as sports, food, or musical instruments. In the recording, you will hear the items in the first list in the same order in which they appear on the page.
- When you listen the first time, try to understand the general meaning of the conversation and think about the best option for each answer. If you aren't sure, don't worry. The second time you listen, you can check your first answer or make another choice.
- The first time you listen, you can also try to identify the items in the second list that are not needed. You can then cross these out so you can focus only on the other items when you listen the second time.
- When you listen the second time, focus more on specific information and check your answers carefully.

REMEMBER!

It's important to know when to stop focusing on a question you're not sure about so that you don't miss the next question. Don't spend too long on one item – try and follow the conversation. You can revise your answers when you listen the second time or at the end.

Listening Practice: Matching

> **Tip!**
> Always read the instructions and question carefully before you listen to the conversation. This will help you to think about the context and anticipate what you are going to hear.

E.01 **1 Read the instruction and question, and answer the questions below. Then listen and check your ideas.**

You will hear Josh and Stella talking about the band for a new school musical. Which musical instrument is each person going to play?

1 Why do you think they're talking about the band for the school musical?

____

2 What kinds of words do you think you will hear in the conversation?

____

3 Where do you think they are having their conversation?

____

E.02 **2 Listen to the conversations. Which item is mentioned but <u>isn't</u> the correct answer in each conversation? Put a cross (✗) next to the incorrect options.**

> **Tip!**
> When you listen, you may hear an item from the second list mentioned in the conversation that isn't necessarily the correct answer. Listen carefully and try to eliminate items which aren't the correct option.

1 Sally enjoys watching …	a comedies.	☐	b dramas.	✗	c soap operas.	☐
2 For the picnic, Joe needs to bring …	a a cake.	☐	b fruit.	☐	c sandwiches.	☐
3 Pippa wants to volunteer as a …	a nurse.	☐	b caregiver.	☐	c paramedic.	☐
4 For sports day, Marcus is going to compete in …	a swimming.	☐	b tennis.	☐	c volleyball.	☐
5 Jessie's favorite subjects are …	a math.	☐	b science.	☐	c geography.	☐

3 Look at the lists of words (a–d). Which vocabulary group does each list belong to?

1 Where did Martin go on Saturday?

a swimming pool b park c theater d restaurant *places in a town*

2 What did Monica's grandfather do when he was younger?

a paramedic b police officer c vet d firefighter ______

3 What did Tim have after his accident?

a bruises b a cut head c a broken leg d a sprain ______

4 How does Luke get to school?

a bus b on foot c car d bike ______

5 What things does Mina have in her bedroom?

a armchair b closet c desk d wardrobe ______

E.03 **4 Listen and choose the correct options in Exercise 3. You will hear all the options (a–d) mentioned, but only two are correct.**

Simple Present

Affirmative	Negative
I / You / We / They play the piano.	I / You / We / They do not (don't) play the piano.
He / She / It plays the piano.	He / She / It does not (doesn't) play the piano.

- We use the simple present to talk about facts, habits, and routines.
  I speak Italian. *He goes to college.*
- The third person form (*he / she / it*) of the simple present ends in ***-s***.
  eat – he eats *read – she reads*
- With verbs ending in **consonant** + ***-y***, we replace the ***-y*** with ***-ies*** for the *he / she / it* forms.
  study – she studies
- The *he / she / it* form of verbs ending in ***-ss***, ***-sh***, ***-ch***, ***-x***, and ***-o*** is ***-es***.
  kisses finishes teaches relaxes goes
- Some verbs have an irregular spelling in the third person.
  have – she has *be – he is*
- We form the negative of the simple present with the **subject** + ***don't/doesn't*** + **infinitive**.
  They don't speak Italian.
- We use ***doesn't*** in the third person (*he / she / it*).
  He doesn't play on the school team.

Questions	Short Answers
Do I / you / we / they like soccer?	Yes, I / you / we / they do. No, I / you / we / they don't.
Does he / she / it like soccer?	Yes, he / she / it does. No, he / she / it doesn't.

- We form simple present ***Yes/No*** questions with ***do/does*** + **subject** + **infinitive**.
  Do you read magazines?
- We use short answers with ***do/does*** to reply. We don't repeat the main verb.
  A: *Do you write a blog?* ***B:*** *Yes, I do.* (NOT ~~*Yes, I write*~~.)

Adverbs of Frequency

never sometimes often usually always

0% ⟵⟶ 100%

- Adverbs of frequency say how often we do something. They go after the verb ***to be*** but before all other verbs.
  She's always late. *He sometimes chats online.*
- In questions, adverbs of frequency always come after the subject.
  Do you always watch TV online?

Love, Like, Don't Mind, Hate + -ing

- We use the ***-ing*** form of the verb after ***like***, ***don't like***, ***don't mind***, ***love***, and ***hate***.
  She loves making cakes. (NOT ~~*She loves make cakes*~~.)
- We can also use nouns after these verbs.
  He doesn't mind basketball, but he loves tennis.

To Have

Affirmative	Negative
I / You / We / They have a phone.	I / You / We / They do not (don't) have a phone.
He / She / It has a phone.	He / She / It does not (doesn't) have a phone.

- We use ***have*** to talk about possession and relationships.
  I have five brothers.
- We usually use contractions in conversation.
  He doesn't have any cousins.
- We use the full form to be more formal.
  He does not have any cousins.
- To make the negative, we put ***n't*** (*not*) after ***do*** and before ***have***.
  We don't have a portable charger.

Questions	Short Answers
Do I / you / we / they have a laptop?	Yes, I / you / we / they do. No, I / you / we / they don't.
Does he / she / it have a laptop?	Yes, he / she / it does. No, he / she / it doesn't.

- We use ***do*** + **subject** + ***have*** + **object** in questions.
  Do you have headphones?
- In spoken English, we reply to questions with short answers.
  A: *Do you have a tablet?*
  B: *Yes, I do.* (NOT ~~*Yes, I do have*~~.) / *No, I don't.* (NOT ~~*No, I don't have*~~.)

Simple Present

1 Complete the table with the verbs in the box in the third person.

fly get up go ~~play~~ try watch

-s	-es	-ies
1 plays	3	5
2	4	6

2 Complete the sentences with the simple present form of the verbs in parentheses.

1 Marta and Matt like sports. (like)
2 I do my homework during the week, but my best friend ______ it on Sundays. (do)
3 They ______ hockey on Saturdays. (play)
4 My sister ______ English in college. (study)
5 My dad ______ the bus to work every day. (catch)

3 Write sentences with the simple present.

1 I / not like / swimming
I don't like swimming.
2 Harry / read / the school magazine / every week
3 My sister / not hang out / with friends in the evening
4 My friends / love / my new blog
5 Laura and Luis / not play / hockey on Saturdays
6 We / do / homework / at the homework club

4 Write *Yes*/*No* questions and short answers.

1 Molly / get up / at 6 a.m. / every day / ? (✓)
Does Molly get up at 6 a.m. every day? Yes, she does.
2 Dan / read / your blog / ? (✗)
3 you / play computer games / with your friends / ? (✓)
4 your sister / write / good stories / ? (✗)
5 Ruth and Ben / go to / the same school / ? (✓)

Adverbs of Frequency

5 Circle the correct options.

1 Carlos *always does* / *does always* his homework in front of the TV.
2 They *often are* / *are often* at the park on the weekend.
3 Gina and Martin *usually go* / *go usually* to the movies on Saturdays.
4 I *sometimes get* / *get sometimes* DVDs from the library.
5 My sister *never is* / *is never* late for school.
6 Alex *usually listens* / *listens usually* to music in the evening.

Love, Like, Don't Mind, Hate + -ing

6 Write sentences with *love*, *like*, *don't mind*, *hate* + *-ing*.

1 I / love / watch / movies
I love watching movies.
2 Molly / not mind / get up / early
3 We / like / go / to the gym
4 My dad / hate / listen / to the radio
5 Jen / not mind / do / homework

To Have

7 Complete the text with the correct form of *have*.

I [1] have a new friend. Her name's Isabel. She [2] ______ brown hair and blue eyes. She [3] ______ (not) any brothers, but she [4] ______ three sisters. Her mom and dad [5] ______ a house next to ours! I really like her because we [6] ______ the same hobbies, and we like the same things! What about you? [7] ______ you ______ a good friend in your class? [8] ______ your friend ______ the same hobbies as you?

Present Continuous

Affirmative	Negative
I am ('m) watching TV.	I am ('m) not watching TV.
You / We / They are ('re) watching TV.	You / We / They are not (aren't) watching TV.
He / She / It is ('s) watching TV.	He / She / It is not (isn't) watching TV.

- We use the present continuous to talk about actions in progress at the time of speaking.
  You are learning about the present continuous.
- For the affirmative, we use **subject** + ***be*** + **infinitive** + **-*ing***.
  Tom's watching a reality show. We're reading a blog.
- For the negative, we put ***not*** after ***be***.
  She is not (isn't) downloading songs.

Questions	Short Answers
Am I watching TV?	Yes, I am. No, I'm not.
Are you / we / they watching TV?	Yes, you / we / they are. No, you / we / they aren't.
Is he / she / it watching TV?	Yes, he / she / it is. No, he / she / it isn't.

- To form questions, we use ***be*** + **subject** + **infinitive** + **-*ing***.
  Are you watching cartoons?
- We don't use the **infinitive** + ***-ing*** in short answers.
  Yes, I am. (NOT ~~*Yes, I am watching*~~.)
- We form information questions with a ***Wh-*** question word before *be*.
  Who are you reading about?
  What are you watching on TV?
- With most verbs, we add ***-ing*** to the **infinitive**.
  speak – speaking read – reading drink – drinking
- For verbs ending in ***-e***, we remove the ***-e*** and add ***-ing***.
  write – writing have – having give – giving
- For verbs ending in a vowel and a consonant, we double the final consonant and add ***-ing***.
  stop – stopping shop – shopping plan – planning

Simple Present and Present Continuous

- We use the simple present to talk about facts, habits, and routines.
  Water freezes at 0 °C.
  I listen to music when I walk to school.
  She always goes shopping on Fridays.
- We use the present continuous to talk about actions in progress at the time of speaking.
  I watch a lot of TV. At the moment, I'm watching a great streaming series.
  He usually works in an office, but he's working at home today.
- Some verbs are not usually used in the continuous form: ***know***, ***understand***, ***like***, ***love***, ***prefer***, ***hate***, ***need***, ***remember***, ***think***, ***want***.
  I like this show. (NOT ~~*I'm liking this show*~~.)
- We use expressions like ***at the moment*** and ***right now*** with the present continuous.
  He's doing his homework at the moment.
- We use adverbs of frequency with the simple present.
  He always does his homework after dinner.

Adverbs of Manner

- We use adverbs of manner to say how we do something.
  Carl can run very fast.
- Adverbs of manner come after the verb or the object if the sentence contains one.
  They don't speak clearly.
  Lia can draw animals well.
- To form regular adverbs, we add ***-ly*** to the adjective.
  nice – nicely loud – loudly
- For adjectives ending in ***-y***, we remove the ***-y*** and add ***-ily***.
  happy – happily noisy – noisily
- For adjectives ending in ***-l***, we add ***-ly***.
  careful – carefully beautiful – beautifully
- Some adverbs of manner are irregular.
  good – well hard – hard late – late

GRAMMAR PRACTICE UNIT 1

Present Continuous

1 Complete the chart with the verbs in the *-ing* form.

~~do~~ run shop take walk write

Add *-ing*	Remove the *-e* and Add *-ing*	Double the Consonant and Add *-ing*
1 doing	3 ______	5 ______
2 ______	4 ______	6 ______

2 Complete the sentences with the present continuous form of the verbs in parentheses.

1 My best friends *are reading* in the library. (read)
2 I ______ for a new camera. (look)
3 My mom ______ in the café. (sit)
4 She ______ coffee. (not drink)
5 My dad ______ a chocolate cake in the kitchen. (make)
6 Rosie and Dan ______ online. (not chat)

3 Write present continuous questions and short answers about the people in the chart.

	Watch a Movie	Study Grammar
Jack	(1) ✗	(4) ✓
Rory and Holly	(2) ✓	(5) ✗
Alicia	(3) ✗	(6) ✓

1 *Is Jack watching a movie?*
No, he isn't.
2 ______
3 ______
4 ______
5 ______
6 ______

Simple Present and Present Continuous

4 Put the words in the correct order to make sentences in the simple present or present continuous.

1 isn't / She / documentary / watching / the
She isn't watching the documentary.
2 makes / My mom / always / for the show / the costumes
______
3 English / We / studying / aren't / today
______
4 to / the / best friend / to go / doesn't / want / movies / My
______
5 weekend / I / with / friends / on / the / chat / my / online
______
6 moment / I'm / helping / my / mom / the / at
______

5 Complete the sentences with the simple present or present continuous form of the verbs in the box.

listen make not do not talk visit ~~watch~~

1 We *'re watching* a comedy show right now.
2 I ______ my homework at the moment.
3 They often ______ their aunt on Saturdays.
4 My grandma usually ______ to the news on the radio in the morning.
5 My mom sometimes ______ the food we see on cooking shows.
6 Ryan ______ on his phone to his best friend at the moment.

Adverbs of Manner

6 Complete the text with the adverb form of the adjectives in parentheses.

My brother doesn't make friends [1] *easily* (easy). He only has two really good friends. They usually play computer games at home. I don't play with them because they do everything really [2] ______ (quick), and I play [3] ______ (slow) and [4] ______ (bad)! My brother loves drawing, and he can draw [5] ______ (good). Sometimes he teaches me how to draw. I think he's a good teacher because he explains everything [6] ______ (careful).

Simple Past

Affirmative	Negative
I / You / He / She / It / We / They went to a museum.	I / You / He / She / It / We / They did not (didn't) go to a museum.
To Be	
I / He / She / It was bored.	I / He / She / It was not (wasn't) bored.
You / We / They were bored.	You / We / They were not (weren't) bored.

- We use the simple past to talk about completed events and actions in the past.
  He watched a history documentary last night.
  We were tired after the trip.
- Most verbs in the simple past end in ***-ed***.
  want – wanted need – needed show – showed
- For verbs ending in ***-e***, *add* ***-d***.
  live – lived hate – hated practice – practiced
- For verbs ending **consonant** + ***-y***, we remove the ***-y*** and add ***-ied***.
  study – studied carry – carried marry – married
- For verbs ending **consonant** + **vowel** + **consonant**, we double the final consonant and add ***-ed***.
  shop – shopped chat – chatted stop – stopped
- Some simple past verbs are irregular.
  become – became come – came put – put
- See the irregular verbs list on page 143.
- To form the simple past negative, we use **subject** + ***did not (didn't)*** + **infinitive** without ***to***.
  Mario didn't finish his homework last night.
- To form the past negative of ***be***, add ***not (n't)***.
  Mom wasn't very happy about my exam scores.

Questions	Short Answers
Did I / you / he / she / it / we / they go to a museum?	Yes, I / you / he / she / it / we / they did. No, I / you / he / she / it / we / they didn't.
To Be	
Was I / he / she / it bored?	Yes, I / he / she / it was. No, I / he / she / it wasn't.
Were you / we / they bored?	Yes, you / we / they were. No, you / we / they weren't.

- To form simple past questions, we use ***Did*** + **subject** + **infinitive** without ***to***.
  Did Tom enjoy the concert yesterday?
- We put question words before ***did***.
  What did you do last weekend?
- To form past questions with ***be***, change the word order.
  Were you late to class this morning?

There Was/Were

	Affirmative	Negative
Singular	There was a bowl / some food.	There was not (wasn't) a bowl / any food.
Plural	There were some forks.	There were not (weren't) any forks.

- We use ***there was*** and ***there were*** to talk about what existed in the past.
- We use ***there was*** with singular countable and uncountable nouns.
  There was a book here. There was milk in the cup.
- We use ***there were*** with plural countable nouns.
  There were a lot of tourists in our town last weekend.
- We use ***some*** after ***there was/were*** with uncountable and plural countable nouns.
  There was some water in the bottle.
  There were some houses here years ago.
- We use ***any*** after ***there wasn't/weren't*** with uncountable and plural countable nouns.
  There wasn't any money in the purse.
  There weren't any cups.

	Questions	Short Answers
Singular	Was there a bowl / any food?	Yes, there was. No, there wasn't.
Plural	Were there any forks?	Yes, there were. No, there weren't.

- In questions, we usually use ***any*** with uncountable and plural countable nouns.
  Was there any bread at home?
  Were there any interesting objects at the museum?
- We don't repeat ***any*** in short answers.
  A: *Was there any news about Laura?*
  B: *No, there wasn't.* (NOT ~~*No, there wasn't any.*~~)

GRAMMAR PRACTICE

Simple Past

1 Complete the chart with the simple past form of the verbs in the box.

cry like plan smile stay stop study ~~wait~~

Add -*ed*	Ending in -e, Add -*d*	Remove -*y*, Add -*ied*	Double Final Consonant, Add -*ed*
1 waited	3 ______	5 ______	7 ______
2 ______	4 ______	6 ______	8 ______

2 Write sentences with the simple past.

1 Tom / wait / three hours / for the train
Tom waited three hours for the train.
2 Joanna / not go / to school / last week
______
3 Megan and Sarah / not feel / tired after the trip
______
4 The trip / take / ten hours!
______
5 I / buy / some / new shoes
______

3 Write simple past questions and short answers about the people in the chart.

	Beth	Maria and Sam	Ivan
go movies	(1) ✗	(3) ✓	(5) ✓
eat pizza	(2) ✓	(4) ✗	(6) ✗

1 Did Beth go to the movies?
No, she didn't.
2 ______
______
3 ______
______
4 ______
______
5 ______
______
6 ______
______

4 Complete the question for each answer.

1 **A:** What did you drink?
B: I drank some soda.
2 **A:** Where ______?
B: He went to a concert.
3 **A:** When ______?
B: They started school in January.
4 **A:** Who ______?
B: She met her sister.
5 **A:** What ______?
B: He ate a hotdog.
6 **A:** Why ______?
B: They stayed at home because it was foggy.

There Was/Were

5 Complete the text with *there was(n't)/were(n't)*.

When I was in elementary school, [1] there weren't a lot of exams and [2] ______ a lot of students in my class – I think [3] ______ only nine or ten of us. In my classroom, [4] ______ an internet connection or an electronic board, but my classroom was beautiful. [5] ______ pictures and stories on the walls, and [6] ______ a storytelling hour every day. [7] ______ any computers or laptops in our class in those days, but we loved writing on the board!

6 Circle the correct options.

1 Were there *a* / *some* / *any* posters on the walls? (*any* circled)
2 There wasn't *an* / *some* / *any* exam every week.
3 There weren't *a* / *some* / *any* computers.
4 Was there *a* / *some* / *any* board in the classroom?
5 There wasn't *a* / *some* / *any* window in the classroom.
6 There were *an* / *some* / *any* interesting storybooks.

7 Complete the questions with *Was there* or *Were there*.

1 Were there many people at the party?
2 ______ any good TV shows on last night?
3 ______ a party at your house last night?
4 ______ an exam at school last week?
5 ______ three or four students at the library?

Past Continuous: Affirmative and Negative

Affirmative	Negative
I / He / She / It was traveling.	I / He / She / It was not (wasn't) traveling.
You / We / They were traveling.	You / We / They were not (weren't) traveling.

- We use the past continuous to talk about actions in progress at a specific time in the past, or actions interrupted by another action.
  We were doing homework at 5 p.m. yesterday.
  Chloe was reading when James texted her.
- We form affirmative sentences with **subject** + ***was*/*were*** + **infinitive** + ***-ing***.
  He was walking to school.
- To form the negative, we put ***n't*** (***not***) after ***was*/*were*** and before the **infinitive** + ***-ing***. ***Not*** is usually contracted.
  They weren't listening to the teacher.

Past Continuous: Questions

Questions	Short Answers
Was I / he / she / it traveling?	Yes, I / he / she / it was. No, I / he / she / it wasn't.
Were you / we / they traveling?	Yes, you / we / they were. No, you / we / they weren't.

- We form questions with ***Was*/*Were*** + **subject** + **infinitive** + ***-ing***.
  Were you reading in bed last night?
- We don't use **infinitive** + ***-ing*** in short answers.
  A: Was he chatting online?
  B: Yes, he was. (NOT ~~*Yes, he was chatting.*~~)
- For information questions, we put the ***Wh-*** question word before ***be***.
  What were you doing this morning?

Simple Past and Past Continuous

- We often use the simple past and past continuous together. We use the simple past for shorter actions that interrupt longer actions in the past continuous.

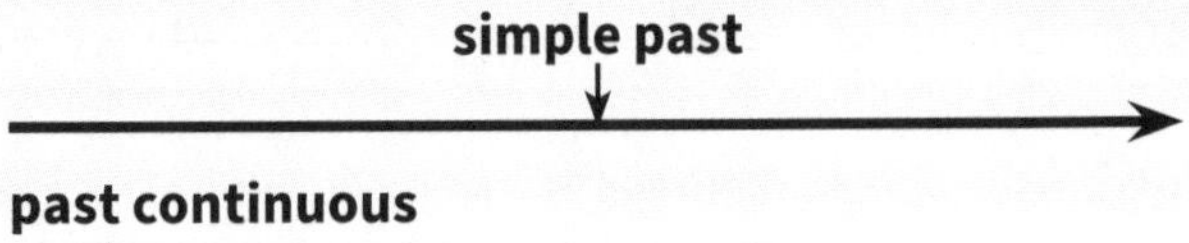

  I was cycling to school when I saw Lily.
  He was walking through the park when he fell and hurt his knee.
- We often use ***when***, ***while***, and ***as*** with the past continuous.
  Their computer broke when they were studying.
  While she was having breakfast, she got a text from Madeline.
  As we were leaving the party, Lucas arrived.
- We use ***when*** with the simple past for shorter actions.
  When I saw Tom, he was arguing with Adele in the street. (NOT ~~*While I saw Tom …*~~)

GRAMMAR PRACTICE

Past Continuous: Affirmative and Negative

1 Complete the sentences with the past continuous form of the verbs in the box.

chat get hide ~~play~~ take watch

At 5 p.m. yesterday afternoon …

1 Peter *was playing* the piano.
2 Hugo ______ a shower.
3 Finn and Olivia ______ with friends.
4 We ______ a drama series on TV.
5 My sister ______ dressed.
6 The children ______ under the bed!

2 Complete the sentences with the negative past continuous form of the verbs in parentheses.

1 Aaron *wasn't playing* soccer. (play)
2 Diana ______ emails. (write)
3 Kate and Denise ______ in the backyard. (sit)
4 We ______ our bikes. (ride)
5 I ______ a sandwich. (eat)
6 The children ______ any noise. (make)

Past Continuous: Questions

3 Write questions with the past continuous.

1 What / you / do / yesterday / ?
What were you doing yesterday?
2 Where / they / go / last night / ?
______
3 Who / she / talk to / ?
______
4 Why / he / laugh / at me / ?
______
5 Where / you and your mom / stay / ?
______
6 What / your / friends / say / ?
______

4 Circle the correct options.

1 **A:** Was he reading the story?
B: Yes, he *(was)* / *were*.
2 **A:** Were they playing soccer at 4 p.m.?
B: No, they *was* / *weren't*.
3 **A:** Were you talking on the phone to your friend at 10 p.m. last night?
B: No, I *wasn't* / *weren't*.
4 **A:** Was your mom making breakfast at 7 a.m.?
B: Yes, she *was* / *were*.
5 **A:** Were you watching TV at 9 p.m. yesterday?
B: Yes, we *was* / *were*.
6 **A:** Was Susan doing her homework at 6 p.m.?
B: Yes, she *was* / *were*.

Simple Past and Past Continuous

5 Complete each sentence with the simple past or the past continuous form of the verbs in parentheses.

1 While we *were walking* (walk) home, we *saw* (see) eight or nine cats crossing the street!
2 He ______ (go) to bed when the phone ______ (ring).
3 I ______ (fall) down while I ______ (walk) to school.
4 When I ______ (arrive) home, my dad ______ (dance) in the kitchen!
5 As the man ______ (take) the money, the police ______ (arrive).
6 While I ______ (chat) online, my mom ______ (come) into my room to turn the light off.

6 Complete the story with the simple past or the past continuous form of the verbs in parentheses.

I [1] *was getting* (get) into bed last night when I [2] ______ (see) a light in the backyard. While I [3] ______ (go) downstairs, I [4] ______ (hear) someone outside! I [5] ______ (try) to close the door when my dad [6] ______ (shout), "Let me in! It's me, your dad!"

Could

Affirmative	Negative
I / You / He / She / It / We / They could swim.	I / You / He / She / It / We / They could not (couldn't) swim.

- We use ***could/couldn't*** to talk about ability and possibility in the past and to make a polite request.
  When I was four I could swim ten meters.
  He couldn't call earlier because he was at work.
- ***Could*** is the same for all persons. The third person (*he / she / it*) form doesn't end in **-*s***.
  She could sing "Happy Birthday" in three languages.
- To form the negative, we put ***n't*** (***not***) after ***could***.
  He couldn't pay for his college books.

Questions	Short Answers
Could I / you / he / she / it / we / they swim?	Yes, I / you / he / she / it / we / they could. No, I / you / he / she / it / we / they couldn't.

- To form questions, we change the order of ***could*** and the subject.
  Could you speak English in elementary school?

Comparative and Superlative Adjectives

Comparatives	
Short adjectives: *smart*	add -***er***: *smarter*
Short adjectives ending in vowel + consonant: *big*	double the final consonant and add -***er***: *bigger*
Adjectives ending in -*e*: *safe*	add -***r***: *safer*
Adjectives ending in -*y*: *easy*	remove the -*y* and add -***ier***: *easier*
Long adjectives: *interesting*	put ***more*** before the adjective: *more interesting*
Irregular adjectives *good bad*	*better worse*

- We use comparative adjectives to compare one thing or person with another.
- We use the verb ***be*** + **comparative adjective** + ***than***.
  Riley is taller than Amelia.

Superlatives	
Short adjectives: *smart*	add -***est***: *the smartest*
Short adjectives ending in vowel + consonant: *big*	double the final consonant and add -***est***: *the biggest*
Adjectives ending in -*e*: *safe*	add -***st***: *the safest*
Adjectives ending in -*y*: *easy*	remove the -*y* and add -***iest***: *the easiest*
Long adjectives: *interesting*	put ***the most*** before the adjective: *the most interesting*
Irregular adjectives *good bad*	*the best the worst*

- We use superlative adjectives to say a thing or person has the most of a particular quality.
- We use ***the*** with a **superlative adjective**.
  Riley is the tallest person in her family.

Too, Too Much, Too Many

- We use ***too***, ***too much***, and ***too many*** to say that there is an excess of something.
- We use ***too*** with **adjectives**.
  I'm too excited to sleep – it's my birthday tomorrow!
- We use ***too much*** with **uncountable nouns**.
  I have too much homework, so I can't go out tonight.
- We use ***too many*** with **plural countable nouns**.
  Daniel has too many plans for the weekend – he doesn't know which one to choose.

(Not) Enough + Noun

- We use ***enough*** when we have the right amount of something or something is sufficient.
  My brother has enough experience to work there.
- We use ***not enough*** when we need more of something or something is insufficient.
  I don't have enough time to do volunteer work on the weekend.

GRAMMAR PRACTICE

Could

1 Complete the sentences with *could* or *couldn't* and the verb in parentheses.

1 I *could speak* French when I was five. (speak)
2 She ______ a shower because there wasn't any water. (not take)
3 My grandparents ______ a house when they were young because they were poor. (not buy)
4 Tyler ______ all the questions on his English test because they were easy. (answer)
5 We ______ him because he spoke very quietly. (not hear)
6 Lynn ______ a bike when she was six, but I couldn't. (ride)

2 Put the words in the correct order to make questions with *could*.

1 five / read / Could / were / you / when / you / ?
Could you read when you were five?
2 his / brother / Could / Spanish / speak / ?
______
3 his / understand / Amy and David / accent / Could / ?
______
4 six / Jeff / skate / was / he / when / Could / ?
______
5 yesterday / you / understand / Could / science / the / class / ?
______

Comparative and Superlative Adjectives

3 Complete the sentences with the comparative form of the adjectives in parentheses.

1 Math is *more boring* (boring) than history.
2 Ava's homework is ______ (good) than Tim's homework.
3 Our new house is ______ (big) than the old one.
4 The weather in December is ______ (bad) than the weather in August.
5 I think my brother is ______ (intelligent) than me.

4 Circle the correct options.

1 **A:** I think being a firefighter is *more dangerous* / *the most dangerous* job in the world!
B: I don't agree. I think a police officer's job is *more dangerous* / *the most dangerous* than a firefighter's job.
2 **A:** What is the *best* / *better* way to travel?
B: People think it's traveling by plane, but I think going by train is *better* / *the best* than traveling by plane.
3 **A:** I think history is *easier* / *the easiest* subject.
B: I don't agree. I think science is *easier* / *the easiest* than history.

Too, Too Much, Too Many; (Not) Enough + Noun

5 Put the words in the correct order to make sentences.

1 to / go / to / I'm / too / park / busy / the
I'm too busy to go to the park.
2 work / My / too / mom / has / much
______
3 clothes / have / I / too / in / many / wardrobe / my
______
4 enough / don't have / money / I / buy / to / a / new laptop
______
5 doesn't have / enough / to / study / She / time
______

6 Complete the text with the words in the box.

enough	not enough	too (x2)	too many	too much

I went to my first concert last week. I didn't like it. It was [1] *too* noisy, and there were [2] ______ people there. I wanted to have something to eat, but there was [3] ______ food for everybody. After two hours, I was [4] ______ hungry to stay and asked my mom to take me home. When we arrived home, Dad had [5] ______ work and didn't have [6] ______ time to cook dinner, so we had pizza and then I went to bed!

(Not) As … As

- We use (***not***) ***as*** … ***as*** to compare one thing or person with another.
  This tablet is as expensive as a laptop.
- We use ***not as*** + **adjective** + ***as*** to say that two things or people are not equal in some way.
  *Being a nurse is**n't as** dangerous **as** being a firefighter.* (= Being a firefighter is more dangerous than being a nurse.)
- We use ***as*** + **adjective** + ***as*** to say two things or people are the same.
  *Being a nurse is **as** hard **as** being a doctor.* (= Being a doctor is as hard as being a nurse.)

(Not) … Enough

- We use ***not*** + **adjective** + ***enough*** when we need more of something or something is insufficient.
  I'm not old enough to drive a car. I'm only 15.
- We use **adjective** + ***enough*** when we have the right amount of something or something is sufficient.
  This carpet is big enough to cover the floor.

Have To

Affirmative	Negative
I / You / We / They have to do the ironing.	I / You / We / They do not (don't) have to do the ironing.
He / She / It has to do the ironing.	He / She / It does not (doesn't) have to do the ironing.

- We use ***have to*** to say that something is necessary.
  My sister has to empty the dishwasher every day.
  You have to drive on the right side of the road in the U.S.A.
- We use ***don't have to*** to say that something isn't necessary.
  I don't have to help at home, but it makes my parents happy.
  They don't have to do after-school activities at their school.

Questions	Short Answers
Do I / you / we / they have to do the ironing?	Yes, I / you / we / they do. No, I / you / we / they don't.
Does he / she / it have to do the ironing?	Yes, he / she / it does. No, he / she / it doesn't.

- To form questions, we use ***Do/Does*** + **subject** + ***have to*** + **infinitive**.
  Does your mom have to work on the weekend?
- In short answers we repeat **do** or ***does***, not ***have to***.
  A: *Do you have to go to bed early during the week?*
  B: *Yes, I do.* (NOT ~~*Yes, I have to.*~~)

GRAMMAR PRACTICE

(Not) As ... As

1 Complete the second sentence so it has the same meaning as the first sentence. Use (*not*) *as ... as* and the adjectives in parentheses.

1 Her new computer is smaller than her old computer.
Her old computer *isn't as small as* her new computer. (small)

2 This red carpet is the same size as the blue one.
This red carpet ______ the blue one. (big)

3 This chest of drawers is prettier than my wardrobe.
My wardrobe ______ this chest of drawers. (beautiful)

4 These armchairs are the same price as the chairs.
The chairs ______ the armchairs. (expensive)

5 This camera is lighter than my smartphone.
My smartphone ______ this camera. (light)

6 The rooms in our apartment are wider than the rooms in your apartment.
The rooms in your apartment ______ the rooms in our apartment. (wide)

(Not) ... + Enough

2 Match 1–5 with a–e.

1 My bedroom is too small. [d]
2 You're too young. [ ]
3 My shoes are too dirty. [ ]
4 This game is too easy. [ ]
5 It's too cold to go swimming. [ ]

a It isn't difficult enough.
b You aren't enough.
c The weather isn't hot enough.
d It isn't big enough.
e They aren't clean enough to wear to school!

3 Complete the text with the phrases in the box.

as big as	as comfortable as	as small as	~~as wide as~~	big enough

I got a new bed last week because I wanted a big, comfortable bed that was [1] *as wide as* my parents' bed. We bought one that was [2] ______ for five people to sleep in! My bedroom isn't [3] ______ my parents' room (theirs is huge), and it's also smaller than my brother's, so my new bed is too big for my room. I sleep well in the bed because it's [4] ______ my parents' bed, but I can't have any furniture in my room now! My brother wants the new bed because he says his room isn't [5] ______ mine, so there's more space! No way!

Have To

4 Complete the sentences with the correct form of *have to*.

1 My teacher *has to* correct a lot of homework. ✓
2 To send a text message, you ______ have a cell phone. ✓
3 My brother ______ go to school by bus because my dad takes him in the car. ✗
4 David and Maria ______ do a lot of homework on the weekend. ✗
5 They ______ wear uniforms at my sister's school. ✓
6 We ______ cook dinner on Mondays and Fridays because Dad does it then. ✗

5 Circle the correct options.

1 Jake *has to* / *doesn't have to* (circled) wash the dishes because there's a dishwasher.
2 *Do* / *Does* Cindy and Tim have to clean the bathroom?
3 Kim *has to* / *doesn't have to* do the shopping because her parents are too busy.
4 Olly *has to* / *doesn't have to* wash his clothes by hand because there is a washing machine.
5 Mom and Dad *don't have to* / *have to* mop the floor because we do it.
6 **A:** *Do* / *Does* Lauren have to do any chores at home?
B: Yes, she *do* / *does*.

GRAMMAR REFERENCE

Should/Shouldn't

Should/Shouldn't	
Affirmative	**Negative**
I / You / He / She / It / We / They should be careful on the beach.	I / You / He / She / It / We / They should not (shouldn't) swim in cold water.

- We use ***should*** and ***shouldn't*** to give advice and say that we think something is a good or bad idea.
  You should put cold water on a burn.
- ***Should*** doesn't change in the different persons. We use an **infinitive without *to*** after ***should***.
  He should help his parents with the housework.

Must/Mustn't

Must/Mustn't	
Affirmative	**Negative**
I / You / He / She / It / We / They must drive on the left in the UK.	I / You / He / She / It / We / They must not (must not) swim when there is a red flag.

- We use ***must*** and ***must not*** to give strong advice and talk about rules.
  You must watch this TV show; it's great.
  You must be 17 to drive a car.
- ***Must not*** means that something isn't allowed.
  You mustn't use your phone in the theater.
- ***Must*** doesn't change in the different persons. We use an **infinitive without *to*** after ***must***.
  He must remember to take his medicine every day.

Zero Conditional

Action/Situation: simple present	**Result**: simple present
If a bee stings you,	it hurts.
Result: simple present	**Action/Situation:** simple present
It hurts	if a bee stings you.

- We use the zero conditional to talk about situations and their results that are always true.
  If you heat water to 100 °C, it boils.
  When you sprain your ankle, it usually bruises.
- We use a comma to separate the two clauses when the action/situation clause comes first.
  If you work hard, you get results.

First Conditional

Action/Situation: simple present	**Result**: *will* + infinitive
If we see a jaguar,	we 'll take a photo.
Result: *will* + infinitive	**Action/Situation:** simple present
We'll take a photo	if we see a jaguar.

- We use the first conditional to talk about possible situations in the future and their results.
  If we pass all our exams, we'll have a party.
  You'll get cavities if you eat too much sugar.
- We use a comma to separate the two clauses if the action/situation clause comes first.
  If the weather is nice tomorrow, we'll go to the park.

GRAMMAR PRACTICE

UNIT 6

Should/Shouldn't and *Must/Mustn't*

1 Complete the sentences with *should* or *shouldn't* and the verbs in the box.

go (x2) open stay wear (x2)

1 It's cold today. You should wear a warm coat.
2 People say there are sharks in the ocean. You ______ swimming.
3 It's raining. You ______ your umbrella.
4 I have an exam tomorrow. I ______ up too late.
5 **A:** I have a toothache.
B: You ______ to the dentist.
6 **A:** These new shoes are too small for me.
B: You ______ them!

2 Complete the sentences with *must* or *must not* and the verb in parentheses.

1 You must not laugh at other students in class. (laugh)
2 You ______ early to get to school on time. (get up)
3 You ______ sandwiches in the classroom. It isn't allowed. (eat)
4 You ______ loudly in the theater. (talk)
5 You ______ on the chairs. (stand)
6 You ______ your teeth every day. (brush)

3 Complete the text with *must* or *must not* and the verbs in the box.

climb look ~~swim~~ take walk wear

My grandma always thinks of the bad things that can happen to me! When I go to the beach, she says I [1] must not swim in the ocean because it's dirty, I [2] ______ sandals on the beach because there's a lot of broken glass, and I [3] ______ out for sharks in the water! When I go to the mountains, she says I [4] ______ near animals that bite or sting, I [5] ______ my phone with me so she can call me, and I [6] ______ any mountains in case I break my leg!

Zero Conditional

4 Match 1–6 with a–f.

1 If it rains, c
2 When you read books, ☐
3 If my friend is feeling sad, ☐
4 When a snake bites you, ☐
5 You make the color green ☐
6 If I don't understand something in class, ☐

a I try to make her laugh.
b if you mix yellow and blue.
c the grass gets wet.
d you learn things.
e I ask my teacher for help.
f you need to go to the hospital.

First Conditional

5 Circle the correct options.

1 If *you go* / *you'll go* online, *I* / *I'll* show you my new website.
2 *We* / *We'll* learn which plants are dangerous if *we go* / *we'll go* to the classes.
3 If *they swim* / *they'll swim* in the ocean at night, *they are* / *they'll be* in danger.
4 If you *don't come* / *won't come*, *I'm not* / *I won't be* your friend anymore!
5 If *he sees* / *he'll see* a tarantula, *he's* / *he'll be* frightened!

6 Complete the conditional sentences with the correct form of the verbs in the box.

call eat not go not have ~~take~~

1 If the computer doesn't work, I'll take it to the store.
2 Sally will play games online if she ______ any homework.
3 They ______ us if they are late.
4 If Harry doesn't get the job, he ______ on vacation.
5 If you ______ something, you'll feel better.

Present Perfect: Affirmative and Negative

Affirmative	Negative
I / You / We / They have ('ve) finished.	I / You / We / They have not (haven't) finished.
He / She / It has ('s) finished.	He / She / It has not (hasn't) finished.

- We use the present perfect to talk about actions with a present result and actions within an unfinished time period.
  I've found my favorite hat!
  Logan hasn't been to the dentist this year.
- To form affirmative sentences, use **subject** + ***have/has*** + **past participle**.
  I've burned my hand.
- To form negative sentences, we put ***n't*** (***not***) after ***have/has*** and before the past participle. ***Not*** is usually contracted.
  Smartphones haven't replaced human interaction completely.
- Most verbs in the past participle form end in ***-ed***.
  want – wanted   need – needed   play – played
- For verbs ending in ***-e***, add ***-d***.
  love – loved   hope – hoped   live – lived
- For verbs ending in **consonant** + ***-y***, remove the final ***-y*** and add ***-ied***.
  study – studied   try – tried   copy – copied
- For verbs ending in **consonant** + **vowel** + **consonant**, double the final consonant and add ***-ed***.
  slip – slipped   shop – shopped   drop – dropped
- Some past participles are irregular and don't follow any pattern.
  see – seen   find – found   put – put
- See the irregular verbs list on page 143.

Will/Won't, *May*, and *Might*

Will/Won't	
Affirmative	**Negative**
I / You / He / She / It / We / They will ('ll) survive.	I / You / He / She / It / We / They will not (won't) survive.

- We use ***will*** and ***won't*** to make certain predictions about the future.
  Computers will control our lives in the future.
  The laptop will help me with my homework.

Will/Won't	
Questions	**Short Answers**
Will I / you / he / she / it / we / they survive?	Yes, I / you / he / she / it / we / they will. No, I / you / he / she / it / we / they won't.

- To form questions, we change the order of ***will*** and the subject.
  Will we travel in cars in the future?

May and *Might*	
Affirmative	**Negative**
I / You / He / She / It / We / They may have a flying car.	I / You / He / She / It / We / They may not have a flying car.
I / You / He / She / It / We / They might have a flying car.	I / You / He / She / It / We / They might not have a flying car.

- We use ***may*** and ***might*** to make uncertain predictions about the future.
  Rhinos may become extinct in the future; no one knows for sure.
  I might go to Bridget's house this weekend; I don't know yet.

Infinitive of Purpose

- We use ***to*** + **infinitive** to express a purpose for doing something.
  I use a car to get to work.
  She bought a tablet to watch videos when she travels.
  They saved money to pay for the wedding.
  (NOT ~~*They saved money for pay for the wedding.*~~)

GRAMMAR PRACTICE

Present Perfect: Affirmative and Negative

1 Complete the chart with the past participle of the verbs in the box.

change drop plan study try ~~upload~~

Add -*d* or -*ed*	Remove -*y*, Add -*ied*	Double Final Consonant, Add -*ed*
1 *uploaded*	3 ______	5 ______
2 ______	4 ______	6 ______

2 Write the past participle of the verbs.

1 have *had*
2 do ______
3 ride ______
4 write ______
5 forget ______
6 see ______

3 Complete the sentences with the correct form of *have*.

1 I*'ve* joined an online club at school.
2 Ava ______ fallen off her bike.
3 Luke ______ broken his wrist.
4 We ______ sent them a message.
5 My brother ______ won an internet competition.
6 Laptops ______ made homework easier!

4 Complete the sentences with the present perfect form of the verbs in parentheses.

1 I think I*'ve lost* my new phone. (lose)
2 I can't use my laptop because I ______ my password! (forget)
3 My brother ______ his bed this morning. (not make)
4 Ruth ______ her ankle! (break)
5 My grandpa ______ a new computer! (buy)
6 My teacher says smartphones ______ how we speak to each other. (change)

Will/Won't, May, and *Might*

5 Complete the text with *will* and the verbs in the box.

be (x2) do ~~go~~ study work

In the future, I think I [1]*'ll go* to college, and I [2] ______ computer technology. I think that computer technology [3] ______ very important in the future because there [4] ______ a lot of new developments in science and technology. Then I think I [5] ______ research at a university in the U.S.A. or Australia. After that, I think I [6] ______ at a company which invents new technology.

6 Circle the correct options.

1 In the future, children *will* / *won't* go to school because they'll study at home.
2 Quinn *might* / *will* be in his bedroom, but I don't know. Go and look.
3 We *will* / *won't* all have electric cars in 100 years because there won't be any gasoline.
4 I *will* / *may* meet Tom tonight, but I haven't decided yet.
5 The library *won't* / *may not* let you borrow more than four books – I'm not sure. Let's ask.
6 People won't work in factories in the future because robots *will* / *won't* do all of the work.

Infinitive of Purpose

7 Complete the text with the infinitive of purpose. Use the verbs in the box.

~~buy~~ change have show speak take

Yesterday, my mom went shopping [1] *to buy* a new smartphone. I went with her [2] ______ my new tablet for a different one because it was broken. When we were going home, we stopped at a café [3] ______ some coffee and then we stopped again [4] ______ to some neighbors we saw at the park. Mom used her new phone [5] ______ some photos of us [6] ______ my dad at home. It was really late when we got home, but my dad loved the photos!

Present Perfect for Experience

Affirmative	Negative
I / You / We / They have ('ve) seen this movie.	I / You / We / They have not (haven't) seen this movie.
He / She / It has ('s) seen this movie.	He / She / It has not (hasn't) seen this movie.

- We use the present perfect to talk about experiences.
  He's visited every country in Europe.
  Jayden and Layla haven't met Mia.

Questions	Short Answers
Have I / you / we / they seen this movie?	Yes, I / you / we / they have. No, I / you / we / they haven't.
Has he / she / it seen this movie?	Yes, he / she / it has. No, he / she / it hasn't.

- We form ***Yes/No*** questions with ***have/has*** + **subject** + **past participle**.
  Has your mom been to Spain?
- We repeat ***have/has*** in short answers.
  A: *Have you tried Portuguese food?*
  B: *Yes, I have.*
- When we talk about experience, we can use ***ever*** in questions to mean "at any time," and ***never*** in affirmative sentences to mean "at no time."
  Have you ever seen a crocodile in real life?
  I've never traveled outside of my country.

Reflexive Pronouns

I – myself	I saw **myself** on TV.
you – yourself	You saw **yourself** on TV.
he – himself	He saw **himself** on TV.
she – herself	She saw **herself** on TV.
it – itself	It saw **itself** on TV.
we – ourselves	We saw **ourselves** on TV.
you (plural) – yourselves	You saw **yourselves** on TV.
they – themselves	They saw **themselves** on TV.

- We use reflexive pronouns when the subject and the object of a sentence are the same, or to emphasize the subject of an action.
  My dad talks to himself when he's nervous.
  I made dinner myself because Dad was late.
- The pronoun usually goes directly after the verb.
  We enjoyed ourselves at Liam's birthday party.
  (NOT ~~*We enjoyed at Liam's birthday party ourselves.*~~)

Indefinite Pronouns

	People	Things	Places
Some... : to talk about one person / thing / place in a positive sentence	**Someone** / **Somebody** called me earlier.	I want **something** to eat.	I want to go **somewhere** hot on vacation.
Every... : to talk about all people, things, or places	**Everyone** / **Everybody** likes chocolate.	**Everything** in your flat is beautiful.	I've been **everywhere** in Chicago.
Any... : to talk about one person, thing, or place in a negative sentence or question	I don't know **anyone** / **anybody** at this party.	I don't have **anything** to wear to the party.	I don't want to go **anywhere** tonight.
No... : to indicate no people, things, or places	**No one** / **Nobody** called me yesterday.	**Nothing** happened last night.	**Nowhere** is open for dinner tonight.

- We use indefinite pronouns to talk about people, things, and places without specifying those people, things, and places.
- Indefinite pronouns take a singular verb.
  Everyone is excited about the wedding. (NOT ~~*Everyone are excited about the wedding.*~~)
- We usually use an affirmative verb with ***no one***, ***nothing***, and ***nowhere***.
  There's nothing to do here! (NOT ~~*There isn't nothing to do here!*~~)
- We usually use a negative verb with ***anyone***, ***anything***, and ***anywhere***.
  I don't have anything to do today. (NOT ~~*I've got anything to do today.*~~)

GRAMMAR PRACTICE

Present Perfect for Experience

1 Complete the sentences with the correct words.

~~'ve~~ ever has have haven't never

1 I've flown on a plane.
2 He's ______ been to Iceland, but he wants to go in the future.
3 **A:** ______ you ever ridden a camel?
B: No, I ______.
4 **A:** Has your grandpa ______ used a laptop?
B: Yes, he ______!

2 Write questions and short answers with the present perfect and *ever*.

1 you / climb / a mountain / ?
Have you ever climbed a mountain?
No, I haven't.
2 Christina / sprain / her ankle / ?
______
Yes, she ______.
3 Tony / eat / Japanese food / ?
______
No, he ______.
4 your parents / travel / to a different country / ?
______
No, they ______.
5 your sister / learn / a new language / ?
______
Yes, she ______.
6 you / spend / too much money / ?
______
Yes, I ______.

3 Underline and correct one mistake in each sentence.

1 Have ever you driven a car? you ever
2 I've never invent anything! ______
3 Has your brother ever win a prize? ______
4 She haven't been to a different country. ______
5 I haven't never seen a waterfall. ______

Reflexive Pronouns

4 Circle the correct options.

1 She wrote the song *herself* / *himself*.
2 He only thinks about *herself* / *himself*.
3 People with talent usually believe in *yourself* / *themselves*.
4 My dad says we should always defend *ourselves* / *themselves*.
5 I taught *myself* / *himself* how to play chess.
6 The laptop switches *itself* / *himself* off when you stop using it.

5 Complete the sentences with the correct reflexive pronouns.

1 Do you like looking at yourself in the mirror?
2 Monica taught ______ to play the guitar.
3 I don't like taking photos of ______ because I look terrible in them!
4 These lights turn ______ on when it's dark.
5 Jack hurt ______ when he was climbing.
6 We enjoyed ______ at the concert.

Indefinite Pronouns

6 Circle the correct options.

1 *Someone* / *No one* lives in that house – the last family moved out two weeks ago.
2 There's *something* / *nothing* better than helping other people.
3 My uncle loves traveling. He's been *everywhere* / *nowhere* except Australia and New Zealand!
4 *Somewhere* / *Someone* told me it's better to dress well if you want to make a good impression.
5 I have *nothing* / *no one* to tell you.
6 She doesn't have *anywhere* / *nowhere* to stay when she begins her new job in Miami.

Going To

Affirmative	Negative
I am ('m) going to dance.	I am ('m) not going to dance.
You / We / They are ('re) going to dance.	You / We / They are not (aren't) going to dance.
He / She / It is ('s) going to dance.	He / She / It is not (isn't) going to dance.

- We use ***going to*** to talk about future plans and intentions.
  I'm going to work in another country in the future.
- To form the affirmative, we use ***be*** + ***going to*** + **infinitive**.
  We're going to travel around Europe before college.
- To form the negative, we use ***be*** + ***not*** + ***going to*** + **infinitive**.
  Ryan isn't going to study French in France.

Questions	Short Answers
Am I going to dance?	Yes, I am. No, I'm not.
Are you / we / they going to dance?	Yes, you / we / they are. No, you / we / they aren't.
Is he / she / it going to dance?	Yes, he / she / it is. No, he / she / it isn't.

- We form questions with ***be*** before the subject.
  Are they going to get married this year?
- We repeat ***be*** in short answers.
  A: *Are you going to learn the keyboard?*
  B: *Yes, I am.*

Will and Going To

- We use ***will*** for predictions and ***going to*** for future plans and intentions.
  Lidia will be the best singer in the school show.
  We're going to write the school play next year.

Present Continuous for Future

- We use the present continuous to talk about fixed arrangements in the future, especially plans we've agreed with other people.
  I'm meeting my friends at 8 p.m. tomorrow. We're seeing a concert.
  We're having lunch with my aunt next Saturday.
- We often use future time expressions such as ***tonight***, ***tomorrow***, ***this weekend***, ***this summer***, ***next week***, ***next month,*** and ***after class/school*** with the present continuous for future.
  Aria and I are practicing for the school talent show this weekend.

Simple Present for Future

- We use the simple present to talk about scheduled events in the future.
  The concert starts at 10 p.m. tomorrow. It ends at midnight.
  My plane leaves tomorrow morning at nine.
  Their train arrives at 8:45 in the morning.
  Our summer vacation starts on June 24.

GRAMMAR PRACTICE UNIT 9

Going To

1 Complete the sentences with the correct form of *going to* and the verbs in the box.

buy	not go	not work	perform	~~study~~

1 I *'m going to study* music and dance in college.
2 Anne ______ in her dad's store this summer.
3 My brother ______ in a musical next week.
4 My parents ______ a new house next year.
5 We ______ to summer camp this year.

2 Write questions with *going to*. Use the words in parentheses.

1 What *are you going to do* (you / do) this summer?
2 Where ______ (Tina / work) next year?
3 When ______ (your parents / start) salsa classes?
4 What ______ (brother / do) on the weekend?
5 ______ (you / learn) the guitar next year?
6 ______ (your sister / buy) tickets for the pop concert tomorrow?

Will and *Going To*

3 Decide if the sentences are predictions or intentions. Then circle the best options.

1 I think you (*will*) / *are going to* need an umbrella today because it might rain.
2 We *will* / *are going to* buy the tickets tomorrow for the show.
3 They *will* / *are going to* watch ballroom dancing tomorrow night.
4 I think it *will* / *is going to* be difficult to find a good job in the future.
5 I'm sure you *will* / *are going to* pass the exam – with a bit of luck.

Present Continuous for Future

4 Write present continuous sentences about the people in the chart.

	Jess	Marta and Adam
tonight	(1) study for a test	(3) go out for pizza with their friends
this weekend	(2) watch ballet	(4) go to a concert

1 *Jess is studying for a test tonight.*
2 ______
3 ______
4 ______

5 Complete the conversation with the present continuous form of the verbs in the box.

~~do~~	go (x2)	have	make	meet

MIA What [1] *are you doing* tonight?
MASON I [2] ______ dinner at Josh's house at about six, but nothing after that. Why?
MIA Anna and I [3] ______ skating at the park.
MASON Sounds interesting. What time [4] ______ you ______ to the park?
MIA Well, the first dancers are always there at eight, but I [5] ______ Anna at 7:30 In the café in front of the park first. Why don't you ask Josh to come, too?
MASON He can't. He [6] ______ a video with his classmates for a school project.

Simple Present for Future

6 Complete the sentences with the simple present form of the verbs in parentheses.

1 The bus *leaves* at 3 p.m. this afternoon. (leave)
2 When ______ this year's opera season ______? (begin)
3 The tap dancing class tomorrow ______ for more than three hours! (last)
4 My brother ______ his first concert next week! (have)
5 The show ______ at about 10 p.m. (end)
6 When ______ the new theater ______? (open)

LANGUAGE BANK

STARTER

Vocabulary

Free Time and Hobbies

a bike ride   a blog   books/magazines
cookies/videos   friends   an instrument
music   online   photos   shopping   songs

Sports

basketball   gymnastics   hockey
rugby   sailing   swimming   table tennis
track and field   volleyball   windsurfing

Personal Possessions

bus pass   camera   headphones   keys
laptop   money   passport   phone
portable charger   tablet

Grammar in Action

Simple Present
Adverbs of Frequency
Love, *Like*, *Don't Mind*, *Hate* + *-ing*
To Have

Writing

Useful Language

Using Commas and Apostrophes

We use apostrophes:

- for contractions / short forms: *name's*
- to show possession: *My cat's name is Tiger.*

We use commas to indicate a pause: *I live with my mom and dad, my grandma, and my cat.*

UNIT 1

Vocabulary

TV Shows

cartoon   comedy   cooking show
documentary   drama   game show
reality show   soap opera   sports show
streaming series   talk show   the news

Making Movies

actor   camera operator   costume
(digital) camera   director   lights
makeup artist   script   set   sound engineer

Grammar in Action

Present Continuous
Simple Present and Present Continuous
Adverbs of Manner

Speaking

Everyday English

Actually …
It's really cool!
Let's see.
Well?

Useful Language

I prefer watching …
I'm not really into it/them.
It's great/good/not bad/awful.
What do you think of …?

Writing

Useful Language

Giving Similar or Contrasting Information

and to add similar information
but to show different information
or when there is a choice of two or more things

LANGUAGE BANK

UNIT 2

Vocabulary

The Weather

cloudy cold dry foggy hot
icy rainy snowy stormy sunny warm
wet windy

Useful Objects

blanket bowl comb cup fork
hairbrush knife lamp mirror pillow
plate scissors spoon toothbrush

Grammar in Action

Simple Past
There Was/Were

Speaking

Everyday English

Nothing much.
Sounds good!
That's a shame.
You learn something new every day!

Useful Language

How was your weekend?
It was (OK/good/great/amazing/awful), thanks.
What about you?
What did you do?
What was the weather like?
Where did you stay?

Writing

Useful Language

Writing an Account of a Journey

At first, …
Finally, …
(He) set off on …
There were a lot of problems.

UNIT 3

Vocabulary

Adjectives of Feeling

afraid angry bored embarrassed
excited lonely nervous surprised tired
worried upset

Prepositions of Movement

across along between down
into off out of over past through
under up

Grammar in Action

Past Continuous: Affirmative and Negative
Past Continuous: Questions
Simple Past and Past Continuous

Speaking

Everyday English

Go on.
No idea.
What a great story!
You're kidding!

Useful Language

Guess what happened (yesterday)?
It happened to …
Really?
That's amazing/incredible!
What was (he) doing (at) …?

Writing

Useful Language

Sequencing Words and Phrases

At first, …
In the afternoon, …
Suddenly, …
The next day, …
The next morning, …
The other day, ...

UNIT 4

Vocabulary

Money Verbs

borrow change cost earn lend owe pay save sell spend

Caring Jobs

caregiver firefighter garbage collector lawyer lifeguard nurse paramedic police officer preschool teacher surgeon vet volunteer

Grammar in Action

Could
Comparative and superlative Adjectives
Too, *Too Much*, *Too Many*
(*Not*) *Enough* + Noun

Speaking

Everyday English

cute
I owe you one.
There you go.
What's up?

Useful Language

Could you do me a favor?
I'm sorry, I can't.
It depends.
Sure.
Would you mind … + *-ing* … ?

Writing

Useful Language

Giving Your Opinion

First of all, …
I believe that …
In my opinion, …
Personally, I think that …
In conclusion, …

UNIT 5

Vocabulary

Furniture

armchair bookcase carpet ceiling chest of drawers cupboard desk floor fridge picture shelves sink wardrobe

Household Chores

do the dishes do the ironing do the laundry dust (the furniture) load/empty the dishwasher make the bed mop the floor sweep the floor vacuum (the carpet)

Grammar in Action

(*Not*) *As* … As
(*Not*) … *Enough*
Have To

Speaking

Everyday English

I'm not convinced.
It looks awesome!
Me neither.
Me too.

Useful Language

at the bottom/top
in the background
on the left/right
What's that … ?

Writing

Useful Language

Adding Information

also
as well
as well as
too

LANGUAGE BANK

UNIT 6

Vocabulary

Accidents and Injuries

break bruise burn cut fall off
get bitten get stung hit scratch
slip sprain trip over

Parts of the Body

cheek chest chin elbow
forehead heel knee neck
shoulder teeth toe wrist

Grammar in Action

Should/Shouldn't and *Must/Must not*
Zero Conditional and First Conditional

Speaking

Everyday English

Awesome
Buddies
I'll have a go at it.
Good job

Useful Language

How about … + *-ing* … ?
Make sure you don't …
Why don't you … ?
You should definitely …

Writing

Useful Language

Giving Advice

I'd say …
If you ask me, …
Make sure …
That's why …

UNIT 7

Vocabulary

Communication and Technology

app chip device download emoji
message screen social media
software upload video chat

Getting Around

catch/take get into get off
get on get out of go by go on

Grammar in Action

Present Perfect: Affirmative and Negative
Will/Won't, May, and *Might*
Infinitive of Purpose

Speaking

Everyday English

Got it?
Like this?
Not quite.
That's it.

Useful Language

Before you start, …
It's really important that …
Make sure that …
Remember (not) to …

Writing

Useful Language

Giving Examples

For example,
For instance,
such as

Adding More Information

In addition, …
What's more, …

UNIT 8

Vocabulary

Exceptional Jobs and Qualities

athlete businessman/businesswoman composer engineer inventor mathematician scientist writer

creativity determination intelligence skill strength talent

Phrasal Verbs: Achievement

come up with give up keep up with look up to set up show off take part in work out

Grammar in Action

Present Perfect for Experience
Reflexive Pronouns
Indefinite Pronouns

Speaking

Everyday English

Tell me more.
that kind of thing
the main thing is
you know

Useful Language

I've learned the basics of …
I'm passionate about …
I've had plenty of experience of …
I've learned how to …

Writing

Useful Language

Talking about Achievements

after a lot of effort
How did I do it?
My advice to you is …
My greatest achievement is …

UNIT 9

Vocabulary

Musical Instruments and Genres

bass drums guitar keyboard microphone saxophone trumpet violin

classical folk hip-hop jazz reggae rock

Dance Styles

ballet dancing ballroom dancing breakdancing disco dancing folk dance modern dance salsa dancing swing tap dancing Zumba

Grammar in Action

Going To
Will and *Going To*
Present Continuous for Future
Simple Present for Future

Speaking

Everyday English

all day long
Never mind.
That's no good.
That's too bad.
What are you up to?

Useful Language

Do you feel like …?
I'd love to, but …
(She's) welcome to …
Thanks for asking, though.
Would you like to …?

Writing

Useful Language

Writing a Review

All in all, …
If you love (dance), this (show) is a must-see.
I was impressed by …
On the downside, …
The highlight of the show is …